MW01628866

Making CONNECTIONS Intro

Skills and Strategies for Academic Reading

Jessica Williams | David Wiese

Shaftesbury Road, Cambridge CB2 8EA, United Kingdom

One Liberty Plaza, 20th Floor, New York, NY 10006, USA

477 Williamstown Road, Port Melbourne, VIC 3207, Australia

314–321, 3rd Floor, Plot 3, Splendor Forum, Jasola District Centre, New Delhi – 110025, India

103 Penang Road, #05–06/07, Visioncrest Commercial, Singapore 238467

Cambridge University Press & Assessment is a department of the University of Cambridge.

We share the University's mission to contribute to society through the pursuit of education, learning and research at the highest international levels of excellence.

www.cambridge.org
Information on this title: www.cambridge.org/9781108651431

© Cambridge University Press & Assessment 2016, 2022

This publication is in copyright. Subject to statutory exception and to the provisions of relevant collective licensing agreements, no reproduction of any part may take place without the written permission of Cambridge University Press & Assessment.

First published 2016

20 19 18 17 16 15 14 13 12 11

Printed in Malaysia by Vivar Printing

A catalogue record for this publication is available from the British Library

Library of Congress Control Number: 2015948232

ISBN 978-1-108-65143-1 Student's Book with Integrated Digital Learning
ISBN 978-1-107-51609-0 Teacher's Manual

Additional resources for this publication at www.cambridge.org/makingconnections

Cambridge University Press & Assessment has no responsibility for the persistence or accuracy of URLs for external or third-party internet websites referred to in this publication, and does not guarantee that any content on such websites is, or will remain, accurate or appropriate. Information regarding prices, travel timetables, and other factual information given in this work is correct at the time of first printing but Cambridge University Press & Assessment does not guarantee the accuracy of such information thereafter.

TABLE OF CONTENTS

6

COMMUNICATION 163

7

MONEY 195

8

SPACE 225

Making CONNECTIONS

MAKING CONNECTIONS INTRO is a high-beginning academic reading and vocabulary skills book. It is intended for students who need to improve their strategic reading skills and build their academic vocabulary.

SKILLS AND STRATEGIES 3

Finding the Meanings of Words: Examples

As you learned in Skills and Strategies 1 on page 2, writers often give definitions for difficult words. Sometimes writers give examples, not direct definitions. Examples give additional information to show what a word means. If you can understand a word by looking at examples, you do not need to stop reading and check a dictionary.

Examples & Explanations

Almost every week a new **diet** becomes popular. For example, people try to lose weight by eating no rice or bread, or by eating fish instead of red meat.

The reader may not know what *diet* means. The writer shows the meaning with examples of diets in the next sentence: *eating no rice or bread* and *eating fish instead of red meat*. These examples are introduced by a signal: *for example*. Writers also use the signals *such as* and *like* to introduce examples.

diet = a plan to eat only a small amount of special types of food in order to lose weight

You often hear about health topics in **the media**. Newspapers, TV, and websites talk about how to be healthy.

The writer gives examples of the media without using a signal word or phrase. Notice that the examples form a list: *newspapers, TV*, and *websites*. Lists often contain examples.

the media = all the organizations – like newspapers, TV, and websites – that give people news and information

Strategies

These strategies will help you find the meanings of words while you read.

- When you see a word you do not know, do not stop reading. Finish reading the sentence with the unknown word, and read the next sentence as well.
- Look for examples in those sentences. Remember that writers use signals like *for example, such as*, and *like* to introduce examples.
- Look for a list. A list could contain examples of an unknown word.
- Use the examples to help you understand the unknown word.

34 • UNIT 2

Each unit begins with an in-depth study of key skills and strategies for reading academic texts, helping students to learn how and when to use them.

Skill Practice 1

Read the following sentence pairs. Highlight the examples that are given for each word in bold. The first one is an example.

1 Some people believe cold weather makes them sick. They put on warm **garments** like coats and sweaters every time they go outside.

2 There is an old saying "an apple a day keeps the doctor away." In fact, apples are good for **organs** such as the heart and brain.

3 There are many different **treatments** for colds, for example, chicken soup, orange juice, and extra sleep. Which one works best?

4 Children need **nutritious** food, like fruit, nuts, and vegetables. It makes them stronger and healthier.

5 Is it true that **stressful** situations can give you health problems? I sometimes feel sick during important exams, presentations, and job interviews.

6 Some people think **spicy** food causes stomach problems. They will not eat things such as hot red peppers.

7 Psychologists say it is good for our health to **complain**. After we talk about our problems at work or in marriage, we usually feel better.

8 My parents **warn** me about health problems. They always say, "don't do this," "be careful about that," or "that's bad for you."

Skill Practice 2

Read the sentences from Skill Practice 1 again. What do the words in bold mean? Write your answers on the blank lines. The first one is an example.

1 Some people believe cold weather makes them sick. They put on warm **garments** like coats and sweaters every time they go outside.

garments = *pieces of clothing*

2 There is an old saying "an apple a day keeps the doctor away." In fact, apples are good for **organs** such as the heart and brain.

organs = ____________

3 I have heard about many different **treatments** for colds, for example, chicken soup, orange juice, and extra sleep. Which one works best?

treatments = ____________

SKILLS AND STRATEGIES 3 • 35

Students learn strategies for approaching academic texts and skills for consciously applying the strategies.

FEATURES

- Critical thinking skills
- Real-time practice of skills and strategies
- Study of the Academic Word List

Before You Read

Connecting to the Topic

Discuss the following questions with a partner.

1 Did you ever learn a "fact" about science that was not really true? Explain your answer.

2 Did you ever learn a "fact" about health or medicine, for example, what kinds of things can make you sick, that was not really true? Explain your answer.

3 People often pass on inaccurate information about science and health. Why do you think these ideas are repeated over and over?

Previewing and Predicting

One way to preview is to notice the way the reading looks. Do any words or sentences appear in bold or italics? These are probably important. Are any sections of the reading set apart with numbers or bullets? If they are short, it is a good idea to preview them.

A Read the title of Reading 1. Then look in the reading for words or sentences that look special. Read the sentences that are in italics or set apart with bullets. Then put a check (✓) next to the statements below that you think are true.

____ 1 All of the sentences with bullets are true.
____ 2 Some of the sentences with bullets are true.
____ 3 None of the sentences with bullets is true.
____ 4 All of the sentences in italics are true.
____ 5 Some of the sentences in italics are true.
____ 6 None of the sentences in italics is true.

B Compare your answers with a partner's.

C Discuss what you think the reading will be about with your partner.

While You Read

As you read, stop at the end of each sentence that contains a word in bold. Then follow the instructions in the box in the margin.

READING 1 • 3

Predicting the content of a text is critical for reading college books, and students practice this skill extensively before beginning each reading.

Each unit contains 3 readings providing students with multiple opportunities to practice applying the skills and strategies.

Students learn how to use the skills and strategies by applying them to each text while they read it.

READING 

Fact or Fiction – Science

1 Maybe your mother or father told you. Maybe it was a teacher or a friend. You have heard these things since you were a child:

- If you drop a **coin**, like a penny, from a very tall building, you could kill a person who is standing below.
- Lightning never hits the same place twice.
- If you touch a baby bird or an egg, the mother will abandon it.

In fact, none of these is true. They are all science **myths**, that is, common beliefs that are actually false. Yet, these myths have persisted across generations, and many people continue to believe them. Probably the greatest number of these science myths are about our health. Here are a few that may be familiar.

2 *You can catch a cold if you go outside with wet hair or without a coat, or sleep near an open window.* In fact, there is no evidence – no supporting facts – for any of these beliefs. Colds are caused by a virus, not by temperature or weather. People who live in cold places don't catch more colds than people who live in warm places do. In fact, the opposite is true. Studies show that people resist colds better in cold weather. You are more likely to catch a cold in a warm house with a lot of other people than outside on a cold day.

WHILE YOU READ 1

Find a clue in this sentence that signals an example of a coin. Highlight the clue and example.

WHILE YOU READ 2

Find a clue in this sentence that signals the definition of *myths*. Highlight the clue and definition.

Lightning never hits the same place twice: true or false?

38 • UNIT 2

FROM THE SERIES AUTHORS

"Reading is an interactive process, in which readers use their knowledge of language, text organization, and the world to understand what they read."

"Reading is goal-oriented and strategic; good academic readers know when to use the right reading skills."

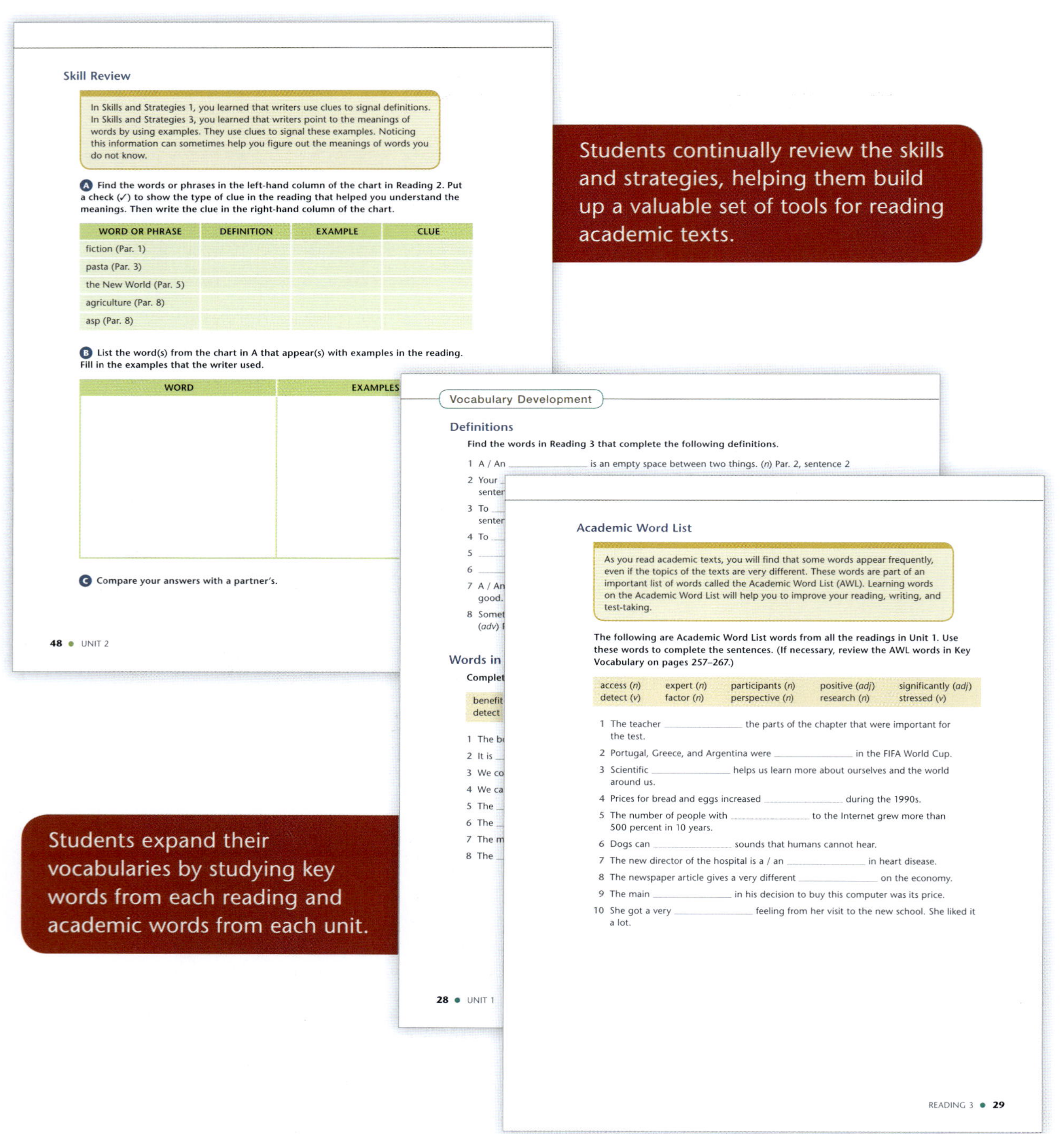

Skill Review

In Skills and Strategies 1, you learned that writers use clues to signal definitions. In Skills and Strategies 3, you learned that writers point to the meanings of words by using examples. They use clues to signal these examples. Noticing this information can sometimes help you figure out the meanings of words you do not know.

A Find the words or phrases in the left-hand column of the chart in Reading 2. Put a check (✓) to show the type of clue in the reading that helped you understand the meanings. Then write the clue in the right-hand column of the chart.

WORD OR PHRASE	DEFINITION	EXAMPLE	CLUE
fiction (Par. 1)			
pasta (Par. 3)			
the New World (Par. 5)			
agriculture (Par. 8)			
asp (Par. 8)			

B List the word(s) from the chart in A that appear(s) with examples in the reading. Fill in the examples that the writer used.

WORD	EXAMPLES

C Compare your answers with a partner's.

48 • UNIT 2

Students continually review the skills and strategies, helping them build up a valuable set of tools for reading academic texts.

Vocabulary Development

Definitions

Find the words in Reading 3 that complete the following definitions.

1 A / An ______________ is an empty space between two things. (*n*) Par. 2, sentence 2

2 Your ___ sentenc

3 To ___ sentenc

4 To ___

5 ___

6 ___

7 A / An good.

8 Somet (*adv*)

Words in

Complet

benefit detect

1 The b

2 It is

3 We co

4 We ca

5 The

6 The

7 The m

8 The

28 • UNIT 1

Academic Word List

As you read academic texts, you will find that some words appear frequently, even if the topics of the texts are very different. These words are part of an important list of words called the Academic Word List (AWL). Learning words on the Academic Word List will help you to improve your reading, writing, and test-taking.

The following are Academic Word List words from all the readings in Unit 1. Use these words to complete the sentences. (If necessary, review the AWL words in Key Vocabulary on pages 257–267.)

access (*n*)	expert (*n*)	participants (*n*)	positive (*adj*)	significantly (*adj*)
detect (*v*)	factor (*n*)	perspective (*n*)	research (*n*)	stressed (*v*)

1 The teacher ______________ the parts of the chapter that were important for the test.

2 Portugal, Greece, and Argentina were ______________ in the FIFA World Cup.

3 Scientific ______________ helps us learn more about ourselves and the world around us.

4 Prices for bread and eggs increased ______________ during the 1990s.

5 The number of people with ______________ to the Internet grew more than 500 percent in 10 years.

6 Dogs can ______________ sounds that humans cannot hear.

7 The new director of the hospital is a / an ______________ in heart disease.

8 The newspaper article gives a very different ______________ on the economy.

9 The main ______________ in his decision to buy this computer was its price.

10 She got a very ______________ feeling from her visit to the new school. She liked it a lot.

READING 3 • 29

Students expand their vocabularies by studying key words from each reading and academic words from each unit.

THE APPROACH

The *Making Connections* series offers a skills-based approach to academic reading instruction. Throughout each book, students are introduced to a variety of academic reading and vocabulary-building skills, which they then apply to high-interest, thematically related readings.

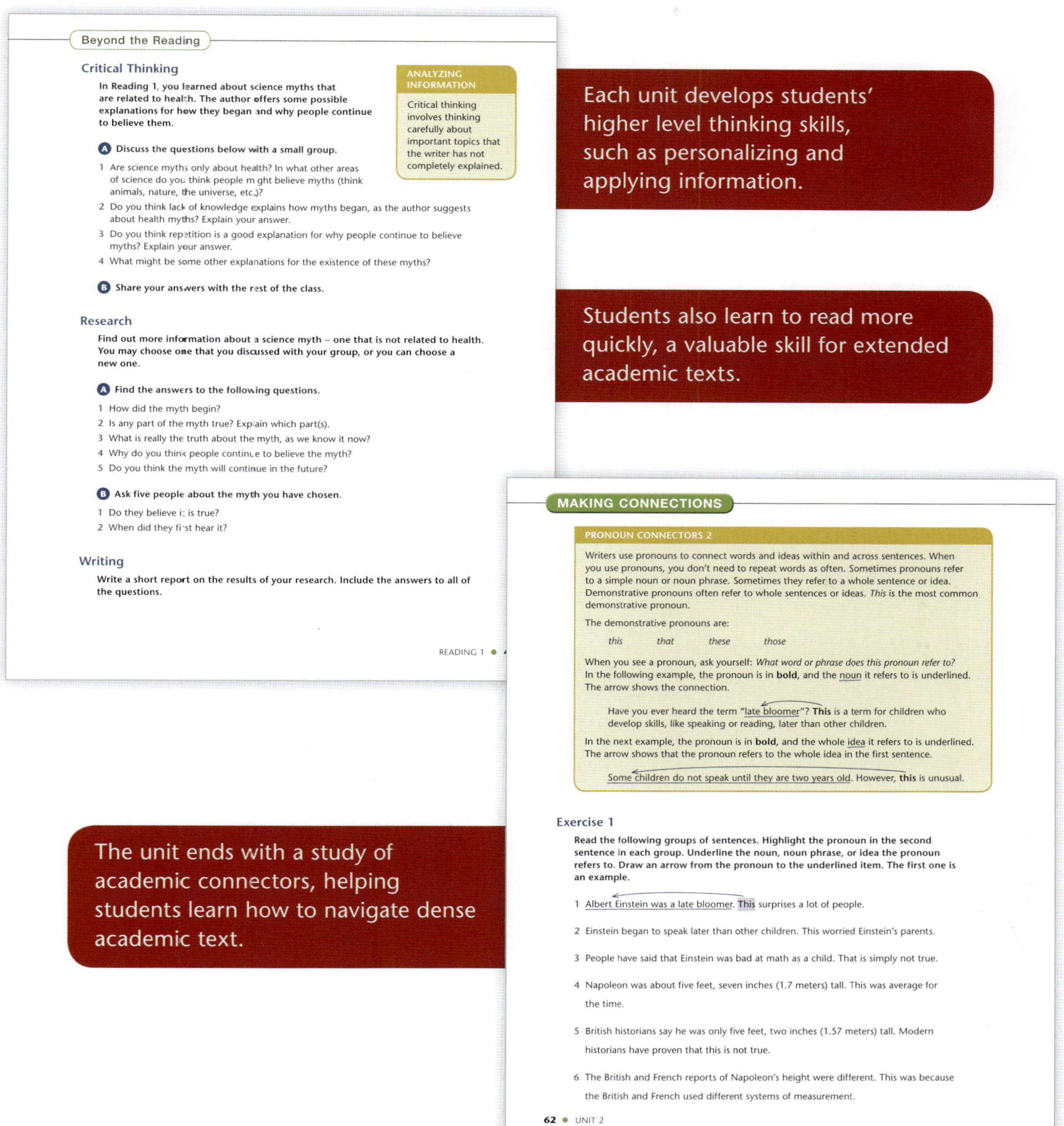

About the Authors

Jessica Williams is Professor and Head of the Department of Linguistics at the University of Illinois at Chicago, where she has taught in the MA TESOL program for almost 30 years. Her research area is second language acquisition, particularly the acquisition of academic literacy. She is an author of Cambridge University Press's *Making Connections* and *Academic Encounters* series.

David Wiese is a lecturer and materials developer at the University of California Berkeley and an adjunct professor at the University of San Francisco. He specializes in academic reading and writing for English language learners, and holds a master's degree in TESOL from Columbia University. He is the author of several texts on reading and writing for English language learners.

1 HUMAN BEHAVIOR

SKILLS AND STRATEGIES

- Finding the Meanings of Words: Definitions
- Finding the Topic of a Paragraph

SKILLS AND STRATEGIES 1

Finding the Meanings of Words: Definitions

Writers sometimes give definitions for difficult words. Definitions are explanations of words. They tell you what a word means. If you can find definitions in a reading, you do not need to stop reading and look up words in the dictionary.

Examples & Explanations

Psychology **means** "the study of human thinking and behavior."

Sometimes a writer gives a definition after a difficult word. In this sentence, the writer uses the verb *means* to signal the definition. Another important signal is the verb *be*.

psychology = the study of human thinking and behavior

There are many scientific words that students need to memorize, **that is**, learn and remember perfectly.

A phrase can also introduce a definition. A phrase is a group of words. In this sentence, the writer uses the phrase *that is*. Writers also use the phrase *in other words* to introduce definitions.

memorize = to learn something so that you remember it perfectly

The world of psychology is changing rapidly **(**very quickly**)** these days.

Sometimes punctuation shows definitions. This writer uses parentheses ( ) to show the definition. Commas (,) and dashes (–) can also show definitions.

rapidly = very quickly

Psychologists say you will learn faster if you have a good attitude. **This** is the opinions and feelings that you often have about something.

A definition can come in the next sentence. The writer introduces the definition with a pronoun, *this*. Writers also use the pronoun *these* to introduce definitions.

attitude = the opinions and feelings that you often have about something

Strategies

These strategies will help you find definitions while you read.

- When you find a difficult word, look for a definition in the reading.
- Look for words, phrases, and punctuation that writers often use to show definitions.
- Remember that a definition may not be in the same sentence as the difficult word. It might be in the next sentence.

Skill Practice 1

Read the following sentences. There is a definition for each word in bold. Highlight the word, phrase, or punctuation that shows the definition. The first one is an example.

1 Students go to school, belong to clubs, help their families and friends, and maybe even work part-time. They have a lot of **obligations**, in other words, things that they need to do for other people.

2 Because they are so busy, students often feel **pressure**. *Pressure* means "the feeling of having too many things to do."

3 A busy student can make an **agenda**. This is a list of the student's tasks and problems along with the date or time to deal with each one.

4 Agendas are helpful. Students can work **efficiently**, in other words, without wasting time.

5 Students will feel less pressure if they make agendas. They know when they will **complete** (finish) each obligation.

6 Many students **insist** – say something strongly and often – that they do not need an agenda. These students should think again.

7 Scientists did some research on agendas. They say that students who make agendas feel **exhausted**, that is, very tired, less often.

8 Scientists say that students who make agendas get better **grades**. These are their marks on tests and exams.

Skill Practice 2

Read the sentences in Skill Practice 1 again. What do the words in bold mean? Write a short definition on the blank line. Use the information you highlighted in Skill Practice 1 to help you. The first one is an example.

1 Students go to school, belong to clubs, help their families and friends, and maybe even work part-time. They have a lot of **obligations**, in other words, things that they need to do for other people.

obligations = *things that someone needs to do for other people*

2 Because they are so busy, students often feel pressure. *Pressure* means "the feeling of having too many things to do."

pressure = ______________________________

3 A busy student can make an **agenda.** This is a list of the student's tasks and problems along with the date or time to deal with each one.

agenda = ______________________________

4 Agendas are helpful. Students can work **efficiently**, in other words, without wasting time.

efficiently = ______________________________

5 Students will feel less pressure if they make agendas. They know when they will **complete** (finish) each obligation.

complete = ______________________________

6 Many students **insist** – say something strongly and often – that they do not need an agenda. These students should think again.

insist = ______________________________

7 Scientists did some research on agendas. They say that students who make agendas feel **exhausted**, that is, very tired, less often.

exhausted = ______________________________

8 Scientists say that students who make agendas get better **grades**. These are their marks on tests and exams.

grades = ______________________________

Before You Read

Connecting to the Topic

Read the definition of *procrastinate*. Then discuss the following questions with a partner.

procrastinate (*v*) to delay doing something that you don't want to do

1 Do you ever procrastinate? If so, describe a situation when you are likely to procrastinate.
2 How do you procrastinate? Do you watch television? Play a game on your computer?
3 Why do you think people procrastinate?
4 Do you think procrastination is bad? Are there any good reasons to procrastinate?

Previewing and Predicting

It is a good idea to look at parts of a reading quickly before you read it carefully. This is called *previewing*. Previewing gives you information about what you are going to read. If you know a little bit about the topic, it will be easier to understand the reading. One way to preview is to read the title and the first sentence of each paragraph.

A Read the title of Reading 1. Below are the first sentences of paragraphs 1–5 in Reading 1. Read these sentences. Then put a check (✓) next to the topics, listed below the sentences, that you think might be in the reading. Check three topics.

1 Your English assignment is due tomorrow, and you have not started it yet. (Par. 1)
2 In general, procrastination is postponing tasks that you should do now until sometime in the future. (Par. 2)
3 Most people feel guilty when they procrastinate. (Par. 3)
4 There is another positive perspective on procrastination. (Par. 4)
5 So, if you are postponing a task, ask yourself if you are procrastinating well. (Par. 5)

_____ a Scientific studies of procrastination
_____ b Good and bad things about procrastination
_____ c Reasons for procrastination
_____ d Instructions for procrastination
_____ e The history of procrastination
_____ f Stories about procrastination

B Compare your answers with a partner's.

While You Read

As you read, stop at the end of each sentence that contains words in bold. Then follow the instructions in the box in the margin.

Procrastination

1 Your English assignment is due tomorrow, and you have not started it yet. You should call your grandmother to thank her for the gift she sent last month. Your broken bicycle is leaning against the wall. It has been there for weeks. You should really repair it. But you are not doing any of those things. Instead, you are watching your favorite television program. You will do all those other things when the program is over – maybe. You are procrastinating. We all do it sometimes. Some of us do it more than others. Why do we procrastinate? Is it really so bad?

2 In general, procrastination is postponing tasks that you should do now until sometime in the future. Some psychologists say postponing – delaying – is the most important factor in procrastination, but they say it is not the only one. Usually, when you procrastinate, you postpone tasks even though you know that this could make things worse. There are several reasons why we do this. First, we prefer to do something **pleasant** – that is, something we enjoy – before something that is difficult or unpleasant. We often do this even when the difficult task is more important. Second, some people believe they only do their best work if they feel the pressure of meeting a deadline. To *meet a deadline* means to complete a task by the time it needs to be done. Finally, some people may postpone tasks because they are afraid they will not do a good enough job.

WHILE YOU READ 1

Find a clue in this sentence that signals the definition of *pleasant*. Is something that is pleasant (a) good or (b) bad?

3 Most people feel guilty when they procrastinate. They know they should not put off their tasks. They may miss a deadline, or they may not have enough time to do the task well. However, John Perry, a professor of philosophy, says that sometimes putting off tasks is a good idea. He has written a lot about procrastination. He says that people complete a lot of other important tasks while they are procrastinating. For example, you might clean the kitchen, pay your bills, or do another assignment instead of writing your English paper. This is sometimes called active procrastination. Active procrastinators often accomplish a lot.

4 There is another positive perspective on procrastination. Another expert in the field, Professor Frank Partnoy, says that when you postpone a task or decision, you may do a better job. When you procrastinate, you have time to consider the task carefully – really think about it hard – and make a plan for the best way to do it. You also have time to set **priorities**, that is, to decide which things are more important and which things are less important. You may not realize you are making plans or setting priorities. They happen while you are doing other tasks, like cleaning the kitchen or paying the bills. Or maybe they happen while you are taking a shower or exercising. We could say that they happen while are you are procrastinating. Professor Partnoy says we must accept procrastination as part of modern life. We will never have enough time to do everything we need to do, so we have to make choices. Since we all procrastinate, he says, we should learn to procrastinate well. Procrastinating well can often lead to thoughtful and creative work.

WHILE YOU READ 2

Find a clue in this sentence that signals the definition of *priorities*. Is setting priorities a (a) good idea or (b) bad idea?

5 So, if you are postponing a task, ask yourself if you are procrastinating well. Are you considering the task while you are doing other things? Are you getting some ideas about how to do it? If so, you may be procrastinating well, and you should not feel guilty about it. If you are just playing video games or eating pizza, you are probably not procrastinating well. You are just procrastinating. And you probably should feel guilty about it.

Reading Skill Development

Main Idea Check

The main idea of a reading is what the whole reading is about.

Which example shows the main idea of Reading 1?

a Kimi takes the bus home from work every day. It leaves her bus stop at 5:35. Kimi had a lot of work to do on Friday. She had to finish a report. She worked until 5:30 and ran to the bus. When she arrived at the bus stop at 5:37, the bus had just left.

b Mr. Xu, the head of the company, is going to visit Clara's office in two days. She has to write a very important sales report. She will give it to Mr. Xu when he comes. Clara has not started on the report. She is organizing the papers on her desk.

c Anwar has a meeting with his professor at 10:00 this morning. They are going to discuss his performance in class. The class has been very difficult for Anwar, and he is not doing very well. It is 9:45. Anwar is taking a shower.

A Closer Look

Look back at Reading 1 to answer the following questions.

1 According to psychologists, what are the two main factors in procrastination? Choose two answers. (Par. 2)

a Feelings of guilt about postponing tasks
b Postponing important tasks
c Knowing that postponing tasks is not a good idea
d Missing important deadlines

2 Procrastination makes most people feel guilty. **True or False?** (Par. 3)

3 What is something people do when they procrastinate actively? (Par. 3)

a They meet important deadlines.
b They don't worry about pressure.
c They work on other important tasks.
d They finish the task that they put off.

4 What is an example of setting priorities? (Par. 4)

a I will finish my math homework before I check my Facebook page.
b I will pay my bills today.
c I will not procrastinate anymore.
d I will organize my desk because it is hard to find the things I need.

5 What is Professor Partnoy's view? (Par. 4)

a We should all try to be more thoughtful and creative.
b We must accept our procrastination and try to do it well.
c We would be happier and more productive if we stopped procrastinating.
d People who procrastinate should feel guilty and try to improve.

Skill Review

In Skills and Strategies 1, you learned several strategies to help you figure out the definitions of words you do not know. You should look for words, phrases, and punctuation that signal a definition.

A **Find the words and phrases in the left-hand column of the chart in Reading 1. Put a check (✓) next to the type of clue in the reading that helped you understand the meanings.**

WORD OR PHRASE	*THAT IS* + DEFINITION	*MEANS* + DEFINITION *IS* + DEFINITION	PUNCTUATION
procrastination (*n*) Par. 2	✓		
postponing (*n*) Par. 2			✓
pleasant (*adj*) Par. 2	✓		
meet a deadline (*v*) Par. 2		✓	
consider (*v*) Par. 4			✓
set priorities (*v*) Par. 4	✓		

B **Find the words and phrases in the left-hand column of the chart in Reading 1. Write their definitions in the right-hand column.**

WORD OR PHRASE	DEFINITION
procrastination (*n*) Par. 2	posponing tasks
postponing (*v*) Par. 2	delaying
pleasant (*adj*) Par. 2	that is something we enjoy
meet a deadline (*v*) Par. 2	to complete a task.
consider (*v*) Par. 4	
set priorities (*v*) Par. 4	

Definitions

Find the words in Reading 1 that

1 ____________ are individua
sentence 1

2 To ____________ somethin 2

3 A / An ____________ is som nce 2

4 To ____________ somethin ng else.
(*v*) Par. 2, sentence 5

5 A / An ____________ is the day or time that you have to finish something. (*n*) Par. 2, sentence 7

6 A / An ____________ feeling is hopeful and happy. (*adj*) Par. 4, sentence 1

7 A / An ____________ is a point of view or a way of thinking about something. (*n*) Par. 4, sentence 1

8 A / An ____________ is a person who knows a lot about a subject. (*n*) Par. 4, sentence 2

Words in Context

Complete the sentences with words from Reading 1 in the box below.

accomplish	bill	guilty	put off
assignment	due	leaning	repair

1 We need to pay our electricity ____________ by Tuesday.

2 The children do not have a homework ____________ because it is a weekend.

3 She was tired so she was ____________ against the wall while she waited for the bus.

4 I feel ____________ because I forgot my friend's birthday.

5 You can ____________ a lot if you plan carefully and use your time well.

6 This window has been broken for a long time. You should ____________ it before the cold weather starts.

7 They decided to ____________ their vacation until they saved more money.

8 The library books are ____________ on February 17. You must return them by that date.

Critical Thinking

> **PERSONALIZING**
>
> Thinking about how new information applies to your own life can help you understand the text better.

In Reading 1, you learned about some of the reasons for procrastination. You also learned about a new concept – active procrastination.

Work with a partner to answer the following questions.

1 Do you procrastinate often? Describe the last time you procrastinated on a task.

2 What do you think are the most important reasons for your procrastination?

3 Do deadlines affect how you work? Explain your answer.

4 When you procrastinate on a task, what do you usually do instead of the task?

5 Are you an active procrastinator? Explain your answer.

6 Do you think postponing tasks results in better work in the end? Explain your answer based on your own experience.

Research

A **Do some research into your own procrastination. Fill in the chart for your activities for 48 hours. An example is done for you.**

TASK	FORM OF PROCRASTINATION	HOW LONG DID I PROCRASTINATE?	HOW LONG DID THE TASK TAKE?	WAS THIS ACTIVE PROCRASTINATION?
My physics homework	*Watching a movie*	*2 hours*	*45 minutes*	*No*

B **Share your results with your classmates.**

Writing

Write a short report on what you found out about procrastination among your classmates. What kind of procrastination was most common? Are your classmates active procrastinators?

Before You Read

Connecting to the Topic

Discuss the following questions with a partner.

1 What do you think is the best way to remember a name or a fact? Do you have a special way to do this?
2 What do you do when you forget a fact, a name, or an important number?
3 Do you take a lot of photographs at important events? What do you do with them after the event is over?
4 What do you think is the purpose of photographs?

Previewing and Predicting

> Remember that reading the first sentence in each paragraph can help you to predict what the reading will be about.

A Below are the first sentences of paragraphs 1–5 in Reading 2. Read these sentences. Then put a check (✓) next to the topics, listed below the sentences, that you think might be in the reading. Check four topics.

1 Who directed the 1954 Godzilla movie? (Par. 1)
2 Before we had access to digital technology, we had different ways to remember things. (Par. 2)
3 Some psychologists thought technology might be causing some important changes in how we store information in our minds. (Par. 3)
4 The impact of technology goes beyond our ability to remember facts and written information. (Par. 4)
5 A recent study suggests that taking photographs may affect our visual memory. (Par. 5)

_____ a How we remember things
_____ b The effect of computers on memory
_____ c The best movies in history
_____ d The history of computers
_____ e The psychology of memory
_____ f The effect of photographs on memory
_____ g The best way to take photographs

B Compare your answers with a partner's.

While You Read

As you read, stop at the end of each sentence that contains words in bold. Then follow the instructions in the box in the margin.

READING 2

Memory and New Technology

1 Who directed the 1954 Godzilla movie? What is the largest city in Kenya? Who is the author (the writer) of the Harry Potter books? What is your sister-in-law's phone number? If you are not sure of the answers, you will probably consult your computer to find out. With access to digital technology and the Internet, we can get all kinds of information right away. This instant access to information is interesting to scientists who study human memory. *Memory* means "the ability to remember facts, events, and **people**." Is digital technology changing the way our memory works?

WHILE YOU READ 1

Find a clue in this sentence that signals the definition of *memory*. Highlight the clue and the definition.

2 Before we had access to digital technology, we had different ways to remember things. First, we depended on other people to remember things for us. For example, perhaps, in the past, you depended on your wife or your mother to remember birthdays in your family. Perhaps someone in your office remembered important information for your business. In addition, in the past, we depended more on printed material – books, magazines, and newspapers. If we forgot something, we could just go back to them. We did not keep all of this information in our heads. Information was stored in these materials just as information is now stored on the Internet.

3 Some psychologists thought technology might be causing some important changes in how we store information in our minds. So they did an experiment, that is, a scientific study, to find out. In this experiment, the psychologists asked two groups of people to find the answers to questions. They told the first group they would have access to this information later. They told the other group they would not have access. The researchers discovered that people who knew they would be able to find information again did not remember it very well. They remembered more about where they found the information than what they found. The people who knew they would not have access to the information again remembered more. The scientists called this the Google Effect. They stress that these changes are not necessarily negative. In fact, knowing where to find information is a very important skill.

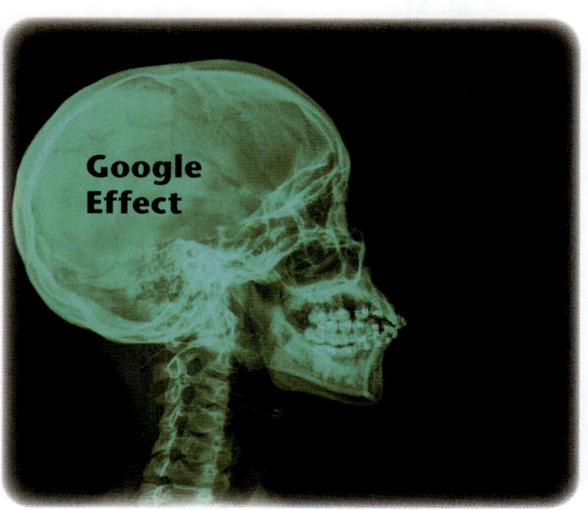

4 The impact of technology goes beyond our ability to remember facts and written information. It also affects our memory of visual information. Today, many phones have cameras, so we take photographs more

often than we did in the past. We take pictures when we want to preserve a memory, for example, an important event or a party. But we also use photographs to support our memory. If we want to remember a hairstyle or the color of a dress in the store, we take a picture. We even take photographs of words. Instead of copying a list or a sentence, we just take a picture of it.

5 A recent study suggests that taking photographs may affect our visual memory. In the study, the researcher took two groups of people to an art **gallery** – a small museum. She asked them to notice some details about the works of art. She told the first group to look at the art for a few minutes. She told the second group to notice the same details, but she told them to take photographs. Later, she asked both groups to remember these details. The people who took photographs did not remember the details as well the group that only looked at the art. Based on her findings, the scientist offered some advice. The next time you are enjoying yourself and you want to remember the people or the place, don't use your camera. Just open your eyes.

WHILE YOU READ 2

Find a clue in this sentence that signals the definition of *gallery*. Highlight the clue and the definition.

Using cell phone cameras may affect our visual memory.

Reading Skill Development

Main Idea Check

> The main idea of a reading is what the whole reading is about.

Which example shows the main idea of Reading 2?

a Marco is writing a paper for his political science class. He has done a lot of research, but he has not taken very good notes. Now he needs some information to support the argument in his paper. He remembers that he read an article online last week. It had a lot of useful facts. He looks up the article and adds the facts to his paper.

b Olga had a birthday party last week. More than 40 people came, but a few could not come. Everyone had a lot of fun. Many of her guests took pictures with their cell phones. The day after the party, everyone posted photos on Facebook and Instagram. The photographs helped Olga share her birthday with the people who could not come to her party.

c Mr. Cho always forgets people's names. It embarrasses him when he meets people at work and he can't remember what their names are. He decided to use his computer to help him. He collected photographs of all the people at the company where he works. He studies the photographs and the names for five minutes every day. His memory is improving, and now he is not embarrassed as often.

A Closer Look

Look back at Reading 2 to answer the following questions.

1 How did people remember things before computers and the Internet? Choose two answers. (Par. 2)

a They stored information in lists.
b They looked things up in books.
c They had better memories in the past.
d They relied on other people.

2 Match the group in the experiment with what they did. One of the groups matches with two letters. (Par. 3)

	Group	Performance
____	1 The group knew that they would have access to information again.	a remembered less information
____	2 The group knew that they would *not* have access to information again.	b remembered where they found information
		c remembered more information

3 Find one good thing and one bad thing about the Google Effect in the statements below. Mark one item with + (good) and one item with – (bad) in the blanks. (Par. 3)

____ a People don't pay close attention to what they read.
____ b People don't try to remember things as well as in the past.
____ c People spend more time on their computers than with other people.
____ d People don't have to work as hard anymore.
____ e People have become very good at finding information on the Internet.

4 Taking photographs helps us remember details. **True or False?** (Par. 5)

5 Why does the author include the information in paragraph 5?

a To demonstrate the importance of cameras
b To provide clear examples of situations in which people take photographs
c To compare photographs with computers
d To show the impact of technology on different kinds of memory

6 Human memory can change under different conditions and in different situations. **True or False?** (whole reading)

Skill Review

In Skills and Strategies 1, you learned that writers sometimes include the definitions of words they use. They may also include signals of these definitions. You also learned that you may need to look in the sentence after the new word to find its definition.

A Find the words and phrases in the left-hand column of the chart in Reading 2. Decide whether the definition is in the same sentence as the word or in the next sentence. Put a (✓) in the correct column.

WORD OR PHRASE	SAME SENTENCE	NEXT SENTENCE
author (*n*) Par. 1		
memory (*n*) Par. 1		
experiment (*n*) Par. 3		
gallery (*n*) Par. 5		

B Find the words in the left-hand column in Reading 2. Write their definitions in the right-hand column.

WORD OR PHRASE	DEFINITION
author (*n*) Par. 1	
memory (*n*) Par. 1	
experiment (*n*) Par. 3	
gallery (*n*) Par. 5	

Vocabulary Development

Definitions

Find the words in Reading 2 that complete the following definitions.

1 A / An ________ answer to a question comes immediately after it is asked. (*adj*) Par. 1, sentence 7

2 To ________ is to keep something for use in the future. (*v*) Par. 2, sentence 8

3 To ________ something means to give it special importance. (*v*) Par. 3, sentence 10

4 Something that is ________ is not hopeful or happy. It shows a bad side. (*adj*) Par. 3, sentence 10

5 A / An ________ is a strong effect. (*n*) Par. 4, sentence 1

6 To ________ something means to have an influence on it. (*v*) Par. 4, sentence 2

7 ________ is related to seeing. (*adj*) Par. 4, sentence 2

8 Something that is ________ happened just a short time ago. (*adj*) Par. 5, sentence 1

Word Families

A word family is a set of different parts of speech, or word forms, that have similar meanings. Some parts of speech are *verbs*, *nouns*, and *adjectives*. When you learn a word, learn the other words in its word family, too. This will help you increase your vocabulary.

A The words in bold in the chart are from Reading 2. The words next to them are from the same word family. Study and learn these words.

NOUN	VERB
access (Par. 1)	*access*
advice (Par. 5)	*advise*
consultation	***consult*** (Par. 1)
preservation	***preserve*** (Par. 4)
support	***support*** (Par. 4)

B Choose the correct form of the words from the chart to complete the following sentences. Use the correct singular and plural noun forms.

1 After a ________ with his doctor, he decided to take the new medicine.

2 The president thanked the people in the crowd for their ________.

3 In many parts of the country, people do not have ________ to the Internet.

4 I asked my friends for ________ about hotels in London.

5 We should ________ an expert before we make this important decision.

6 The preservation of old buildings has become important in many cities.

7 My parents always support me even when I make bad decisions.

8 I don't know anything about computers, so I cannot advise you about how to fix yours.

9 I can access the files on my office computer from my computer at home.

10 There are many ways to preserve food, including freezing and drying.

Beyond the Reading

Critical Thinking

In Reading 2, you learned about the possible changes in memory and behavior in response to new technology. One claim is that we behave differently when we have easy access to information.

> **APPLYING INFORMATION**
>
> You use critical thinking skills when you apply information you have just learned to new situations.

A Discuss the following questions with a partner or small group of classmates.

1 How has easy and rapid access to information changed the way people study and learn in school?

2 How has this access changed the way people do their jobs?

3 What kinds of jobs have changed or will change the most as a result of easy and rapid access to information?

4 What kinds of other activities have changed? Give some examples and explain why you think they have changed.

B Share your answers and examples with the rest of the class.

Research

Do your own experiment on visual memory. You will need a camera.

A Invite two friends to join you in your research. Choose a place, such as a museum, café, or park. Ask both friends to try to remember the details they see. Ask only one of them to take a picture of it.

B Later, you will ask them both to remember some details. Write three questions to ask them:

____

____

____

C The following day, ask them both to remember the details of what they saw. Ask them the questions you wrote.

Writing

Write a short summary of your research. Include the answers to these questions:

- Who remembered more details?
- Did they remember different details?
- What do you conclude about visual memory from this experiment?

Finding the Topic of a Paragraph

Most paragraphs have one topic. The topic is what the paragraph is all about. It is the general idea that connects all the sentences in the paragraph. Knowing the topic of a paragraph helps you understand the whole paragraph.

Examples & Explanations

People tell lies all the time. But not all lies are the same. In fact, there are three types of lies.

The topic of this paragraph is *lies*. It is what the paragraph is all about.

One type of lie is a half-truth. A half-truth combines some information that is true with some that is not. For example, we tell a story from our lives but change some details. We may leave out the parts of the story that we do not like. We may make ourselves sound smarter, stronger, or more skilled than we really are. With a half-truth, we are lying, but not completely.

The topic of this paragraph is *half-truths*. Writers often give the topic in the beginning of a paragraph.

Another type of lie is a white lie. We tell white lies when we do not want to hurt someone's feelings. For example, we tell our friend that his bad haircut looks great or that he is a better singer than he really is. People tell white lies like these all the time.

The topic of this paragraph is *white lies*. The topic is often a key term that the writer repeats many times in the paragraph. For example, in this paragraph, the writer says *white lies* three times.

White lies and half-truths might not cause serious problems. They may not hurt anyone. However, another type of lie – a fabrication – often causes serious trouble, especially if it is about another person. A fabrication is not true at all. We usually tell fabrications to protect ourselves. For example, we might break a window and say that someone else did it. We might go to a party but say we went to the library. When we tell fabrications, we often feel uncomfortable. That is because they are the biggest type of lie.

The topic is often in the first sentence of a paragraph, but not always. In this paragraph, the topic is *fabrications*. The writer states the topic in the third sentence. We know this is the topic because the rest of the paragraph is about fabrications and why they are serious.

Strategies

These strategies will help you find the topics of paragraphs while you read.

- As you read a paragraph, ask yourself: *What is this paragraph all about?*
- Pay attention to the first sentence of the paragraph. It often states the topic.
- Find a key term that the writer repeats often. Key terms are usually nouns and verbs.
- Remember that writers do not always tell the topic in the first sentence of the paragraph.

Skill Practice 1

Read the paragraphs. Then look at the three choices for possible topics. Choose the one that best states the topic of each paragraph. Discuss your answers with a partner.

1 Do you want to know if someone is telling the truth or not? Just look at his or her behavior. Experts say people's behavior changes when they lie. Here are a few common behaviors that you can look for.

Topic:

a Truth
b Behavior
c Experts

2 One common behavior is not answering a question. When people do not want to tell the truth about something, they may change the subject or stop to think for a long time. By not answering the question immediately, they give themselves time to think of a good lie.

Topic:

a Changing the subject
b Thinking of a good lie
c Not answering a question

3 Another common behavior is giving too much information. If someone talks for a long time and gives a lot of unnecessary details, it may mean he or she is lying. Liars think that all the talk and details make them seem honest and open.

Topic:

a Giving too much information
b Talking for a long time
c Seeming honest and open

4 We can often know that people are lying just from the way that they answer a question. However, the best way to tell if people are lying is from their voice. When people lie, their voice often changes. They speak in a slightly higher voice than normal. Experts say that this is the best way to know that someone is lying.

Topic:

a The way that people answer a question

b Experts' opinions on lying

c Changes in the voice

Skill Practice 2

Read the paragraphs. What is the topic of each paragraph? Write your answers on the blank lines. Discuss your answers with a partner.

1 The company Honest Tea makes cold tea drinks. Honest Tea wanted more people to try its products. Many companies make tea drinks, so Honest Tea had to do something special to get people's attention.

Topic: ____________________

2 The company decided to do an experiment (a test to get information) in cities around the United States. They left bottles of Honest Tea in public places along with a box with a sign that said, "Please pay $1." People could choose to pay, or they could just take the tea. The idea of the experiment was to test people's honesty.

Topic: ____________________

3 So what did the experiment show? The results were very surprising. Almost everyone paid for the tea. In some places, 100 percent of people paid! Honest Tea was happy with the results. They did not expect people to be so honest. What's more, their tea got a lot of attention. For Honest Tea, that was the best result of all.

Topic: ____________________

Before You Read

Connecting to the Topic

Discuss the following questions with a partner.

1 How many lies do you think the average person tells every day?
2 Why do you think most people lie?
3 Are there some situations in which you think it is better to lie than tell the truth?
4 Can you tell when someone else is lying? Explain your answer.

Previewing and Predicting

Skills and Strategies 2 discussed the topics of paragraphs. Longer readings sometimes have sections as well as paragraphs. A section can be made up of one or more paragraphs. When you preview a longer reading, look to see if it has sections. Each section may have a heading. These headings can help you predict what the reading will be about. Remember that reading first sentences can also help you make predictions about the reading.

A Read the headings for the three sections of Reading 3. Then read the first sentence in each paragraph. Decide what you will read about in each section. Then write the number of the section (*I–III*) next to the topics that you think will be in those sections.

SECTION	TOPIC
	A professor who studies lies
	What makes people lie more
	What makes people lie less
	Why people lie
	Why lying is sometimes easier than telling the truth

B Compare your answers with a partner's.

While You Read

As you read, stop at the end of each sentence that contains words in bold. Then follow the instructions in the box in the margin.

Lying

1 As children, we are told that we should not lie. Yet, experts say that most of us lie all the time. We even lie about lying when we say we don't lie very much. Children begin to lie when they are very young – perhaps as young as two years old. And we keep lying throughout our lives. Telling two or three lies in a 10-minute conversation is not unusual. They are usually not big, serious lies. We tell ourselves that they **don't matter** – that they are not so important. We call them *white lies* because they don't really hurt anyone.

WHILE YOU READ 1

Find a clue in this sentence that signals the definition of the phrase *don't matter*. Highlight the clue and definition.

I. Reasons for Lying

2 We say we should not lie, but most of us lie quite a lot. Why is there a big gap between *should* and *do*? Probably because lying is very useful – so useful that we are willing to break our own rules. We lie for many reasons, but the primary reason is to protect someone or something. We lie to protect ourselves, to protect our interests, and to protect our image. We lie to avoid punishment and to make others think we are intelligent or important. However, another reason we lie is to protect others. We lie because the truth would be too difficult or painful for them. People don't want to hear that they look old or that they did a bad job. They don't want to hear that their new shirt is ugly. Telling the truth all the time can be rude or unkind. Lying helps us maintain and protect our relationships. For these reasons, we even teach our children that it is sometimes necessary to tell these white **lies**.

WHILE YOU READ 2

What is the topic of paragraph 2? Highlight the sentence that contains the topic.

II. Research on Lying

3 However, protecting ourselves and others is not the whole story. The decision to tell a lie is not always logical. You might think, for example, that people are less likely to lie if they believe someone will discover their lie. You might also think that people are more likely to lie if they will receive money as a result. Yet, research suggests that these are not the situations in which people are most likely to lie.

4 Psychology professor Dan Ariely has studied more than 30,000 people in an effort to discover what factors are most important in lying. He has conducted several experiments. In the first experiment, he gave participants a piece of paper with 20 sets of numbers. (See Figure 1.1.) He asked them to try to find two numbers with a sum of 10 in each set. Participants had five minutes to complete the task. Then they had to report how many sums of 10 they found. Ariely paid them for each one. Most participants found four. Then he told participants in one group to tear up their papers after the experiment but before they reported their results. Suddenly everyone in that group became a little bit smarter. They found an average of six sums. If they had an opportunity to lie, they did.

Figure 1.1 Which two numbers in each set add up to ten?

1.69	1.82	2.91
4.67	4.81	3.05
5.82	5.06	4.28
6.36	5.19	4.57

1.00	1.82	2.01
4.87	4.81	3.05
5.82	5.08	4.26
8.38	5.19	4.57

III. Factors That Increase or Decrease Lying

5 Then, in a second experiment, Ariely changed the conditions to find out what would influence participants to lie more or less. He found that some conditions made very little difference. Almost everyone lied a bit to get a little more money, but very few people lied a lot to get a lot more money. In fact, participants were more likely to lie if the reward was plastic money. The probability of discovery did not matter to them either. In a third experiment, they tore up only half of their scores. This condition increased the probability of discovery, but the amount of lying did not decrease significantly.

6 Some conditions did affect the amount of lying, however. Ariely conducted a final set of experiments and found the following results: If participants saw that someone else lied and got more money, they lied more. If Ariely told them that someone else would benefit if they performed well, they lied more. Participants were also more likely to lie if they were tired. On the other hand, when the researcher told participants in the beginning of the experiment that it was important to be honest about their performance, they lied much less. They also lied less when they had to sign a paper that said their answers were the **truth**.

7 So, with all of these lies, how can you know if someone is lying to you? We are actually better at lying than at realizing when other people are lying. Most people can detect lies only about half the time. However, if the research on lying is correct, it is likely that you hear many lies every day without realizing it.

WHILE YOU READ 3

What is the topic of paragraph 6? Highlight the sentence that shows the topic.

Main Idea Check

The main idea of a reading is what the whole reading is about.

Read the statements below. Which of these statements are important ideas from Reading 3? Choose two answers.

a Lying is bad.
b Most people lie.
c People lie for many different reasons.
d People lie more now than in the past.
e Adults lie more than children.

A Closer Look

Look back at Reading 3 to answer the following questions.

1 Very young children already know how to lie. **True or False?** (Par. 1)

2 Which of the following statements explain why people lie? Choose three answers. (Par. 2)
 a People lie to be kind to others.
 b People lie because they are scared of what might happen if they tell the truth.
 c People lie because their parents did not teach them to tell the truth.
 d People lie to show they are important.
 e People lie to get money.

3 According to Professor Ariely's research, when do people lie? (Par. 4)
 a They lie when they think no one will find out.
 b They lie when it doesn't matter if someone will find out.
 c They lie when they get a chance to lie.
 d They lie when they feel guilty.

4 The math problems in Professor Ariely's experiment were difficult to finish in five minutes. Why do you think he chose this task for his research? (Par. 4)
 a He believed that math skills are related to lying.
 b He didn't want his participants to become bored.
 c He wanted to test the participants' math skills.
 d He wanted to give participants a chance to lie.

5 What was one surprising result of Professor Ariely's second experiment? (Par. 5)
 a Money did not make much difference in how much people lie.
 b People are more likely to lie to someone they like than to someone they don't like.
 c People are not afraid to lie.
 d Most people lie several times every day.

6 People can detect when a person is lying most of the time. **True or False?** (Par. 7)

7 What are two pieces of evidence that people lie not for themselves, but for others? Choose two answers. (whole reading)

a They lie when they don't want to be unkind to others.
b They lie when they want others to respect them.
c They lie more when they think it will help others.
d They lie less when they think others will find out.

Skill Review

In Skills and Strategies 2, you learned that every paragraph has a topic. Knowing the topic can help you understand the paragraph.

A 1 Reread paragraph 2 of Reading 3. Aside from the words *lie* and *lying* and the verb *be*, what are the most frequent noun and the most frequent verb in this paragraph?

noun ______________________ verb ______________________

2 Reread paragraph 5 of Reading 3. What are the two most frequent nouns in this paragraph?

______________________ ______________________

B Reread the beginning of each paragraph of Reading 3. Based on this information and what you learned in A, match the topics of paragraphs 2–7 to the list below. Write the number of the correct paragraph on the blank line.

1 ____ Factors that don't affect lying
2 ____ Protection as a reason for lying
3 ____ An experiment to find out about lying
4 ____ Conditions that increase or decrease lying
5 ____ Detecting lies
6 ____ Some unexpected results of research into lying

C Compare your answers with a partner's.

Vocabulary Development

Definitions

Find the words in Reading 3 that complete the following definitions.

1 A / An ______________ is an empty space between two things. (*n*) Par. 2, sentence 2

2 Your ______________ is the way that other people think of you. (*n*) Par. 2, sentence 5

3 To ______________ something is to stay away from it or not do it. (*v*) Par. 2, sentence 6

4 To ______________ something is to continue to have it. (*v*) Par. 2, sentence 12

5 ______________ is serious study about a topic. (*n*) Par. 3, last sentence

6 ______________ are people who take part in an activity. (*n pl*) Par. 4, sentence 3

7 A / An ______________ is something that you get in exchange for doing something good. (*n*) Par. 5, sentence 4

8 Something that decreases ______________ goes down by a large amount. (*adv*) Par. 5, last sentence

Words in Context

Complete the sentences with words from Reading 3 in the box below.

benefit	logical	probability	rude
detect	primary	punishment	sum

1 The boy's mother took away his toy as a ______________ after he hit his sister.

2 It is ______________ to speak when someone else is talking.

3 We could ______________ the smell of gas in the house, so we did not go in.

4 We can all ______________ from this experience and learn from our mistakes.

5 The ______________ of snow in Toronto is higher in January than in April.

6 The ______________ of 13 and 27 is 40.

7 The most ______________ place to put the sign is where many people can see it.

8 The ______________ reason for our trip is to visit our grandparents.

Academic Word List

As you read academic texts, you will find that some words appear frequently, even if the topics of the texts are very different. These words are part of an important list of words called the Academic Word List (AWL). Learning words on the Academic Word List will help you to improve your reading, writing, and test-taking.

The following are Academic Word List words from all the readings in Unit 1. Use these words to complete the sentences. (If necessary, review the AWL words in Key Vocabulary on pages 257–267.)

access (*n*)	expert (*n*)	participants (*n*)	positive (*adj*)	significantly (*adj*)
detect (*v*)	factor (*n*)	perspective (*n*)	research (*n*)	stressed (*v*)

1 The teacher __________ the parts of the chapter that were important for the test.

2 Portugal, Greece, and Argentina were __________ in the FIFA World Cup.

3 Scientific __________ helps us learn more about ourselves and the world around us.

4 Prices for bread and eggs increased __________ during the 1990s.

5 The number of people with __________ to the Internet grew more than 500 percent in 10 years.

6 Dogs can __________ sounds that humans cannot hear.

7 The new director of the hospital is a / an __________ in heart disease.

8 The newspaper article gives a very different __________ on the economy.

9 The main __________ in his decision to buy this computer was its price.

10 She got a very __________ feeling from her visit to the new school. She liked it a lot.

Beyond the Reading

Critical Thinking

In Reading 3, you learned about the reasons why people lie and the conditions under which they are more likely to lie.

> **CLARIFYING CONCEPTS**
>
> Critical thinking includes exploring an idea in a text by thinking about how it would fit into a different context.

A Work with a partner. Read the list of lies below. Then rank them on a scale of 1–3. A ranking of 1 means that this kind of lie is always acceptable. A ranking of 2 means it is sometimes acceptable. A ranking of 3 means it is never acceptable.

1 Mr. A tells his boss that he finished an important project.
2 Ms. B tells her friend that she likes her new haircut.
2 Mr. C tells a police officer that he did not see anything.
3 Ms. D tells her parents that she got home by 10:00 the night before.
3 Mr. E tells his teacher he cannot take a test because he is sick.

B Explain your rankings to the rest of the class.

Research

Make a chart that shows your class results. Look at the example:

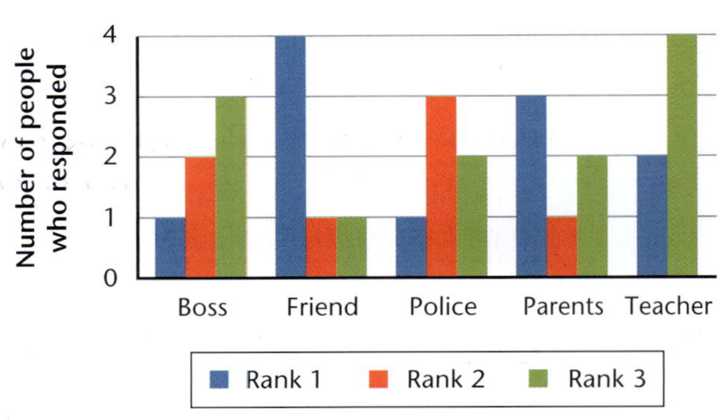

Writing

Write a short summary of your results. Explain why you think each lie was ranked in a particular way.

> **Improving Your Reading Speed**
>
> Good readers read quickly and still understand most of what they read.
>
> **A** Read the instructions and strategies for Improving Your Reading Speed in Appendix 3 on page 270.
>
> **B** Choose one of the readings in this unit. Read it without stopping. Time how long it takes you to finish the text in minutes and seconds. Enter the time in the chart on page 271. Then calculate your reading speed in number of words per minute.

PRONOUN CONNECTORS

Writers use pronouns to connect words and ideas w
When you use a pronoun, you don't need to repeat
using pronouns gives the reader extra work to do b
find the words that the pronouns refer to.

Some common pronouns are:

he *she* *it* *they* *him* *her* *then*

When you see a pronoun, ask yourself: *What word c*
back to find it. In the following example, the prono
or noun phrase it refers to is underlined. The arrow

Sometimes older people have trouble remembering. **They** may forget the names of people and places.

As people grow older, sometimes **their** memories are not as strong as in the past.

Exercise 1

Read the following groups of sentences. Highlight the pronoun(s) in the second sentence in each group. Underline the noun or noun phrase each pronoun refers to. Draw an arrow from the pronoun to the underlined items. The first one is an example.

1 Some people have incredible memories. They can remember long lists of numbers.

2 Every year, there is a World Memory Championship. People come from all over the world to participate in it.

3 Dominic O'Brien won the first championship in 1991. He won again the next year it was held in 1993, but another person beat him in 1994.

4 O'Brien won the Championship several more times. His record remains the best.

5 In 2011, a 21-year-old Chinese man won the championship. He listened to 400 numbers and remembered 300 of them.

6 You may not have a good memory now. However, if you practice, you can improve it and perhaps participate in the championship next year.

Exercise 2

Make a clear paragraph by putting sentences A, B, and C into the best order after the numbered sentence. Look for pronouns to help you choose the order. Write the letters in the correct order on the blank lines.

1 You have probably seen a polygraph on television or in a movie. ___ ___ ___

- **A** It can help them find out who is lying and who is telling the truth.
- **B** The police use it with people who they think are criminals.
- **C** It is a machine that is sometimes called a lie detector.

2 The first polygraph appeared in the beginning of the twentieth century. ___ ___ ___

- **A** He wanted officers in his department to try out his invention.
- **B** They tested it for the first time in 1921.
- **C** It was invented by John Larson, who was a police officer.

3 The first polygraph machine was quite simple. ___ ___ ___

- **A** It only measured users' blood pressure.
- **B** Later, more advanced machines could take other measurements.
- **C** They measured breathing, heart rate, and perspiration.

4 The polygraph test is an important tool. ___ ___ ___

- **A** He killed at least 48 people, but he fooled the polygraph.
- **B** They can pass the test even when they lie, as Gary Ridgeway did in 1987.
- **C** However, it does not always work on good liars.

5 Long ago in China and India, grains of rice were used to detect lies. ___ ___ ___

- **A** If his mouth was dry, the rice stuck to his tongue.
- **B** They were placed in a man's mouth.
- **C** People thought his dry mouth showed he was a liar.

2 FACT OR FICTION

SKILLS AND STRATEGIES

- Finding the Meanings of Words: Examples
- Finding the Main Idea of a Paragraph

Examples: (definition) such as, for example, like

Definition: means, in another words, that is.

eanings of Words:

es 1 on page 2, writers often give
times writers give examples, not direct
l information to show what a word means.
oking at examples, you do not need to

The reader may not know what *diet* means. The writer shows the meaning with examples of diets in the next sentence: *eating no rice or bread* and *eating fish instead of red meat*. These examples are introduced by a signal: *for example.* Writers also use the signals *such as* and *like* to introduce examples.

diet = a plan to eat only a small amount of special types of food in order to lose weight

You often hear about health topics in **the media**. Newspapers, TV, and websites talk about how to be healthy.

The writer gives examples of the media without using a signal word or phrase. Notice that the examples form a list: *newspapers, TV,* and *websites.* Lists often contain examples.

the media = all the organizations – like newspapers, TV, and websites – that give people news and information

Strategies

These strategies will help you find the meanings of words while you read.

- When you see a word you do not know, do not stop reading. Finish reading the sentence with the unknown word, and read the next sentence as well.
- Look for examples in those sentences. Remember that writers use signals like *for example, such as,* and *like* to introduce examples.
- Look for a list. A list could contain examples of an unknown word.
- Use the examples to help you understand the unknown word.

Skill Practice 1

Read the following sentence pairs. Highlight the examples that are given for each word in bold. The first one is an example.

1 Some people believe cold weather makes them sick. They put on warm **garments** like coats and sweaters every time they go outside.

2 There is an old saying "an apple a day keeps the doctor away" In fact, apples are good for **organs** such as the heart and brain.

3 There are many different **treatments** for colds, for example, chicken soup, orange juice, and extra sleep. Which one works best?

4 Children need **nutritious** food, like fruit, nuts, and vegetables. It makes them stronger and healthier.

5 Is it true that **stressful** situations can give you health problems? I sometimes feel sick during important exams, presentations, and job interviews.

6 Some people think **spicy** food causes stomach problems. They will not eat things such as hot red peppers.

7 Psychologists say it is good for our health to **complain**. After we talk about our problems at work or in marriage, we usually feel better.

8 My parents **warn** me about health problems. They always say, "don't do this," "be careful about that," or "that's bad for you."

Skill Practice 2

Read the sentences from Skill Practice 1 again. What do the words in bold mean? Write your answers on the blank lines. The first one is an example.

1 Some people believe cold weather makes them sick. They put on warm **garments** like coats and sweaters every time they go outside.

garments = *pieces of clothing*

2 There is an old saying "an apple a day keeps the doctor away" In fact, apples are good for **organs** such as the heart and brain.

organs = ______________________

3 I have heard about many different **treatments** for colds, for example, chicken soup, orange juice, and extra sleep. Which one works best?

treatments = ______________________

4 Children need **nutritious** food, like fruit, nuts, and vegetables. It makes them stronger and healthier.

nutritious = ______________________________

5 Is it true that **stressful** situations can give you health problems? I sometimes feel sick during important exams, presentations, and job interviews.

stressful = ______________________________

6 Some people think **spicy** food causes stomach problems. They will not eat things such as hot red peppers.

spicy = ______________________________

7 Psychologists say it is good for our health to **complain**. After we talk about our problems at work or in marriage, we usually feel better.

complain = ______________________________

8 My parents **warn** me about health problems. They always say "don't do this," "be careful about that," or "that's bad for you."

warn = ______________________________

Before You Read

Connecting to the Topic

Discuss the following questions with a partner.

1 Did you ever learn a "fact" about science that was not really true? Explain your answer.

2 Did you ever learn a "fact" about health or medicine, for example, what kinds of things can make you sick, that was not really true? Explain your answer.

3 People often pass on inaccurate information about science and health. Why do you think these ideas are repeated over and over?

Previewing and Predicting

One way to preview is to notice the way the reading looks. Do any words or sentences appear in bold or italics? These are probably important. Are any sections of the reading set apart with numbers or bullets? If they are short, it is a good idea to preview them.

A Read the title of Reading 1. Then look in the reading for words or sentences that look special. Read the sentences that are in italics or set apart with bullets. Then put a check (✓) next to the statements below that you think are true.

_____ 1 All of the sentences with bullets are true.

_____ 2 Some of the sentences with bullets are true.

_____ 3 None of the sentences with bullets is true.

_____ 4 All of the sentences in italics are true.

_____ 5 Some of the sentences in italics are true.

_____ 6 None of the sentences in italics is true.

B Compare your answers with a partner's.

C Discuss what you think the reading will be about with your partner.

While You Read

As you read, stop at the end of each sentence that contains a word in bold. Then follow the instructions in the box in the margin.

Fact or Fiction – Science

1 Maybe your mother or father told you. Maybe it was a teacher or a friend. You have heard these things since you were a child:

- If you drop a **coin**, like a penny, from a very tall building, you could kill a person who is standing below.
- Lightning never hits the same place twice.
- If you touch a baby bird or an egg, the mother will abandon it.

In fact, none of these is true. They are all science **myths**, that is, common beliefs that are actually false. Yet, these myths have persisted across generations, and many people continue to believe them. Probably the greatest number of these science myths are about our health. Here are a few that may be familiar.

2 *You can catch a cold if you go outside with wet hair or without a coat, or sleep near an open window.* In fact, there is no evidence – no supporting facts – for any of these beliefs. Colds are caused by a virus, not by temperature or weather. People who live in cold places don't catch more colds than people who live in warm places do. In fact, the opposite is true. Studies show that people resist colds better in cold weather. You are more likely to catch a cold in a warm house with a lot of other people than outside on a cold day.

WHILE YOU READ 1

Find a clue in this sentence that signals an example of a coin. Highlight the clue and example.

WHILE YOU READ 2

Find a clue in this sentence that signals the definition of *myths*. Highlight the clue and definition.

Lightning never hits the same place twice: true or false?

3 *You should always wait 30–60 minutes after a meal before you go swimming.* If you swim immediately, you might get a pain in your stomach and drown. Mothers have been telling their children this for years. This idea first appeared in a book about outdoor sports, like swimming and boating, in 1908. Many people still believe it today. However, there is no scientific evidence that swimming after eating is dangerous.

4 *Hair and fingernails continue to grow after death.* It is possible that this idea came from books or movies, which often show dead bodies with long fingernails and wild hair. However, this cannot happen in real life. When a person dies, the heart stops working. This means that the body does not receive oxygen or energy. Without these, nothing in the body can grow, including hair and nails.

5 Why do people continue to believe these ideas when science shows that they are not true? This is an important question because false information about health can be dangerous. Experts have studied this problem. They believe that two factors are important in keeping myths alive. First and most important is repetition. If you hear something often, you are likely to believe it. You will continue to believe it even when you hear evidence that it is false. Second, your first ideas about something are often the most powerful. Most people first heard these myths about health when they were children. Finally, there may be another explanation for why there are so many myths about health. Most of these ideas originated when very little was known about health or diseases, such as measles, or the flu, or even colds. Yet, health and safety are deeply relevant and important to daily life. If people don't understand something so important, they will accept explanations that make sense to them. Once these myths begin, it is easy to pass them on without questioning them. It is likely that these myths will persist even when there is evidence against **them**.

WHILE YOU READ 3

What is the topic of paragraph 5?
a) Health advice
b) Why people believe myths
c) Health myths

6 However, not all old ideas about health are myths. Scientists say that chicken soup really is good for you when you are sick, and eating fish really is beneficial for your brain. So, the next time you hear advice about your health, stop before you follow it. Ask yourself if it makes sense. You may want to check what experts say.

Main Idea Check

The main idea of a reading is what the whole reading is about.

Read the statements below. Which of these statements is the most important idea from Reading 1?

a Some health myths are based on truth.
b If you hear something many times, you are likely to believe it.
c People always remember and believe the first thing they hear about something.
d A lot of health advice you hear is not really true.
e We hear a lot of myths about our health when we are very young.

A Closer Look

Look back at Reading 1 to answer the following questions.

1 Which of the statements below describe myths? Choose three answers. (Par. 1)
 a They are not true.
 b They are partly true.
 c Many people believe them.
 d They may persist for many years.
 e They can offer good advice.

2 Lightning never hits the same place twice. **True or False?** (Par. 1)

3 You are more likely to catch a cold when you are inside than when you are outside. **True or False?** (Par. 2)

4 What is one likely explanation for why myths about health continue? (Par. 5)
 a People often do not believe what their parents tell them.
 b People are afraid not to follow the advice in the myths.
 c People repeat them over and over.
 d They help people remember important information.

5 Which statement do you think is most likely to be true? (Par. 5)
 a Most of these myths began before modern medicine.
 b Most of these myths will probably disappear soon.
 c Most of these myths began in a far-away place.
 d Most of these myths began when children believed what their parents told them.

6 For which of these statements does the reading suggest there is scientific evidence? (whole reading)
 a Fingernails continue to grow after death.
 b People with a cold should eat chicken soup.
 c You will catch a cold if you don't wear a coat in cold weather.
 d You should not swim right after lunch.

Skill Review

In Skills and Strategies 1, you learned that writers use clues to signal definitions. In Skills and Strategies 3, you learned that writers also point to the meanings of words by using examples. They use clues to signal these examples. Noticing this information can sometimes help you figure out the meanings of words you do not know.

A **Read the sentences below from Reading 1. Decide if the writer is providing a definition or an example to explain the words in bold. Write *D* (for definition) or *E* (for example) on the blank lines, and underline the clue. Then highlight the part of each sentence that contains either the definition or the examples.**

E 1 If you drop a **coin**, like a penny, from a very tall building, you could kill a person who is standing below.

D 2 They are all science **myths**, that is, common beliefs that are actually false.

D 3 In fact, there is no **evidence** – no supporting facts – for any of these beliefs.

E 4 The idea first appeared in a book about **outdoor sports**, like swimming and boating, in 1908.

E 5 Most of these ideas originated when very little was known about health or **diseases**, such as measles, or the flu, or even colds.

B **Compare your answers with a partner's.**

Definitions

Find the words in Reading 1 that complete the following definitions.

1 To do something twice is to do it two times. (*adv*) Par. 1, bulleted list

2 To abandon something is to leave it forever. (*v*) Par. 1, bulleted list

3 To persive is to continue, often for longer than the expected time. (*v*) Par. 1, 3rd sentence after the bulleted list

4 A / An generation is all of the people who were born at about the same time. (*n*) Par. 1, last sentence

5 A / An virus is a very small organism that lives in the body and can make you sick. (*n*) Par. 2, sentence 3

6 To dronw is to die because you are under water and cannot breathe. (*v*) Par. 3, sentence 2

7 If something is relevant, it is directly related. (*adj*) Par. 5, sentence 12

8 Something benegition is good for you. (*adj*) Par. 6, sentence 2

Words in Context

Complete the sentences with words from Reading 1 in the box below.

evidence	fingernails	lightning	repetition
familiar	immediately	originated	resist

1 The street looks familiar because I have seen it before.

2 During storms, there are often flashes of lightning and loud thunder.

3 This new fashion originated in Japan and then spread to other countries.

4 Repetition helps me learn. When I hear something over and over, I remember it.

5 If you feel a pain in your chest, you should call a doctor immediately. Don't wait.

6 A scientist found some very old burned bones and wood. They are evidence that humans used fire more than one million years ago.

7 She painted her fingernails a bright red color so that everyone would notice her hands.

8 Many people resist new technology because they don't want to make changes in their lives.

Beyond the Reading

Critical Thinking

In Reading 1, you learned about science myths that are related to health. The author offers some possible explanations for how they began and why people continue to believe them.

ANALYZING INFORMATION

Critical thinking involves thinking carefully about important topics that the writer has not completely explained.

A Discuss the questions below with a small group.

1 Are science myths only about health? In what other areas of science do you think people might believe myths (think animals, nature, the universe, etc.)?

2 Do you think lack of knowledge explains how myths began, as the author suggests about health myths? Explain your answer.

3 Do you think repetition is a good explanation for why people continue to believe myths? Explain your answer.

4 What might be some other explanations for the existence of these myths?

B Share your answers with the rest of the class.

Research

Find out more information about a science myth – one that is not related to health. You may choose one that you discussed with your group, or you can choose a new one.

A Find the answers to the following questions.

1 How did the myth begin?

2 Is any part of the myth true? Explain which part(s).

3 What is really the truth about the myth, as we know it now?

4 Why do you think people continue to believe the myth?

5 Do you think the myth will continue in the future?

B Ask five people about the myth you have chosen.

1 Do they believe it is true?

2 When did they first hear it?

Writing

Write a short report on the results of your research. Include the answers to all of the questions.

Before You Read

Connecting to the Topic

Most countries have stories about their history that are based on facts but are not completely true. For example, in the United States, schoolchildren often learn the story of the first Thanksgiving. In the fall of 1621, the European settlers and native Indians sat down for a friendly dinner to celebrate a good year of farming. Is this story true? Perhaps a little bit, but a lot of it is probably not true.

Discuss the following questions with a partner.

1 What are some stories you learned in school about the history of your country or community?

2 Choose one of the stories. How much of this story do you think is true, and how much is not? Explain your answer.

3 Why do you think people continue to tell these stories? Explain your answer.

Previewing and Predicting

Remember that a good way to preview is to read the title and the first sentence or two of each paragraph.

A **Read the title of Reading 2. Then read the first sentence or two of each paragraph. Thinking about what you have read and what you know, write *T* (true), *F* (false), or *M* (maybe/not sure) on the blank lines.**

_____ 1 Marco Polo was one of the first travelers to Asia.

_____ 2 Marco Polo opened up Asian culture to Europe.

_____ 3 Christopher Columbus was the first person to sail to America.

_____ 4 Christopher Columbus wanted to prove the world was round.

_____ 5 Most people during the time of Columbus believed the world was flat.

B **Compare your answers with a partner's.**

C **Discuss what you think the reading will be about with your partner.**

While You Read

As you read, stop at the end of each sentence that contains words in bold. Then follow the instructions in the box in the margin.

Fact or Fiction – History

1 We all learned about historical events from books in school. However, sometimes these history books mix facts with stories. These stories have often been presented as true, but historians agree that many are not. They may include some truth, which makes them more believable. Others are completely false. They are fiction, that is, somebody invented them. Here are just two examples.

Marco Polo

2 Marco Polo, a thirteenth century explorer, spent many years traveling through Asia. He served the Mongol emperor, Kublai Khan. He brought the art, science, and culture of Asia to Europe. True?

3 Perhaps. Historians disagree on this. Some are certain that this is true. Others believe that he never traveled all the way to China. These historians think he listened to the stories of other travelers and made up his own journey. One story about Marco Polo is well known to schoolchildren. They learn that he brought Chinese noodles back to Europe. In Italy, these noodles were the origins of **pasta** – like spaghetti. This is certainly not true. Pasta was already well established in southern Italy before the thirteenth century. It was probably brought to Italy from the Arab world, not China.

WHILE YOU READ 1

Find a clue in this sentence that signals an example of a type of pasta. Highlight the clue and example.

4 So, why do we often give Marco Polo credit for spaghetti? Here is the reason: In 1929, a business group called the American Pasta Association published an article about the origin of pasta. It told the story of a handsome Italian sailor on Marco Polo's ship. He met a beautiful Chinese girl who was making delicious noodles. She gave him some of the noodles to take home. According to the article, the sailor's name was **Spaghetti**.

WHILE YOU READ 2

What is the topic of paragraph 4? Highlight the sentence that shows the topic.

5 Christopher Columbus's voyage was the first to visit the New World – North and South America. Columbus wanted to prove that the world was round. At the time of his voyage, most people believed that the world was flat. True?

6 In fact, none of these "facts" about Columbus is true. It is certain that there were many earlier visitors to the New World. There were traders and explorers from Northern Europe as early as the tenth century and possibly Arab sailors even before that. In addition, the purpose of Columbus's journey was to find gold, silver, and spices. The belief that the world was round was widespread during the time of Columbus. This knowledge went back as far as ancient Greece (200 BCE) and was also familiar to scholars in both the Islamic world (as early as the ninth century) and non-Muslim Europe.

Christopher Columbus

7 So, what is the origin of these myths about Columbus? Historians have tried to trace them. There is mention of them in books from the seventeenth through nineteenth centuries, but not before that. One book, published in the United States in the 1820s, says that the main purpose of Columbus's voyage was to prove that the world was round. Historians are not sure how or why these myths about Columbus began.

8 There are many other examples of historical myths. The Roman emperor, Nero, played the violin while Rome burned. Chinese history began 5,000 years ago when the Yellow Emperor taught his people about **agriculture**, which is the growing of rice, beans, fruit, and other crops. Cleopatra died when an asp (a kind of snake) bit her. Napoleon was very short. Astronauts saw the Great Wall of China from space. Einstein was not a good math student. How do these myths begin, and why do they continue? Each myth has a different origin, and some of them do contain some facts. But most of them continue for one good reason: they are good stories. Everyone likes a good story, but perhaps not so many of them belong in history books.

WHILE YOU READ 3

Find a clue in this sentence that signals a definition of *agriculture*. Highlight the clue and definition.

Reading Skill Development

Main Idea Check

The main idea of a reading is what the whole reading is about.

Read the statements below. Which of these statements is the most important idea from Reading 2?

a Most myths about history started long ago.
b Some of our beliefs about history are a mix of facts and fiction.
c Historians disagree about many of the events in history.
d We don't know how many history myths began.

A Closer Look

Look back at Reading 2 to answer the following questions.

1 There was no pasta in Italy before Marco Polo went to Asia. **True or False?** (Par. 3)

2 Why do you think the American Pasta Association wrote the story about Marco Polo? (Par. 4)
   a They thought a good story would make people want to buy pasta.
   b They didn't know it was false.
   c They wanted to show the connection between pasta and Chinese food.
   d They believed that history was very important.

3 Columbus was the first European to visit the Americas. **True or False?** (Par. 6)

4 When did people first recognize that the world was not flat? (Par. 6)
   a After Columbus's voyage
   b In the seventeenth century
   c In the ninth century
   d During ancient times in Greece

5 Historians are not sure why the myths about Columbus began. **True or False?** (Par. 7)

6 The Great Wall of China is visible from space. **True or False?** (Par. 8)

7 Which statements are true about historical myths? Choose three answers. (whole reading)
   a They began in ancient times.
   b They are good stories.
   c They are all completely false.
   d Some of them contain some truth.
   e We are often not sure of their origins.

Skill Review

In Skills and Strategies 1, you learned that writers use clues to signal definitions. In Skills and Strategies 3, you learned that writers point to the meanings of words by using examples. They use clues to signal these examples. Noticing this information can sometimes help you figure out the meanings of words you do not know.

A **Find the words or phrases in the left-hand column of the chart in Reading 2. Put a check (✓) to show the type of clue in the reading that helped you understand the meanings. Then write the clue in the right-hand column of the chart.**

WORD OR PHRASE	DEFINITION	EXAMPLE	CLUE
fiction (Par. 1)	✓		that is
pasta (Par. 3)		✓	like
the New World (Par. 5)	✓		–
agriculture (Par. 8)		✓	which is
asp (Par. 8)	✓		

B **List the word(s) from the chart in A that appear(s) with examples in the reading. Fill in the examples that the writer used.**

WORD	EXAMPLES
- fictions	- somebody invested them.
- pasta	- spaghetti

C **Compare your answers with a partner's.**

Vocabulary Development

Definitions

Find the words in Reading 2 that complete the following definitions.

1 To make up a tale is to invent a story that isn't true. (*2-part v*) Par. 3, sentence 5

2 To publish something is to make it available to other people, usually as a book. (*v*) Par. 4, sentence 2 (after the colon)

3 Someone who is hadsome is attractive or good-looking; the word is usually used to describe men. (*adj*) Par. 4, sentence 3

4 To prove something is to make clear that it is / is not true. (*v*) Par. 5, sentence 2

5 Spices are flavorings from plants that we add to food to make it taste better. (*n pl*) Par. 6, sentence 4

6 If something is widespread, it is happening in many places. (*adj*) Par. 6, sentence 5

7 To tace something is to discover how it started. (*v*) Par. 7, sentence 2

8 Astronauts are people who travel in space. (*n pl*) Par. 8, sentence 6

Words in Context

Complete the passages with words from Reading 2 in the box below. Use capital letters if necessary.

ancient	culture	explorer	traders
credit	established	historians	voyage

1 The Silk Road describes several routes that were establish (a) during ancient (b) times (starting in the second century BCE) from China, across Asia, all the way to Europe. Traders (c) used this route to bring silk, gold, and other valuable things from places at one end of the road and sell them at the other end. The route was of great economic importance, but it was equally important for the exchange of culture (d). Europeans learned about life in China and the rest of Asia as result of trade along the Silk Road.

2 Christopher Columbus, the fifteenth-century European explorer (e), often gets credits (f) for making the first European voyage (g) to the Americas. However, historianes (h) have found evidence of a much earlier visit – from the Vikings. They landed in Canada almost 500 years earlier.

Critical Thinking

In Reading 2, the author explored several myths about history that mix fact with fiction.

> **ANALYZING INFORMATION**
>
> Critical thinking involves thinking carefully about important topics that the writer has not completely explained.

A Discuss the questions below with a small group.

1 Why do you think people continue to tell the story about Marco Polo and spaghetti?

2 Why and how do you think the story about the voyage of Christopher Columbus began? Consider the fact that many people already knew that the earth was round at the time of his voyage.

3 Can you think of an explanation for why people continue to believe these stories when most of them are clearly false?

4 Were you familiar with these two stories? When and how did you hear about them?

B Share your answers with the rest of the class.

Research

Do some research on a story from history that mixes fact with fiction. If you can, choose a story about a person or event in the history of your country or community. Perhaps there is a story that you heard when you were a child. Find answers to the following questions.

1 How did the story begin?

2 How much of the story is true? What are the facts?

3 Which parts of the story are not true?

4 Why do you think people continue to believe the story?

5 Did you hear this story when you were young? Explain your answer.

Writing

Write a short report on the results of your research. Include the answers to all of the questions.

SKILLS AND STRATEGIES 4

Finding the Main Ic Paragraph

In Unit 1, you learned that each paragraph has on also has one main idea. The main idea is what the If you can find the main idea of a paragraph, the to understand.

Topic: what the writer is talking about.

Main idea: what the writer is talking about the topic.

Examples & Explanations

Here are two common types of email scams (attempts to trick or cheat you). One is the email banking scam. You receive an email, apparently from your bank. It says there is a problem and asks for your private banking information. Someone then uses that information to take money from your bank account. Another common scam is the "advance-fee" email. In this scam, a person emails you and pretends to be very rich and in need of help. If you just give him a little money now, he explains, he will give you a lot more money later.

The topic of this paragraph is *email scams*. The main idea is what the writer says about email scams. In this paragraph, the writer describes two common types of email scams.

Email scams may seem unbelievable, but they trick many people. In fact, experts say 10 percent of people will believe an email scam at some point in their lives. Even smart people can be fooled. In 2008, a highly educated health-care worker in Oregon lost more than $400,000 in an advance-fee scam. Because of stories like this, people keep creating new email scams.

The topic of this paragraph is also *email scams*. In this paragraph, the writer's main idea is that *they seem unbelievable, but they trick many people.*

So, how can you protect yourself? There are a few ways to tell if an email is a scam. First, if an email offer seems too good to be true, it probably is. Trust your common sense. Second, you can look for language that is too positive. For example, be careful with emails that contain lots of UPPERCASE LETTERS or many exclamation points!!! Finally, pay no attention to statements like "This is NOT a scam." People who write scam emails do not mean what they say, and this statement is just another example.

The main idea is not always in the first sentence. In this paragraph, the first sentence is a question. The answer to the question is the main idea. The topic in this paragraph is *protecting yourself from email scams*. The main idea is *there are a few ways to tell if an email is a scam.*

Strategies

These strategies will help you find the main idea of a paragraph while you read.

- While you read, ask yourself: *What is the topic? What does the writer say about the topic?*
- Pay attention to the first and second sentences of a paragraph. Often, the main idea is in one of these sentences.
- If a paragraph starts with a question, look for the answer to it. The answer may tell you the main idea.
- Read the whole paragraph, and use the other sentences in the paragraph to help you understand the main idea.

Skill Practice 1

Read the following paragraphs. Then look at the three possible main idea choices for each paragraph. Choose the best main idea. Discuss your answers with a partner.

1 Have you ever received an email scam? If you are like most people, you receive them quite often. Experts say the number of email scams increases each year. They affect millions of people, in every part of the world.

Main idea:

a Many people receive email scams.
b Email scams have a long history.
c People write email scams to steal your money.

2 One common email scam is the "Nigerian letter." It is a modern variation of the advance-fee scam. The writer pretends to be a rich Nigerian prince or leader. He writes and asks for a little money to help with a problem. Just send a little money now, the email promises, and you will be rich in the future.

Main idea:

a The Nigerian letter promises to make you rich in the future.
b The Nigerian letter is a common email scam.
c Rich princes and leaders in Nigeria write email scams.

3 Nigerian scam emails are very hard to believe. The emails often have mistakes in spelling and grammar. They make unbelievable promises. They also mention "Nigeria" many times, although many people already know about the Nigerian email scam.

Main idea:

a Nigerian scam emails are very hard to believe.
b Nigerian scam emails often have mistakes in spelling and grammar.
c Many people already know about the Nigerian scam email.

4 Why would anyone write such an unbelievable email? In fact, they have very good reasons to do so. Scammers know that most people will not believe their emails. They want to find the one or two people who *will* believe them. That way, they will

not waste time communicating with people who will never send them money. If just one or two people believe their email, the scammers can still make large amounts of money. That is why they often include bad grammar and misspellings, and why they always mention Nigeria. They want to find people who do not know about the Nigerian scam email and who will believe anything.

Main idea:

a Nigerian scam emails are unbelievable for a reason.
b The people who write Nigerian scam emails are often not Nigerian.
c Some people actually believe Nigerian scam emails.

Skill Practice 2

Read the following paragraphs. Write the main idea of each paragraph on the blank line.

1 Some people try to fight email scammers. They respond to their emails and pretend to believe the scam. They communicate with the scammers for months and give the scammers false information.

Main idea: ______________________

2 People try to fight email scammers for different reasons. Some are angry with the scammers. They feel bad for the people who lose money in scams, and they want to punish the scammers. Other people are just bored. They think fighting against the scammers will be a fun way to spend their time. Either way, the goal is the same: to waste the scammers' time and money.

Main idea: ______________________

3 So just how do you fight the scammers? There are several ways. One way is to waste the scammers' time with unnecessary emails. You communicate with scammers for many months, just to keep them busy. Another way is to make the scammers take unnecessary trips. For example, one professional airline pilot asked a scammer to fly to London and meet him in the airport so he could give him money. The pilot never went to London, of course, but the scammer did!

Main idea: ______________________

4 However, you need to be careful when you fight email scammers. Some email scammers are dangerous people. That is why expert scam fighters never use their real names or email addresses. As one experienced scam fighter says, "The best way to stop email scams is to tell the police and advise your friends and family not to believe them."

Main idea: ______________________

Before You Read

Connecting to the Topic

Read the definition of *hoax*, and then discuss the following questions with a partner.

hoax (*n*) a plan to trick a large group of people

1 Have you ever read a story online or in the newspaper that you thought might be a hoax? Explain your answer.

2 Have you ever received an offer in the mail or in an email that you thought might be a hoax? Explain your answer.

3 Hoaxes are not true, but many people believe them anyway. Why do you think people believe hoaxes are true?

Previewing and Predicting

When you preview a longer reading, remember to look at section headings. These headings can help you predict what the reading will be about. Also remember that reading first sentences can help you make predictions about the reading.

A **Read the section headings that follow the first paragraph in Reading 3. Then read the first sentence in each paragraph. Decide what topics you think will be in each section. Then write the number(s) of the sections (*I*, *II*, or *I and II*) next to the topics that you think will be in those sections.**

SECTION	TOPIC
	Famous hoaxes
	An example of a hoax that made money
	Reasons for hoaxes
	An example of a hoax that was not for money
	Why people believe hoaxes

B **Compare your answers with a partner's.**

C **In a few words, write what you think the reading will be about.**

While You Read

As you read, stop at the end of each sentence that contains words in bold. Then follow the instructions in the box in the margin.

Hoaxes

1 Have you ever received an email with an offer that seemed just a little bit too good? Or have you read a story in the newspaper that you didn't quite believe? It is likely that these were hoaxes. A hoax is an event or a story that is presented as true but is not actually true. However, a hoax is not a mistake; the deception is **intentional**. In other words, the person who creates a hoax is trying to trick people. Most hoaxes don't trick a lot of people, but occasionally there is a hoax that tricks so many people that it becomes familiar all over the world. It may take many years to prove that the story is a hoax. Why do so many people believe hoaxes? There is no easy explanation, but often, there is just enough truth in these hoaxes to trick even intelligent, well-educated people. Also, some people want to believe that strange things are true, even when they are completely false.

WHILE YOU READ 1

Find a clue in this sentence that signals a definition of *intentional*. Highlight the clue and definition.

I. Hoaxes for Fame and Profit

2 Why do people create hoaxes? One reason is that hoaxes give the creator of the hoax an opportunity to become famous and perhaps also to make a profit. One example of this type of hoax is the Tasaday people of the Philippines. In 1971, a government official named Manuel Elizalde claimed he had information about a secret group of people on an island. They had never seen modern civilization. They lived in caves. They had no modern clothing or tools. They did not farm. The world was fascinated by the news. Many newspaper and television reporters traveled to the Philippines to see the Tasaday. Scientists wanted to study them and see how they **lived**.

WHILE YOU READ 2

What sentence answers a question and gives the main idea of paragraph 2?

a) The first sentence
b) The second sentence
c) The last sentence

3 The official, Elizalde, collected money from the public, saying the collection was to protect and assist the Tasaday. Some reports say he collected $35 million. Soon, however, people began to ask questions. Why weren't the Tasaday very thin? Why were the caves so clean? Some people reported that they saw some Tasaday people eating rice and smoking cigarettes. Were the Tasaday really undiscovered? After these reports appeared in the news, the government stopped scientists and reporters from visiting the Tasaday. Questions about the Tasaday continued, but few people had access to their villages. Then, in 1986, a news report revealed that the Tasaday story was a hoax. Although the Tasaday lived very simply in an area far away from other people, they did have contact with the modern world. Some of them admitted that Elizalde told them to dress in leaves and live

The Tasaday

in caves. He promised them money and gifts. By then, Elizalde had left the Philippines.

4 Fame and profit are probably the most common reasons for hoaxes. The Tasaday are just one example. There have been many of them throughout history. They include a man who claimed that his horse could understand human language and a man who said he had discovered a **mermaid** – a creature with the body of a human and the tail of a fish. People were willing to pay money to see these amazing things. Although they were hoaxes, people believed them for a long time. And the creators of the hoaxes made money and became famous – at least for a short time – as a result of public curiosity.

WHILE YOU READ 3

Find a clue in this sentence that signals the definition of *mermaid*. Highlight the clue and definition.

II. Hoaxes as Jokes

5 In other cases, hoaxes have nothing to do with money. Many of these begin as jokes. The people who create them love to fool people. One example is Bigfoot. In the northwestern United States, for many years, people talked about Bigfoot—a huge, hairy creature with big feet. Some people claimed that they had seen Bigfoot, but there was not much real evidence. One morning in 1958, a man found 16-inch (40-centimeter) footprints in the dirt. Many people thought this was finally evidence that Bigfoot was real. In fact, another man created the hoax as a joke. He made big feet out of wood, and then he walked around in them when the ground was wet. He probably never thought that so many people would believe the footprints were real: But he enjoyed the idea that he had fooled everyone. He never revealed the hoax. His family discovered his secret and revealed it after he died in **2002**.

WHILE YOU READ 4

Choose a sentence that gives the main idea of paragraph 5.

a) The first sentence
b) The second sentence
c) The last sentence

6 Hoaxes have occurred throughout history. There is an online museum of hoaxes that describes hundreds of them, beginning in the eighth century. It is not likely that we have seen the end of hoaxes. Somewhere there is always someone who wants to believe them.

Bigfoot?

Reading Skill Development

Main Idea Check

Match the main ideas below to paragraphs 1–5 in Reading 3. Write the number of the paragraph on the blank line.

__3__ A The Tasaday appeared to be a hoax.

__5__ B Some people create hoaxes because they like to fool people.

__2__ C The Tasaday are an example of a hoax for profit or fame.

__1__ D Hoaxes don't fool a lot of people, but they keep occurring.

__4__ E There have been many hoaxes for fame and profit.

A Closer Look

Look back at Reading 3 to answer the following questions.

1 Most hoaxes fool a lot of people. **True or False?** (Par. 1)

2 What are two reasons that may explain why people believe some hoaxes? (Par. 1)

- a People like to believe incredible stories.
- b The creators of hoaxes often pay people to say they believe them.
- c They may include a little bit of truth.
- d People who don't have a lot of education often believe them.

3 What part of the Tasaday story hoax fascinated the public? (Par. 2)

- a They lived on an island that did not have any agriculture.
- b Most of them ate food without cooking it.
- c Their first contact with people outside of their group was very recent.
- d The caves where the Tasaday lived were very clean.

4 Why did the public believe that Elizalde was trying to help the Tasaday? (Par. 3)

- a He helped scientists to study them.
- b He was collecting money for them.
- c He brought them rice and cigarettes.
- d He stopped reporters and scientists from asking them questions.

5 At first the public believed the story about the Tasaday. Later, most people believed it was a hoax. Read the statements about the Tasaday below. If they are evidence that the story was true, write *T* in the blank. If they are evidence that the story was a hoax, write *H* in the blank. (Pars. 2 and 3)

a __H__ They smoked cigarettes.

b __H__ They ate rice.

c __T__ They lived in caves.

d __H__ They were not thin.

e __T__ They had no agriculture.

f __T__ They did not use modern tools.

g __H__ Their caves seemed very clean.

6 How are creators of hoaxes able to make money from them? (Par. 4)

- a Someone pays them to make up the hoax.
- b Newspapers pay them to write their stories.
- c People are willing to pay to satisfy their curiosity.
- d They sell books that explain their hoaxes.

7 The story of Bigfoot began before 1958. **True or False?** (Par. 5)

8 Why did the man create the Bigfoot hoax? (Par. 5)

- a He wanted to be famous.
- b He liked to play jokes on people.
- c He hoped that he could make some money from it.
- d He thought Bigfoot was real.

Skill Review

In Skills and Strategies 4, you learned that most paragraphs have one main idea. You learned that one way to determine the main idea is to ask the questions "What is the paragraph about?" and "What does the writer say about this topic?"

A Look back at Reading 3. For each of the first five paragraphs, the middle column of the chart below contains a brief description of what the paragraph is about. Complete the chart by writing what the writer wants to say about this topic in the last column.

PARAGRAPH NUMBER	WHAT IS THE PARAGRAPH ABOUT?	WHAT DOES THE WRITER SAY ABOUT IT?
1	An introduction to hoaxes	
2	An example that illustrates one reason for hoaxes	
3	The discovery of a hoax	
4	Other hoaxes for profit	
5	An example of another reason for hoaxes	

B Compare your answers with a partner's.

Vocabulary Development

Definitions

Find the words in Reading 3 that complete the following definitions.

1 A / An ______________ is money that you make when you sell something. (*n*) Par. 2, sentence 2

2 ______________ are large holes in the side of a mountain or under the ground (*n pl*) Par. 2, sentence 6

3 ______________ are something you hold in your hand to help you do a job. (*n pl*) Par. 2, sentence 7

4 A / An ______________ is a particular part of a city, country, house, etc. (*n*) Par. 3, sentence 11

5 If you have ______________ with someone, it means you communicate with each other. (*n*) Par. 3, sentence 11

6 ______________ is the strong wish to know something. (*n*) Par. 4, last sentence

7 ______________ are stories or tricks to make people laugh. (*n pl*) Par. 5, sentence 2

8 To ______________ is to happen. (*v*) Par. 6, sentence 1

Word Families

A The words in bold in the chart are from Reading 3. The words next to them are from the same word family. Study and learn these words.

NOUN	VERB
assistance	***assist*** (Par. 3)
collection	***collect*** (Par. 3)
creation	***create*** (Par. 1)
deception (Par. 1)	*deceive*
revelation	***reveal*** (Par. 3)

B Choose the correct form of the words from the chart to complete the following sentences.

1 She couldn't finish the job alone, so she asked for my ______________.

2 He tried to ______________ us with a quick answer, but we could see he was lying.

3 Tomorrow, the mayor will ______________ her plans for a new park near the river.

4 We are going to ______________ money to help people who lost their homes in the fire.

5 Yesterday's ______________ about the president's secret bank account was a surprise to everyone. He may lose the election now.

6 You should not trust this man. He has a history of ______________.

7 We need to ______________ a plan to improve education.

8 Part of this job is to ______________ the manager when she has important meetings.

9 The president announced the ____________ of a committee to study crime.

10 He has a ____________ of books and papers that once belonged to Nelson Mandela.

Academic Word List

The following are Academic Word List words from all the readings in Unit 2. Use these words to complete the sentences. (If necessary, review the AWL words in Key Vocabulary on pages 257–267.)

beneficial (*adj*)	established (*v*)	generation (*n*)	persisted (*v*)	revealed (*v*)
contact (*n*)	evidence (*n*)	occurred (*v*)	published (*v*)	widespread (*adj*)

1 Each ____________ enjoys a different kind of music. My parents and I don't listen to the same thing.

2 When you make an argument, it is very important to provide ____________ to support it.

3 A man in Canada ____________ his first book when he was 100 years old.

4 Exercise is ____________ for your health.

5 There was ____________ resistance to the plan for the new building. No one liked it.

6 After the two sisters had a big fight, they had no ____________ for the rest of their lives.

7 After her surgery, the pain in her legs ____________ for several months.

8 The Romans ____________ the world's first public libraries.

9 This is a very dangerous road. Four accidents ____________ in this spot last year.

10 On television last night, two movie stars ____________ that they plan to marry.

Critical Thinking

Reading 3 offers two reasons why people create hoaxes.

A Discuss the following questions with a partner.

1 Do you think that all hoaxes are intentional deceptions? Explain your answer.

2 What might be an example of an unintentional hoax?

3 Do you think that people who create hoaxes should be punished? Why or why not?

4 Today we have the Internet to check information. Do you think it is harder to create a hoax today? Explain your answer.

B Share your answers with the rest of the class.

EXPLORING OPINIONS

Critical readers form their own opinions about important topics in a text.

Research

Do some research on one of the hoaxes listed below, or choose one of your own. Find the answers to the questions that follow.

- Roswell UFO Incident (USA, 1947)
- Piltdown Man (England, 1912)
- Fiji Mermaid (1842)
- Bonsai Kitten (USA, 2000)
- Jimmy's World (USA, 1980)
- Crop Circles (Europe, 1970s)
- Archaeoraptor (China, 1999)

1 What was the hoax?

2 When did it happen?

3 Who created it?

4 Why did he or she create it?

5 How was it discovered?

Writing

Write a short summary of your research. Include the answers to the questions.

Improving Your Reading Speed

Good readers read quickly and still understand most of what they read.

A Read the instructions and strategies for Improving Your Reading Speed in Appendix 3 on page 270.

B Choose one of the readings in this unit. Read it without stopping. Time how long it takes you to finish the text in minutes and seconds. Enter the time in the chart on page 271. Then calculate your reading speed in number of words per minute.

MAKING CONNECTIONS

words and ideas within and across sentences. When
d to repeat words as often. Sometimes pronouns refer
. Sometimes they refer to a whole sentence or idea.
efer to whole sentences or ideas. *This* is the most common

those

urself: *What word or phrase does this pronoun refer to?*
onoun is in **bold**, and the noun it refers to is underlined.

rm "late bloomer"? **This** is a term for children who develop skills, like speaking or reading, later than other children.

In the next example, the pronoun is in **bold**, and the whole idea it refers to is underlined. The arrow shows that the pronoun refers to the whole idea in the first sentence.

Some children do not speak until they are two years old. However, **this** is unusual.

Exercise 1

Read the following groups of sentences. Highlight the pronoun in the second sentence in each group. Underline the noun, noun phrase, or idea the pronoun refers to. Draw an arrow from the pronoun to the underlined item. The first one is an example.

1 Albert Einstein was a late bloomer. This surprises a lot of people.

2 Einstein began to speak later than other children. This worried Einstein's parents.

3 People have said that Einstein was bad at math as a child. That is simply not true.

4 Napoleon was about five feet, seven inches (1.7 meters) tall. This was average for the time.

5 British historians say he was only five feet, two inches (1.57 meters) tall. Modern historians have proven that this is not true.

6 The British and French reports of Napoleon's height were different. This was because the British and French used different systems of measurement.

Exercise 2

Make a clear paragraph by putting sentences A, B, and C into the best order after the numbered sentence. Look for pronouns to help you. Write the letters in the correct order on the blank lines.

1 The Cottingley Fairies refers to a famous hoax. B A C

A	B	C
A Their names were Elsie Wright and Frances Griffith.	**B** It was a series of five photographs taken by two girls.	**C** The hoax made them famous.

2 Elsie loved to take photographs. C A B

A	B	C
A He loved photography, too.	**B** It was his hobby.	**C** So her father, Arthur, lent her his camera.

3 The girls took a photograph in the woods. A B C

A	B	C
A They asked Arthur to develop it.	**B** In it, he saw four little fairies.	**C** This surprised and puzzled him.

4 The fairies were in the woods. B C A

A	B	C
A That is what a lot of other people thought, too.	**B** They were dancing in Elsie's photograph.	**C** Arthur thought she was playing a trick.

5 Sir Arthur Conan Doyle, the author of the Sherlock Holmes stories, used the photograph in one his stories. C B A

A	B	C
A Many years later, Elsie and Frances admitted it was a hoax.	**B** He thought their photograph of the fairies was real.	**C** He believed the girls.

3 MARKETING

SKILLS AND STRATEGIES

- Finding the Meanings of Words: Contrasts
- Finding the Topic and Main Idea of a Reading

Contrast: however, unlike, but, in contrast.

...eanings of Words:

...s 1 on page 2 and Skills and Strategies 3 ...tions and examples to help you ...way writers help you understand difficult ...trast is a difference between two or more ... help you understand the meaning of a

Examples & Explanations

Our friends decided to **purchase** a new computer. However, we did not buy one.

The writer uses a word that readers may not know: *purchase*. In the next sentence, the writer gives a contrast: *did not buy*. This contrast can help the reader understand the meaning of *purchase*.

purchase = *to buy something*

Advertising in the newspaper is a **bargain**, unlike high-priced TV commercials.

The writer uses another word that readers may not know: *bargain*. In the next sentence, the writer gives a contrast: *high-priced*. The writer introduces the contrast with the signal *unlike*. Other contrast signals are *but*, *however*, and *in contrast*.

bargain = *something that is sold cheaply or at a low price*

Martina's advertising plan will **certainly** work. We are not sure about Joe's plan.

The writer uses the word *certainly*. The next sentence gives a contrast: *not sure*. This time, the writer does not use a signal to introduce the contrast. The reader has to think about the connection between the two ideas.

certainly = *surely; without a doubt; definitely*

The company thought that their new product would do very well. However, it became one of their biggest **failures**.

The writer uses the word *failure* in the second sentence. The contrast comes in the first sentence: *do very well*. As this example shows, the contrast may come in the sentence before the difficult word.

failure = *something that does not do well*

Strategies

These strategies will help you find contrasts and use them to understand word meanings while you read.

- When you see a word you do not know, do not stop reading. Look for contrasts that can help you understand the unknown word.
- Look for signals like *however, but, unlike,* and *in contrast* that can help you identify contrasts.
- Remember that writers may not use a signal to introduce a contrast.
- Remember that the contrast may come in the sentence before or after the sentence with the difficult word.

Skill Practice 1

Read the following sentences. Highlight the contrasts that are given for each word in bold. The first one is an example.

1 Some companies can spend as much as they want on advertising, but most companies have a **budget**.

2 Big businesses do advertising all the time. However, our family business can only do advertising **occasionally**.

3 Electronic advertising is **widespread** these days. In the past, you saw it in only a few places.

4 Many advertisements focus on the idea of **youth**. The advertisers do not want people to connect their products with old age.

5 People **ignore** most of the advertising that they see. But they pay attention when the advertising is funny.

6 The advertising plan came from a low-level worker at the company. It was not created by an **executive**.

7 Sales went up immediately. We thought they would increase only **gradually**.

8 The restaurant's new advertisement is not getting good results, unlike their very **effective** advertisement from last year.

Skill Practice 2

Read the sentences in Skill Practice 1 again. What do the words in bold mean? Write your answers on the blank lines. Use the contrasts to help you. Then check your answers in a dictionary. The first one is an example.

1 Some companies can spend as much as they want on advertising, but most companies have a **budget**.

budget = *a limited amount of money*

2 Big businesses do advertising all the time. However, our family business can only do advertising **occasionally**.

occasionally = is not all the time

3 Electronic advertising is **widespread** these days. In the past, you saw it in only a few places.

widespread = many places

4 Many advertisements focus on the idea of **youth**. The advertisers do not want people to connect their products with old age.

youth = young people

5 People **ignore** most of the advertising that they see. But they pay attention when the advertising is funny.

ignore = don't pay attention

6 The advertising plan came from a low-level worker at the company. It was not created by an **executive**.

executive = high level worker

7 Sales went up immediately. We thought they would increase only **gradually**.

gradually = slowly

8 The restaurant's new advertisement is not getting good results, unlike their very **effective** advertisement from last year.

effective = getting good result.

Before You Read

Connecting to the Topic

Read the definition of *marketing*, and then discuss the following questions with a partner.

> **marketing** (*n*) everything that a company does in order to sell its products or services

1 What are some things that you think a company needs to do to sell its products successfully?

2 Which of these things do you think are most important? Explain your answer.

3 Do you think marketing activities can convince people to buy things? Explain your answer.

Previewing and Predicting

Remember to preview the title and quickly look at any art, such as photos or drawings. If the art has any words below it, you should read them, too. Looking at all of these can help you to predict what the reading will be about.

A Read the title of Reading 1 and look at the photographs below. With a partner, discuss what the advertisements are trying to express.

1

2

3

B Put a check (✓) next to the topic or topics you think will be in the reading.

_____ a The best car advertisements

_____ b The impact of advertisements

_____ c The history of advertisements

_____ d How to find a job writing advertisements

_____ e Why advertisements increase sales

C Compare your answers with a partner's.

While You Read

As you read, stop at the end of each sentence that contains words in bold. Then follow the instructions in the box in the margin.

READING 1

How Do Advertisements Work?

1 Advertisements are everywhere: on television and radio, in the newspapers, on the Internet, and on big signs above buildings and streets. They are an important part of a company's marketing plan, but how do they work? The basic principles are simple. A company wants you to buy its **products** (for example, computers or shoes) or use its services (for example, painting or banking). Many companies use advertisements to achieve these goals. Advertisements must do one or more of these three basic things:

1 Make customers aware of the product or service
2 Make customers like and want the product or service
3 Encourage customers to buy the product or service

WHILE YOU READ 1

Find a clue in this sentence that signals two examples of *products*. Highlight the clue and examples.

2 This seems simple, but how can advertisements make customers want a product? How can they push customers to buy it? The key to this process is a successful *appeal*. An appeal is a way to get a customer's attention and create a desire for a product or service. This is at the heart of all advertising. Most advertisements use two general kinds of appeals. Appeals can be rational or emotional.

3 Advertisements, or "ads," with rational appeals present a logical reason for why you should buy a company's products or use its services. You could say that these are ads for your brain. They try to prove that their company's product is better than other products. Perhaps the ads show the results of a scientific study. The results show a company's medicine is more effective, or their car is faster, or their camera is easier to use. Some ads have an expert, such as a doctor or engineer, who talks about how good the product **is**.

WHILE YOU READ 2

What is the topic of paragraph 3? Highlight the sentence that shows the topic.

4 Unlike ads with rational appeals, which try to show that a product is effective, ads with emotional appeals try to change how you feel. For example, they might make you frightened, envious, or happy. You could say these are ads for your heart. For example, one car company might use fear in its advertisements. They say their cars are very safe. You thought your old car was **safe**, but suddenly, you begin to think that driving it might be dangerous. You feel scared, and you think about buying a new, safer car for your family. A different ad shows a man with a big beautiful car, a big expensive house, and a beautiful wife. Perhaps you want to have a life like that. You want that car, too. It may make you feel envious. In contrast, an ad that shows a big family enjoying a car trip together might make you feel happy and satisfied. It may make you remember family trips from your childhood. Maybe you will want to buy the car that the family in the ad is driving.

WHILE YOU READ 3

Find a clue in this sentence that signals a contrast with the word *safe*. Highlight the clue and the word that means the opposite of *safe*.

5 The purpose of ads like these is usually very clear, but other ads are not so direct. If an advertisement makes you laugh, will it make you want to buy the product in it? What about if a movie star or a famous athlete appears in the ad? Although research on the effects of advertisements does not provide clear answers to these questions, most companies continue to advertise because they believe their ads are effective. Businesses around the world spent more than $550 billion on advertising in 2014, and that figure is expected to increase.

Table 3.1 Spending on Advertising by Region

Major Media (US$M Current Prices)

	2010	2011	2012	2013	2014
North America	162,165	165,104	172,039	178,313	186,344
Western Europe	106,344	108,688	107,885	109,668	112,642
Asia-Pacific	125,059	132,172	140,383	148,423	157,155
Central & Eastern Europe	24,181	26,151	26,631	28,592	31,089
Latin America	31,996	35,344	38,080	41,935	45,600
Middle East & North Africa	4,881	4,155	4,198	4,313	4,412
Rest of World	10,940	11,592	12,321	13,468	14,812
World	**465,566**	**483,206**	**501,536**	**524,712**	**552,054**

Source: Jenni Baker, London

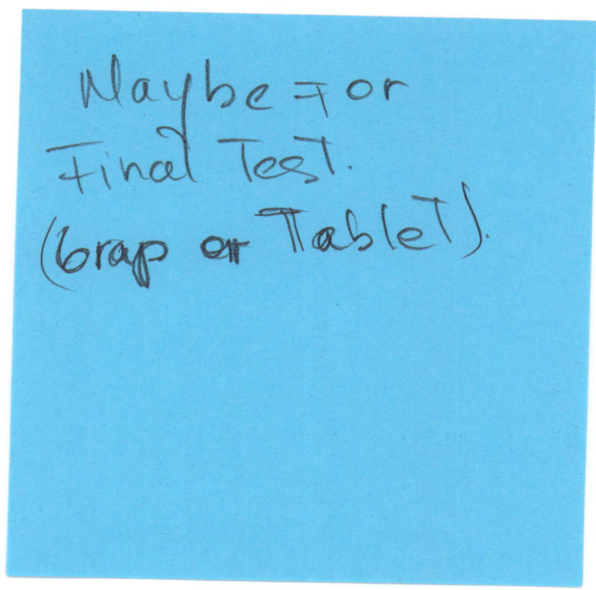

Main Idea Check

Match the main ideas below to paragraphs 1–5 in Reading 1. Write the number of the paragraph on the blank line.

____ A Advertisements are based on appeals.
____ B Emotional appeals try to change how you feel about a product.
____ C Advertisements have three basic goals.
____ D Businesses believe that advertisements are effective.
____ E Rational appeals show why a product is better than others.

A Closer Look

Look back at Reading 1 to answer the following questions.

1 What are the goals of advertisements? Choose two answers. (Par. 1)
- a One goal is to increase the price of products.
- b One goal is to change how people view products.
- c One goal is make products more valuable.
- d One goal is to make people buy things.

2 An appeal is a part of an advertisement. **True or False?** (Par. 2)

3 How do rational appeals encourage the sale of products? (Par. 3)
- a They make people feel positive about products.
- b They provide evidence for why the product is the best.
- c They make people think they need the product.
- d They use humor to sell the product.

4 How do emotional appeals encourage the sale of products? (Par. 4)
- a They use people's past experience with the product.
- b They show that the product is more effective than other similar products.
- c They make people feel safer.
- d They try to influence people's feelings about the product.

5 Why does the author use the example about car safety? (Par. 4)
- a It shows how companies use fear in their advertisements.
- b It shows how much advertisements have changed in recent years.
- c It shows how companies use envy in their advertisements.
- d It shows that customers really pay attention to advertisements.

6 Why do businesses spend so much money on advertisements? (Par. 5)
- a It is very expensive to have athletes and movie stars in advertisements.
- b They believe advertisements are effective.
- c They are not sure if advertisements work or not.
- d Advertisements have become more and more expensive every year.

7 What does the table show about advertising spending? (Table 3.1)

a It is increasing the fastest in Western Europe.
b It has not increased very much.
c In general, it has been rising significantly.
d It will probably slow down in the future.

Skill Review

In Skills and Strategies 5, you learned that writers sometimes give clues to the meanings of words by showing contrasts. Noticing this information can sometimes help you figure out the meanings of unfamiliar words in a text.

A Read the sentences below from Reading 1. Highlight the word in each sentence that signals a contrast. Then underline the words that show the meaning that contrasts with the word or phrase in bold.

1 Unlike ads with rational appeals, which try to show that a product is effective, ads with **emotional appeals** try to change how you feel.

2 You thought your old car was **safe**, but suddenly, you begin to think that driving it might be dangerous.

3 Perhaps you want to have a life like that. You want that car, too. It may make you feel **envious**. In contrast, an ad that shows a big family enjoying a car trip together might make you feel happy and satisfied.

4 The purpose of ads like these is usually very clear, but other ads are **not so direct**.

B Read the following sentences. Each one includes a signal of contrast that helps explain a word that you learned in an earlier unit. Choose the word in bold that best fits the meaning of the sentence.

1 Your plan does have some **benefits** / **assistance**, but I still think it has too many disadvantages.

2 George showed a lot **curiosity** / **support** when he was a child. Today, in contrast, he does not seem to be interested in anything.

3 Last year there was **widespread** / **regular** support for the mayor's plan, but today, very few people think his ideas will work.

4 We planned to work on this project right away; however, we had to **postpone** / **maintain** it because everyone in the office has been sick.

Vocabulary Development

Definitions

Find the words in Reading 1 that complete the following definitions.

1 ________________ are basic rules for how something works. (*n pl*) Par. 1, sentence 3

2 To ________________ something is to do or get something that you worked for. (*v*) Par. 1, sentence 5

3 A / An ________________ is an aim; something that you want to get or achieve. (*n*) Par. 1, sentence 5

4 ________________ are people who buy things. (*n pl*) Par. 1, first numbered phrase

5 To ________________ someone is to make that person want to do something. (*v*) Par. 1, third numbered phrase

6 Something that is ________________ involves thinking. (*adj*) Par. 2, last sentence

7 Something that is ________________ works well. (*adj*) Par. 3, sentence 5

8 A / An ________________ is a number or amount. (*n*) Par. 5, last sentence

Word Families

A The words in bold in the chart are from Reading 1. The words next to them are from the same word family. Study and learn these words.

NOUN	ADJECTIVE
athlete (Par. 5)	*athletic*
awareness	***aware*** (Par. 1)
directness	***direct*** (Par. 5)
emotion	***emotional*** (Par. 2)
envy	***envious*** (Par. 3)

B Choose the correct form of the words from the chart to complete the following sentences.

1 I was not ________________ that he had a new job. When did that happen?

2 The ________________ of the advertisements makes them easy for everyone to understand.

3 A / An ________________ from Uganda won the men's marathon in the 2012 Olympics.

4 The young man was ________________ because his friend had a nicer phone and computer.

5 There is greater ________________ today about how our actions affect the environment.

6 His face doesn't show much ________________ unless he gets very angry.

7 The most ________________ way to find the answer is to ask your teacher.

8 She is very ________________. She runs, swims, and plays tennis.

9 When he saw his neighbor's 80-inch television, he felt tremendous ________________.

10 He gave a very ________________ speech about his good friend who died last week.

Critical Thinking

In Reading 1, you learned about the power of advertising and the reasons behind that power.

> **APPLYING INFORMATION**
>
> You use critical thinking skills when you apply information you have just learned to new situations.

A Find an advertisement in print, on television, or online. Work with a partner or small group. Discuss the following questions.

1 Does the ad use a rational or emotional appeal? Explain your answer.

2 How does the ad make you feel about the product? Does it make you feel differently than you did before?

3 Would you choose this product? Why or why not?

4 In your opinion, what kind of ad would be most effective for this product?

B Share your answers with the rest of the class.

Research

Do some research on effective advertisements.

A Find out about some ads that experts think were very good. What made them effective?

B Based on your research, select a past or recent ad that you think is especially effective.

C Share the ad you selected with the rest of the class.

Writing

Write a short report on your research. Explain some experts' perspectives on effective ads. Then describe your selection and why you found it effective.

Before You Read

Connecting to the Topic

Discuss the following questions with a partner.

1 Do you wait for sales to buy things that you want? Explain your answer.

2 How much does price, that is, how much something costs, affect your decision to buy it? Which do you look at first – the price or the thing you want to buy?

3 How do you decide whether a price is good and fair?

Previewing and Predicting

Remember that you should quickly look at any photos, drawings, tables, or graphs. Read any words or labels, too.

A Read the title of Reading 2 and look at the photographs and other art. Then answer the following questions.

1 How are the title and pictures related?

2 When do businesses advertise prices?

3 Where are the prices in the pictures?

4 Why are these pictures included?

5 How much is the steak on page 78?

B Compare your answers with a partner's.

While You Read

As you read, stop at the end of each sentence that contains words in bold. Then follow the instructions in the box in the margin.

The Psychology of Price

1 Special sale! Low, low prices! Shop now! You have probably seen many signs like these. Most people love sales because they can buy products they want at low prices. They are happy because they feel they got good value, that is, they paid less than what the product was worth. But did they really get good value? Experts who understand the psychology of price say maybe they did not.

2 Businesses are very careful about how they set prices for their products and services. They understand how to use price as a strategy. At the heart of most price strategies is a fundamental principle called *the anchor*. The anchor

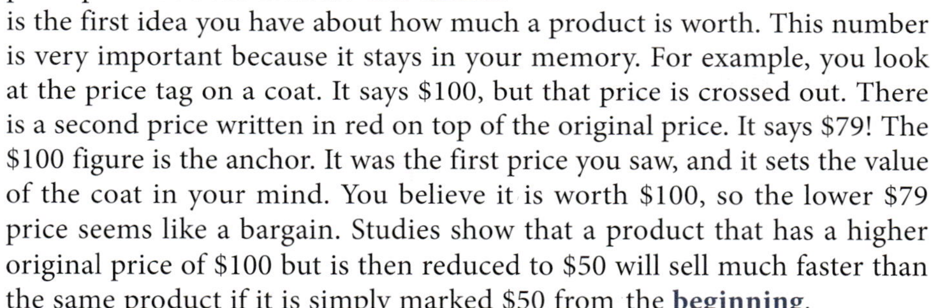

is the first idea you have about how much a product is worth. This number is very important because it stays in your memory. For example, you look at the price tag on a coat. It says $100, but that price is crossed out. There is a second price written in red on top of the original price. It says $79! The $100 figure is the anchor. It was the first price you saw, and it sets the value of the coat in your mind. You believe it is worth $100, so the lower $79 price seems like a bargain. Studies show that a product that has a higher original price of $100 but is then reduced to $50 will sell much faster than the same product if it is simply marked $50 from the **beginning**.

WHILE YOU READ 1

What is the main idea of paragraph 2? Highlight the sentence that shows the main idea.

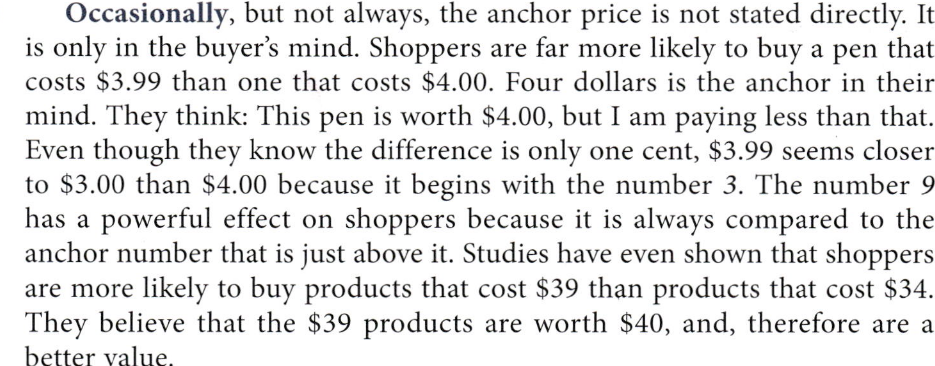

3 **Occasionally**, but not always, the anchor price is not stated directly. It is only in the buyer's mind. Shoppers are far more likely to buy a pen that costs $3.99 than one that costs $4.00. Four dollars is the anchor in their mind. They think: This pen is worth $4.00, but I am paying less than that. Even though they know the difference is only one cent, $3.99 seems closer to $3.00 than $4.00 because it begins with the number *3*. The number *9* has a powerful effect on shoppers because it is always compared to the anchor number that is just above it. Studies have even shown that shoppers are more likely to buy products that cost $39 than products that cost $34. They believe that the $39 products are worth $40, and, therefore are a better value.

WHILE YOU READ 2

Find a clue in this sentence that signals a contrast with the word *occasionally*. Highlight the clue and the word that means the opposite of *occasionally*.

4 The psychology of price is at work in all sorts of places, including on menus. A menu is not just a list of food that a restaurant offers. Many are carefully designed and use anchor pricing. When you open a menu, the first place you usually look is on the top right side. That is where you will

find the item that is most profitable for the restaurant. However, nearby you will also find the most expensive item, like a big steak or lobster. The restaurant does not really believe a lot of people will order the most expensive dish; however, it provides an anchor. The high anchor price makes all the other dishes look like good value, including the dish that is profitable for the restaurant, perhaps a chicken or pasta dish. Restaurant owners have other tricks. They have found if they do not include money symbols like €, $, or ¥, people spend more money. So many restaurants just write the number without the **symbol**.

WHILE YOU READ 3

What is the main idea of paragraph 4? Highlight the sentence that shows the main idea.

5 There are many strategies for pricing, but anchor pricing is probably the most powerful. Even when you know about it, it is sometimes difficult to resist the effect of the anchor on your shopping behavior.

Menu

Porterhouse Steak	49
Lamp Chops	46
Short Ribs	39
Lobster Tail	64
Grilled Salmon	39

Main Idea Check

Match the main ideas below to paragraphs 1–4 in Reading 2. Write the number of the paragraph on the blank line.

3 A The number 9 sets an anchor in customers' brains.
4 B You can see anchor pricing at work in restaurants.
1 C Sale prices may not offer good value.
2 D The anchor is fundamental to pricing strategy.

A Closer Look

Look back at Reading 2 to answer the following questions.

1 The goal of sale prices is to make customers feel they are getting good value. **True or False?** (Par. 1)

2 What is an anchor price? (Par. 2)
a It is the fundamental value of a product.
b It is the price a customer is willing to pay for a product.
c It is the figure that a customer first believes is the product's value.
d It is the lowest price that a customer has seen for the product.

3 One pair of shoes is tagged originally as $80 and then marked as $49. Another pair is simply tagged as $49. Why does the first pair sell faster? (Par. 2)
a The reduced price is better value.
b The original price is cheaper.
c People don't want to spend $80 on a pair of shoes.
d Eighty dollars sets an anchor price.

4 Customers are more likely to pay $94 for a watch than $99 for the same watch. **True or False?** (Par. 3)

5 Why is the number nine so important in pricing? (Par. 3)
a Products with prices that end in nine are good value.
b Prices that end in nine make customers feel they are getting a bargain.
c The number nine has a powerful anchor.
d Customers know that they can save at least one cent.

6 What dish gives the anchor price on a menu? (Par. 4)
a The most expensive dish
b The most profitable dish
c Any dish without a $ symbol
d The first dish on the menu

Skill Review

In Skills and Strategies 5, you learned that writers sometimes give clues to the meanings of words by showing contrasts. In earlier units, you learned they also give clues to the meanings of words by using examples and definitions. Noticing this information can sometimes help you figure out the meanings of unfamiliar words in a text.

A **Read the sentences below from Reading 2. Decide if the writer is using *contrast*, *examples*, or *definitions* to explain the words in bold. Write *C* (for contrast), *E* (for example), or *D* (for definition) on the blank lines. Then highlight the part of each sentence that contains the contrast, the example, or the definition.**

____ 1 They are happy because they feel they got **good value**, that is, they paid less than what the product was worth.

____ 2 At the heart of most price strategies is a fundamental principle called **the anchor**. The anchor is the first idea you have about how much a product is worth.

____ 3 Studies show that a product that has a higher original price of $100 but is then **reduced** to $50 will sell much faster than faster than the same product if it is simply marked $50 from the beginning.

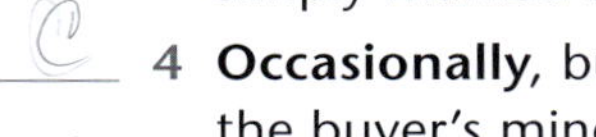

____ 4 **Occasionally**, but not always, the anchor price is not stated directly. It is only in the buyer's mind.

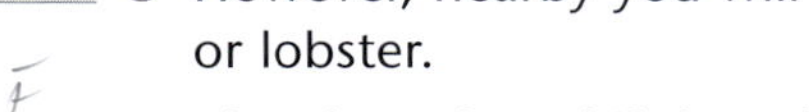

____ 5 However, nearby you will also find the most **expensive** item, like a big steak or lobster.

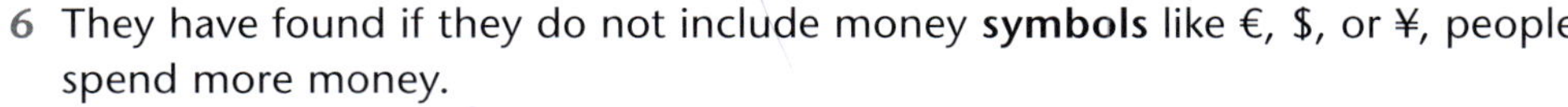

____ 6 They have found if they do not include money **symbols** like €, $, or ¥, people spend more money.

B **Compare your answers with a partner's.**

Vocabulary Development

Definitions

Find the words in Reading 2 that complete the following definitions.

1 Something that is good ________________ is worth the money you paid for it. (*n*) Par. 1, sentence 6

2 Something that is ________________ is basic or most important. (*adj*) Par. 2, sentence 3

3 A / An ________________ is something that gives a base, a foundation, or a starting point. (*n*) Par. 2, sentence 6

4 A / An ________________ is a piece of paper with information on it; a label. (*n*) Par. 2, sentence 6

5 A / An ________________ is something that you can buy at a lower price than usual. (*n*) Par. 2, sentence 12

6 A / An ________________ is a list of things that a restaurant serves. (*n*) Par. 4, sentence 1

7 A / An ________________ is a single thing, usually one that is a part of a group. (*n*) Par. 4, sentence 5

8 A / An ________________ is something that represents something else; for example, π is the symbol for the number pi (3.14). (*n*) Par. 4, sentence 10

Words in Context

Complete the sentences with words from Reading 2 in the box below.

crossed out	effect	reduced	sign
designed	profitable	sale	trick

1 I ________________ the amount of sugar in the cake because it was too sweet.

2 The ________________ in front of the store said "Opening Soon!"

3 He made a mistake, so he ________________ the first answer and wrote the correct one above it.

4 The medicine had an immediate ________________, making her feel better right away.

5 Some people use this ________________ to remember things: They tie a string around their finger.

6 This business is very ________________. It makes lots of money.

7 There was a great ________________ at my favorite store. I bought a coat and a shirt because the prices were so low.

8 A famous artist ________________ the new restaurant. It looks very bright and modern.

Critical Thinking

In Reading 2, you learned about the strategies stores use when they set the prices for their products. One of the primary strategies is anchoring.

CLARIFYING CONCEPTS

A critical thinker might explore a text's ideas by considering how they would fit into a different context.

A Work with a partner or small group. Below is a list of additional marketing strategies that affect price. With your group, discuss which of these strategies you think is most effective. Give reasons for your answers.

1 Prices that include more than one of a product: "Ten oranges for just $3!"

2 Time limits, for example, "This television is available at this price for just two days!"

3 Limits on availability: An ad offers a computer at a very low price but only has a few of them for sale.

4 Free gifts: "Buy a pizza and get a free drink."

5 Gradual payment plans: "Buy a television and pay a little bit each month." However, the total price may be higher than if you paid the whole price in the beginning.

B Think of at least one more marketing strategy that affects price. Share it with the rest of the class.

Research

Do some research on price strategies in your own community. Look at the newspaper, or listen to ads on television. You may also want to visit a street or mall where there are a lot of stores. Take notes on the following questions:

1 What kinds of price strategies do you see in these ads?

2 Which is the most common strategy?

3 Are some strategies more common with specific products? For example, is the first strategy, in **A** above, more common with food?

Writing

Write a short report on the results of your research. Include pictures of the ads if you can.

Finding the Topic and Main Idea of a Reading

In Skills and Strategies 2 on page 20 and Skills
you learned that each paragraph has one topi
reading also has one topic and one main idea.
the whole reading is about. The main idea is t
the writer makes overall about the topic in the
idea of the reading connect all the paragraph

Examples & Explanations

Red Bull, originally from Thailand, is the
popular energy drink in the world. Surprisingly, the
company became famous without spending much money on advertising. How is that possible? The answer: Red Bull found a cheap and effective way to advertise its products.

cheap and effective way to advertise its products. Writers often tell the main idea in the last sentence of the first paragraph.

Red Bull wanted young people to buy its product. The company went to places where young people often go, like schools and shopping malls. At these places, the company put many empty cans of Red Bull in the garbage. Doing this cost the company almost nothing, but it introduced young people to the new drink. They saw the empty cans and thought, "Drinking Red Bull is really popular!"

The topic of the second and third paragraphs is also *Red Bull*. These paragraphs connect to the main idea of the reading. They show how Red Bull's advertising was cheap (the second paragraph) and effective (the third paragraph).

This strategy worked. Almost immediately, young people started talking about Red Bull. Sales of Red Bull increased quickly. Before long, it was the most popular energy drink in the world. Today, many other companies sell energy drinks, but their sales are far behind Red Bull's.

Red Bull's advertising plan was very successful. The company became very famous, and it did not have to spend a lot of money. All Red Bull needed was a creative new idea.

In the first sentence of this paragraph, the writer gives the topic and main idea of the reading again: *Red Bull's advertising plan was very successful.* Writers often repeat the topic and main idea of the reading in the last paragraph. They may tell the main idea in other words than they used before. For example, in the first paragraph, the writer used the words *cheap and effective*. In this paragraph, the writer uses the word *successful.*

Strategies

These strategies will help you find the main idea of a reading.

- As you read, ask yourself: *What is this reading all about? What idea connects all the paragraphs?*
- Look at the last sentence of the first paragraph. Writers often tell the topic and main idea in this sentence.
- Look at the last paragraph. Writers often repeat the topic and main idea there. Remember that writers may not use the same words as before to tell the main idea.

Skill Practice 1

Read the following article. Then answer the questions.

Bob Wagstaff, a doctor from Utah, created a tongue cleaner called the Orabrush. Dr. Wagstaff then spent almost all his money on television commercials for the Orabrush, but no one was buying his product. He was out of ideas, and almost out of money. Desperate, Dr. Wagstaff went to a college business class and asked the students for advice. Most of the students thought his product would not succeed. But one student, named Jeffrey Harmon, had an idea that would make the Orabrush a big success.

Harmon's idea was simple: use the Internet for advertising. He advised Dr. Wagstaff to make a funny video about his product and post it online. If people liked the video, Harmon said, maybe people would start to buy the Orabrush. Harmon did not have much experience in business, but Dr. Wagstaff decided to follow his advice.

With the last of his money, Dr. Wagstaff made a two-minute video about the Orabrush. In the video, an actor said a lot of funny things about bad breath and showed how the Orabrush can stop bad breath. The video became very popular, and before long, so did the Orabrush. Today the Orabrush is sold in stores around the world, and Dr. Wagstaff's company is very successful.

Thanks to Harmon's clever marketing idea, the Orabrush became a big hit. Later, Harmon became the Chief Marketing Officer for Dr. Wagstaff's company. Other companies can learn from his and Dr. Wagstaff's success.

1 What is the topic of the reading? Choose the best answer.

a Bad breath
b The Orabrush
c Jeffrey Harmon

2 Which sentence tells the main idea of the reading? Choose the best answer.

a Bob Wagstaff is the creator of a tongue cleaner called the Orabrush.
b Other companies can learn from the success of Harmon and Wagstaff.
c The Orabrush is successful because of Harmon's clever marketing idea.

Skill Practice 2

Read the following paragraphs. Underline the two sentences in the reading that tell the main idea. Then write the topic and main idea of the reading in your own words on the lines below.

Undercover Marketing

These days, many people ignore traditional advertising. To get their attention, companies have to find new ways to advertise their products. Some companies are using a strategy called *undercover marketing*. With undercover marketing, companies hide their advertising messages in everyday life. They pay regular people to use and talk about products in a way that will get others' attention. Undercover marketing can be very successful, but it must be done carefully.

For some companies, undercover marketing has very positive results. An example is Sony. The company used undercover marketing for its camera phone. Sony paid young people to act like tourists and ask other people to take their picture with the camera phone. Many people became interested in the camera phones, at a very low cost to Sony. Now many companies use this type of undercover marketing to help sell their products.

However, undercover marketing also comes with risks. Walmart had very poor results when it paid writers to speak positively about the company online. People discovered Walmart's plan and complained that the company was dishonest in its online actions. Instead of making people excited about the company, Walmart's plan had the opposite effect.

Clearly, undercover marketing has both benefits and risks. Companies should consider their options carefully before they try this new form of marketing.

Topic of the reading: Undercover Marketing. ______

Main idea of the reading: ______

______

Before You Read

Connecting to the Topic

Discuss the following questions with a partner.

1 Are some things more important than price when you buy a product? Explain your answer.

2 Are you loyal to some products? In other words, do you continue to buy a product from a specific company even if the price is higher than others? If so, why?

3 Do you think marketing can change how people feel about products? Explain your answer.

Previewing and Predicting

When you preview a longer reading, remember to look at section headings. These headings can help you predict what the reading will be about. Also remember that looking at the art and reading first sentences can help you make predictions about the reading.

A Read the title, section headings, and first few sentences of the sections that follow the first paragraph in Reading 3. Look at the art. Then choose the best answers to the questions below.

1 What do you think *guerrilla marketing* is?

a Marketing during wars
b Unusual forms of marketing
c International marketing
d Advertising to large crowds

2 Who uses guerrilla marketing?

a Businesses
b Government and international organizations
c Both of the above
d Neither of the above

B Look at the photographs in Reading 3. How do you think the activities and objects in the photographs are related to marketing? Discuss with a partner.

While You Read

As you read, stop at the end of each sentence that contains words in bold. Then follow the instructions in the box in the margin.

Guerrilla Marketing

1 To sell its products or services, a company may advertise on television, in newspapers, or on the Internet. But marketing is more than just advertising. A company's marketing plan may also include some unusual ways to make people aware of the company and its products. One strategy for doing this is *guerrilla marketing*.

WHILE YOU READ 1

What do you think the topic of the reading will be? Highlight the sentence in the paragraph that gives the topic.

I. Guerrilla Marketing as a Business Strategy

2 The word *guerrilla* comes from Spanish. It means a person who fights in a war, but not in the regular military. Guerrillas use unusual methods, they often fight secretly, and it is difficult to predict when they will appear. Similarly, *guerrilla marketing* uses unusual and often unpredictable methods of marketing.

3 One of these is the *flash mob*. Flash mobs were a popular form of guerrilla marketing in the early years of this century. A flash mob is a crowd of people. They don't look unusual. But suddenly, they begin to sing, dance, or perform together. Flash mobs usually occur in large, public places. The mobile phone company T-Mobile and the French clothing company Moncler Grenoble organized flash mobs in train stations. It was just an ordinary evening, but suddenly there was music, and hundreds of people began to dance. Some people in the crowd started to dance, too. Others took photos and videos on their phones. Everyone was smiling.

A flash mob in an airport

4 This kind of activity may not sell products immediately. However, it certainly increases the public's awareness of these products, even among people who don't like flash mobs. Many people find guerrilla marketing events like flash mobs entertaining. They may feel positive about the products as a result. Just as important, the effect of guerrilla marketing continues long after the events end because videos of them are posted **online**, that is, on the Internet. Nearly 40 million people have watched the T-Mobile flash mob video. In general, the goal of guerrilla marketing is not to make immediate sales. Instead, it is to change how people feel about a company and its products.

WHILE YOU READ 2

Find a clue in this sentence that signals a definition of *online*. Highlight the clue and definition.

5 Flash mobs are not the only form of guerrilla marketing. There are other interesting and unusual methods. Coca-Cola sent "happiness trucks" and "happiness vending machines" to communities all over the world. The happiness trucks offered free bottles of Coke. The vending machines were similar. They gave away free Cokes, but they also gave away flowers, pizza,

and sandwiches! In the videos of these events, you can see people smiling, laughing, and hugging. Coca-Cola succeeded in its goal – to make people feel happy about its product.

II. Guerrilla Marketing in Other Organizations

6 Businesses are not the only organizations that use guerrilla marketing. For example, UNICEF (a United Nations organization that works to improve the health of children) wanted to bring attention to the lack of safe drinking water around the world. UNICEF wanted to do something that was unusual and surprising, so the organization chose a guerrilla marketing strategy. Staff members put dirty water into plastic bottles. Then they put the bottles into vending machines. Instead of a brand name like Orangina or Fanta, the labels on bottles said "Dirty Water" and the machines displayed names of the diseases that dirty water can cause. One said "Cholera." Another said "Typhoid." No one bought the water, but thousands of people gave money to UNICEF. That money helped bring safe drinking water to communities around the world. Thousands more people who saw the video of the dirty water machines also gave money to **UNICEF**.

A vending machine

WHILE YOU READ 3

What is the topic of this paragraph?
a) the use of vending machines for marketing
b) the use of guerrilla marketing by organizations that are not businesses
c) the importance of video in guerrilla marketing

III. Guerrilla Marketing and Technology

7 The Internet and mobile communications make it easier to organize and promote guerrilla marketing events. The Internet increases the impact of the original event because so many people watch the video. They experience the event indirectly, sometimes months or years later. People enjoy watching these videos because they are surprising and unusual, but also entertaining. They share them with friends, and those people share them with other friends. Marketing professionals call this *going viral*. Going viral means that something – an idea, a video, a song – moves very quickly through the population. It reaches more and more people with every step, just like a virus. And this continued attention costs the company nothing.

8 Are these forms of marketing successful? Will you go on the Internet now and look for videos of some of these examples? If you do, it shows just how the effective these methods can be.

Reading Skill Development

Main Idea Check

Match the main ideas below to paragraphs 2–7 in Reading 3. Write the number of the paragraph on the blank line.

____ A Flash mobs can be an effective form of guerilla marketing.

____ B Government and international organizations may choose guerrilla marketing as a strategy.

____ C Other forms of guerrilla marketing can change how people feel about products.

____ D Many guerrilla-marketing strategies depend on the Internet.

____ E The term *guerrilla marketing* comes from a kind of fighting during wars.

____ F Guerrilla marketing can promote a general good feeling, like happiness

A Closer Look

Look back at Reading 3 to answer the following questions.

1 How is the term *guerrilla marketing* related to guerrilla fighters? (Par. 2)

a No one knows about them.
b They both are unexpected and unpredictable.
c Marketing is a little bit like war.
d Both of them began in the early years of this century.

2 Which of the following are characteristics of a flash mob? Choose two answers (Par. 3)

a The members perform together as a group.
b They appear in unexpected places.
c They perform with mobile telephones.
d They take videos and photographs of their performances.

3 The main goal of flash mobs is to increase sales of a product quickly. **True or False?** (Par. 4)

4 What was the goal of the Coke "happiness" marketing strategy? (Par. 5)

a To give people free Coke products
b To let more people know about Coke
c To make people feel positive about Coke
d To spread happiness to communities around the world

5 UNICEF chose the vending machines as their strategy. What was their main reason for doing this? (Par. 6)

a They didn't want to use a flash mob.
b They wanted people to think about the importance of clean water.
c They knew that people are willing to put money in vending machines.
d They wanted people to have a negative response.

6 Why is the Internet so important to guerrilla marketing? (Par. 7)

a It increases the impact of the strategy.
b It makes marketing more entertaining.
c Most people prefer to use the Internet.
d Indirect methods of marketing are more effective.

7 What did the flash mobs, the Coke happiness strategy, and the UNICEF vending machines have in common? Choose two answers. (Pars. 3–6)

a The companies hoped they would make people feel positive about their products.
b They made people smile and laugh together.
c They were unusual and surprising.
d They were fun but not very effective.

Skill Review

In Skills and Strategies 6, you learned that a reading has one main idea. You learned that one way to determine the main idea is to ask questions like: *What is the reading about? What does the writer say about this topic?* and *What idea connects all of the paragraphs?*

A Look back at Reading 3. Review the main ideas you chose for the paragraphs in Main Idea Check on page 89. What is the topic of Reading 3?

____

B **Now think about the three main goals of advertising:**

1 Make customers aware of the product or service
2 Make customers like and want the product or service
3 Encourage customers to buy the product or service

Marketing strategies like *guerrilla marketing* do not always focus directly on the third goal, selling products. Do they try to achieve the other two goals? Complete the chart by putting a check (✓) to show whether the guerrilla marketing strategies in Reading 3 try to achieve these goals.

GUERRILLA MARKETING STRATEGY	MAKES PEOPLE AWARE OF THE COMPANY AND ITS PRODUCTS	MAKES PEOPLE LIKE THE COMPANY AND ITS PRODUCTS
Flash mobs		
Coke happiness		
UNICEF vending machines		

C **Now think about the main idea of the reading. Begin with the whole-reading topic you chose in A. With a partner, discuss what you think the writer says about that topic. One way to answer this question is to make a generalization based on the chart you completed in B.**

Now write a sentence that states the main idea of the reading:

____

Definitions

Find the words in Reading 3 that complete the following definitions.

1 A / An ________________ is a plan for reaching a goal. (*n*) Par. 1, last sentence

2 Something that is ________________ is usual or ordinary. (*adj*) Par. 2, sentence 2

3 A / An ________________ is a group of people who may act in a disorganized or even violent way in public. (*n*) Par. 3, sentence 1

4 To ________________ is to entertain people by singing, dancing, etc. (*v*) Par. 3, sentence 5

5 To ________________ some information, a picture, or a video is to put it on the Internet so other people can see it. (*v*) Par. 4, sentence 5

6 ________________ are groups of people who live in the same area. (*n pl*) Par. 6, sentence 10

7 To ________________ something is to help it develop or grow stronger. (*v*) Par. 7, sentence 1

8 ________________ are people with jobs that require special skills. (*n pl*) Par. 7, sentence 6

Words in Context

A Use context clues to match the first part of each sentence with the best completion for the sentence. Each completion should fit with the meaning of the words in bold.

_____ 1 The **population** of the city

_____ 2 He served in the **military** because he

_____ 3 The two men looked **similar**, and they also

_____ 4 The girl gave her grandmother a **hug** when she

_____ 5 His **lack** of education

_____ 6 He **gave away** most of his furniture when he

_____ 7 The little boy didn't want to **share** his toys when he and his friends

_____ 8 We used a new **method** because it

a saw her at the airport.

b made it hard to find a job.

c wanted to serve his country.

d moved to a smaller house.

e played together.

f increased to more than one million.

g worked better than the old way.

h behaved in the same way.

B Compare your answers with a partner's. Discuss what clues helped you match the parts of the sentences and helped you understand what the words in bold mean.

Academic Word List

The following are Academic Word List words from all the readings in Unit 3. Use these words to complete the sentences. (If necessary, review the AWL words in Key Vocabulary on pages 257–267.)

achieve (*v*)	community (*n*)	principles (*n*)	rational (*adj*)	strategy (*n*)
aware (*adj*)	goal (*n*)	professionals (*n*)	similar (*adj*)	symbol (*n*)

1 The general explained his ________________ for winning the war to the soldiers.

2 The white dove is a / an ________________ of peace.

3 Those two women are wearing ________________ dresses. The only difference is the color.

4 Our ________________ is to collect one million dollars for medical research.

5 Most ________________ have to study for several years before they can begin their jobs.

6 We hope to ________________ economic growth of five percent next year.

7 No one was ________________ of the president's visit until this morning.

8 Everyone in the ________________ came to the meeting to discuss plans to build a new school.

9 One of the basic ________________ of advertising is to keep ads short and simple.

10 Some of my decisions were not ________________ but were based on emotion.

Critical Thinking

Reading 3 makes the claim that guerrilla marketing can be a successful strategy.

> **EXPLORING OPINIONS**
>
> Critical readers form their own opinions about important topics in a text.

A Discuss the following questions with a partner.

1 Do you think guerrilla marketing would change how you feel about a product? Explain your answer.

2 Experts in marketing hope that if they make people feel good, this will result in sales in the future. Do you think this is likely? Why or why not?

3 Have you ever had an experience with guerrilla marketing? Or have you watched a marketing video online? If so, describe it to your partner.

B Share your answers with the rest of the class.

Research

Find some examples of flash mobs on the Internet. There are many examples on YouTube and other video sites. Think about these questions as you do your research.

1 Were all the flash mobs related to a product?

2 Do you think flash mobs have other functions?

3 What is the role of music in flash mobs?

4 How did the people who were watching the flash mob respond?

5 How did you feel when you watched the video?

6 Do you think the creators achieved their goal?

Writing

Write a short report about your research on flash mobs. Include the answers to the questions above.

Improving Your Reading Speed

Good readers read quickly and still understand most of what they read.

A Read the instructions and strategies for Improving Your Reading Speed in Appendix 3 on page 270.

B Choose one of the readings in this unit. Read it without stopping. Time how long it takes you to finish the text in minutes and seconds. Enter the time in the chart on page 271. Then calculate your reading speed in number of words per minute.

MAKING CONNECTIONS

CATEGORY WORDS

Writers often need to connect ideas in a text. They can do this by using *this* or *these* plus a word for a category that includes the original idea.

In the following example, the two phrases in **bold** express connected ideas. The arrows show how they are connected. The arrow starts at the phrase that names the category, and the point of the arrow shows the idea included in the category.

> Sometimes companies try to sell their products by **giving something away**. Surprisingly, **this strategy** can be very effective.
>
> *Strategy* is a category word. *Giving something away* is a type of marketing strategy.

Exercise 1

Read the following groups of sentences. Highlight the phrase that contains *this* / *these* + a category word in the second sentence in each group. Underline the phrase containing the idea it refers to. Draw an arrow from the highlighted phrase to the underlined phrase. The first one is an example.

1 One successful advertising strategy is the slogan, like Nike's "*Just do it.*" These words make customers aware of the product.

2 Some advertisements use musicians, actors, or athletes. These famous people can help sell products.

3 A special song can also help sell a product. Customers hear this music in their heads, and they think about the product.

4 In the last five years, there has been a lot of marketing on social media. These sites include Facebook and YouTube.

5 Some companies prefer more traditional ways of marketing. These methods include newspaper and television ads.

6 Direct marketing can be very effective. An example of this kind of advertising is a text message on your cell phone about a special sale.

Exercise 2

Make a clear paragraph by putting sentences A, B, and C into the best order after the numbered sentence. Look for pronouns and category words to help you. Write the letters in the correct order on the blank lines.

1 A theater owner in Canada wanted to sell more tickets. ___ ___ ___

A	B	C
He decided to give free tickets to taxi drivers.	It worked because the drivers told their passengers good things about the theater.	This idea was very successful.

2 Sometimes businesses lose money on some products. ___ ___ ___

A	B	C
It is to sell other products that make money.	These products have a specific purpose.	This marketing strategy is very common.

3 Think about the printer that is connected to your computer. ___ ___ ___

A	B	C
However, this company probably made a profit on the ink for the printer.	The printer company probably lost money when you bought it.	This machine was probably not very expensive.

4 Printer companies have a found a way to make you buy other products. ___ ___ ___

A	B	C
These products include the ink for their printers.	This strategy has been very effective.	It is very expensive, but it is only available from the printer company.

5 Printer companies have connected the sale of printers and ink. ___ ___ ___

A	B	C
These profits show that a company can make money by first losing money.	This connection has resulted in big profits for them.	Many other companies have copied this idea.

4

TASTE

SKILLS AND STRATEGIES

- Finding the Meanings of Words: Prior Knowledge
- Finding Supporting Details: Facts and Examples

Finding the Meanings of Words: Prior Knowledge

...ies 1 (page 2), 3 (page 34), and
...top reading when they see a difficult
...meaning of the difficult word in the
...uch as definitions, examples, or contrasts.
...erstand difficult words is by using their
...n general. The things that readers already
...nderstand word meanings.

Readers may not know the word *boil*. However, readers probably know what happens when water reaches a temperature of 212°F (100°C). They can use this knowledge to understand the meaning of *boil*.

boils = *reaches the temperature when bubbles and steam appear*

People usually drink coffee from a **mug** so the coffee will stay hot and they won't burn their fingers.

The writer uses a word that readers may not know: *mug*. Readers can use their knowledge to understand the meaning. They can ask themselves, "What do people usually drink coffee from?" and "What kind of cup do people use for hot drinks like coffee?" If readers know the answers to these questions, they can understand the meaning of *mug*.

Readers can also picture the sentence in their mind. They can imagine a person drinking hot coffee, and they can picture the object in the person's hand.

mug = *a big cup with a handle*

Children should have fruit for dessert and only eat candy and ice cream as a **treat**.

The writer uses a word that readers may not know: *treat*. Readers can think about other words to put in the sentence so the sentence still makes sense. From the information in the sentence, readers can guess that a *treat* is a special food that you do not eat very often.

treat = *a special food that you do not eat very often*

Strategies

These strategies will help you find the meanings of words while you read.

- When you see a word you do not know, do not stop reading. Look for information in the reading that you understand because of prior knowledge about the world in general. Try to relate the new word to this knowledge. This can help you understand the meaning of the word.
- If a sentence has an unknown word, make a picture in your mind of the parts of the sentence that you know. This picture may help you understand the unknown word.
- Ask yourself: *What other word can replace the difficult word so the sentence still makes sense?*

Skill Practice 1

Read the following sentences. Write each word in bold next to its meaning in the lettered list below. Do not use a dictionary. Use the strategies above to help you. The first one is an example.

1 The ice cream **melted** in the sun.

2 When bananas are **ripe**, they turn yellow.

3 If you keep fruit in the refrigerator, it will not **spoil** as quickly.

4 Be sure to wash and **peel** the potatoes before you cook them.

5 Some people can eat a whole pizza, but most just have a **slice** or two.

6 It is best to cook pasta in a large **pot** of water.

7 To find out if an egg is fresh, put it in a pot of water; if it **sinks** to the bottom, it is good to use.

8 Those eggs are spoiled; they should be **discarded** immediately.

a *pot* = a round container that you use for cooking

b peel = to remove the outer layers of fruit or vegetables

c discared = thrown away; put in the trash

d spoil = to become too old to eat safely

e melted = changed from a solid to a liquid because of heat

f sinks = goes down below the surface of water or other liquid

g ripe = developed enough and ready to eat

h slice = a flat piece of food that has been cut from a larger piece

Skill Practice 2

Read the following article. Use your prior knowledge to figure out the meanings of the words in bold. Then write their meanings on the blank lines below.

How is coffee produced? There are seven **steps**. First, once a year, workers go from tree to tree and **harvest** the coffee beans. Then, the workers **dry** the coffee beans by leaving them in the sun. After the coffee beans dry, the workers remove the **skins** from the outside of the beans. Only the inside of the beans is used to make coffee. Next, the beans are put over a fire and **roasted**. The heat makes the color of the beans change from green to brown. After that, the workers **grind** the coffee using a special machine. Next, the workers test the coffee. They put it close to their nose and test the **scent**. If the coffee smells good, it is ready for **distribution**. Workers bring the coffee to stores, supermarkets, cafes, and restaurants.

1 *steps* = parts of the proce

2 *harvest* = colect

3 *dry* = is not weath.

4 *skins* = parts the out side

5 *roasted* = to cook

6 *grind* = very small piece

7 *scent* = smell

8 *distribution* = that give something a people

Before You Read

Connecting to the Topic

Discuss the following questions with a partner.

1 What are the five senses? Which one do you think is the most important?

2 What do you know about the sense of taste? Explain what you know to your partner.

3 What happens to your sense of taste when you have a cold? Why do you think this happens?

Previewing and Predicting

One way to preview is to read the title and the first paragraph of a reading. The first paragraph can often tell you what the whole reading will be about.

A Read the first paragraph of Reading 1 below and the title on page 102. Then answer the questions that follow. Write your answers on the blank lines.

> *Delicious, scrumptious, tasteless.* We have lots of words to describe how things taste. But how does taste actually work? How does your brain know that something is tasteless? Also, what makes a food delicious?

1 What do *delicious* and *scrumptious* mean?

____

2 What do you think this reading will discuss next?

____

3 What do you think the whole reading will be about?

____

B Compare your answers with a partner's.

While You Read

As you read, stop at the end of each sentence that contains words in bold. Then follow the instructions in the box in the margin.

Taste – The Least Understood Sense

1 *Delicious, scrumptious, tasteless*. We have lots of words to describe how things taste. But how does taste actually work? How does your brain know that something is tasteless? Also, what makes a food delicious?

2 There has been less research on taste than on our other four senses, but scientists have been aware of the basics of taste for many years. Scientists have identified five distinct tastes: sweet (like ice cream), sour (like lemons), salty (like olives), bitter (like coffee), and savory. Savory is sometimes called umami, which is the Japanese word for this taste. A Japanese scientist first proposed umami as the fifth taste more than 100 years ago. This taste is difficult to describe, but it is in meat and fish as well as mushrooms and cheese.

3 All of those little bumps on your tongue contain structures called taste buds. Each bud has an opening at the top with special cells. The saliva in your mouth dissolves the food. Then, very small pieces of the dissolved

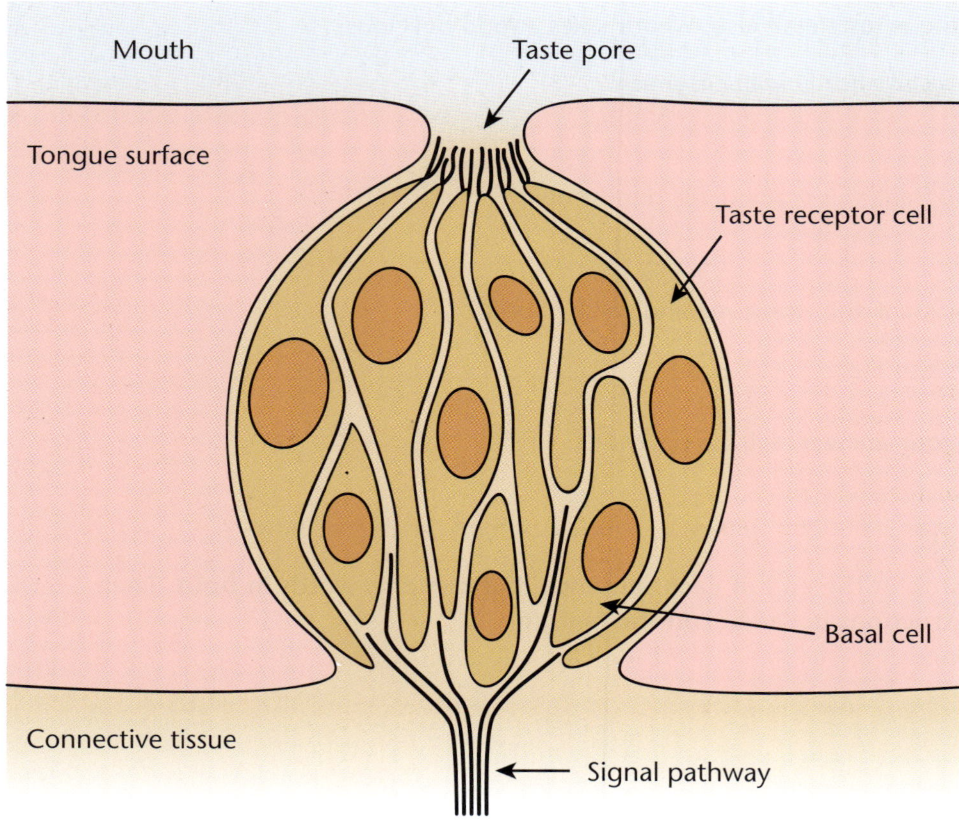

The parts of a human taste bud

food enter the opening at the top of the taste bud. The special cells detect different chemicals in food and send messages about how they taste to the brain.

4 There are several widespread, but incorrect, beliefs about taste buds. First, taste buds are not just on your tongue; they are all over your mouth. Second, you may have learned that there are centers of taste in certain parts of your mouth, for example, sweet at the tip of your tongue. Although some parts of the tongue detect some tastes better than others, you can sense different tastes in every part of your **mouth**.

WHILE YOU READ 1

What is the main idea of paragraph 4? Highlight the sentence that shows the main idea.

5 Scientists believe that each of the five basic tastes developed because it was important for human survival. The sweet taste encourages us to eat food that gives us energy. Salty foods contain important minerals (like sodium and calcium), and sour foods often contain vitamins. Many savory foods contain protein. All of these are essential for good health. Finally, our ability to taste bitter foods may help us avoid foods that are dangerous. Dangerous plants, for example, often have a bitter taste that many people do not like.

6 The taste buds play an important role in our perception of taste, but they are not the only factor. Experts often point out the difference between taste and flavor. Flavor is more complex. It includes basic taste as well as **aroma**, that is, how things smell. When you say a food is delicious, you are describing both the taste and the aroma. You can prove this with a candy test. Close your eyes and hold your nose closed. Then ask a friend to give you two different flavors of candy, for example, strawberry and grape. If you cannot smell them, they both taste sweet, but they taste almost the same. Now, stop holding your nose so you can smell. The air can easily carry the aroma from your mouth to your nose, so now you will be able to taste the difference.

WHILE YOU READ 2

Find a phrase in this sentence that signals a definition of *aroma*. Highlight the phrase and definition.

7 There is one final aspect of flavor. People in many cultures like hot, **spicy** food. This spiciness is not really a taste. Foods that contain ginger, chili, and black pepper all hurt your mouth a little bit – or sometimes a lot! Your brain does not get the signal about this flavor from your taste buds. Instead, the signal of pain that goes to the brain when you eat these foods is received by a sense much closer to touch than taste or smell. So, when you think about whether something is scrumptious or tasteless, remember that the flavor of foods is not just about taste. Our perception of flavor is actually a combination of taste, smell, and touch.

WHILE YOU READ 3

Read the next two sentences to find clues to the meaning of *spicy*. Highlight the words that help you understand the meaning.

Reading Skill Development

Main Idea Check

Match the main ideas below to paragraphs 2–7 in Reading 1. Write the number of the paragraph on the blank line.

_____ A The sense of taste begins with the taste buds and goes to the brain.

_____ B The human ability to detect the five tastes may have helped us survive.

_____ C Spiciness is not related to the sense of taste.

_____ D Humans can sense five different tastes.

_____ E Many people believe things about the sense of taste that are not true.

_____ F The sense of smell is related to how we sense flavor.

A Closer Look

Look back at Reading 1 to answer the following questions.

1 What is umami? (Par. 2)

a A Japanese flavor
b The savory taste
c The flavor of olives
d A mix of salty and sour flavors

2 Provide an example of a food for each taste. (Par. 2)

TASTE	EXAMPLE FOOD
Sweet	
Sour	
Salty	
Bitter	
Umami	

3 All taste buds are located on the tongue. **True or False?** (Par. 4)

4 Match each of the tastes with the benefit they may provide. (Par. 5)

	Taste	Benefit
_____	1 sweet	a protein
_____	2 bitter	b minerals
_____	3 umami	c energy
_____	4 sour	d vitamins
_____	5 salty	e avoiding danger

5 What does the candy test show? (Par. 6)

a It shows that your vision and your sense of taste are connected.
b It shows that smell does not make very much difference.
c It shows it is difficult to tell the difference between flavors.
d It shows that the sense of smell contributes to how things taste.

6 The reading suggests that the sense of touch and pain are closely connected. **True or False?** (Par. 7)

Skill Review

In Skills and Strategies 7, you learned that good readers use context and their own prior knowledge about the world in general to guess the meanings of words they do not know.

A Find the sentences below in Reading 1. Use context and your knowledge of the world in general to figure out the meaning of the words in bold. Choose the word that best fits the meaning of the word in bold.

1 *Delicious,* ***scrumptious****, tasteless.* We have lots of words to describe how things taste. (Par. 1)

a having a good taste
b understandable

2 There has been less research on taste than on our other four **senses**, but scientists have been aware of the basics of taste for many years. (Par. 2)

a parts of the body
b ability to see, hear, touch, taste, and smell

3 Finally, our ability to taste bitter foods may help us **avoid** foods that are dangerous. Dangerous plants, for example, often have a bitter taste that many people do not like. (Par. 5)

a store for the future
b stay away from

4 Close your eyes and **hold your nose** closed. (Par. 6)

a blow hard to open it
b press the sides together to close it

5 Our perception of flavor is actually a **combination** of taste, smell, and touch. (Par. 7)

a several things that are put together into one
b a group of things in a special order

B Review the sentences that you read in A. Consider whether you used the context (*C*) or your own knowledge of the world (*KW*), or both (*B*), to figure out the meaning of the word in bold.

1 _____ *Delicious, **scrumptious**, tasteless*. We have lots of words to describe how things taste. (Par. 1)

2 _____ There has been less research on taste than on our other four **senses**, but scientists have been aware of the basics of taste for many years. (Par. 2)

3 _____ Finally, our ability to taste bitter foods may help us **avoid** foods that are dangerous. Dangerous plants, for example, often have a bitter taste that many people do not like. (Par. 5)

4 _____ Close your eyes and **hold your nose** closed. (Par. 6)

5 _____ Our perception of flavor is actually a **combination** of taste, smell, and touch. (Par. 7)

Vocabulary Development

Definitions

Find the words in Reading 1 that complete the following definitions.

1 To ____________ something is to discover exactly what it is. (*v*) Par. 2, sentence 2

2 ____________ are small, raised areas, especially on the body. (*n pl*) Par. 3, sentence 1

3 ____________ are the smallest units of living things. Your skin and blood are made of these. (*n pl*) Par. 3, sentence 2

4 ____________ is the liquid in your mouth that keeps it wet. (*n*) Par. 3, sentence 3

5 To ____________ a solid thing is to make it become part of a liquid. (*v*) Par. 3, sentence 4

6 ____________ are pieces of information that are sent somewhere. (*n pl*) Par. 3, last sentence

7 ____________ is awareness from the senses. (*n*) Par. 6, sentence 1

8 A / An ____________ is a part of a situation, plan, or idea that has many other parts. (*n*) Par. 7, sentence 1

Words in Context

Complete the passages with words from Reading 1 in the box below.

complex	essential	role	survival
distinct	protein	signal	vitamins

1 ____________ (a) are chemicals that are ____________ (b) for human health. Without them, we would soon get sick and die. Although they are similar in some ways, each has a / an ____________ (c) function. For example, some are important for the health of our eyes, whereas others are important for the skin. Others help us to break down different elements of food, such as fat and ____________ (d), so we can use them for energy and growth.

2 Hunger also plays an important ____________ (e) in human ____________ (f). We need to eat to stay alive, and hunger pushes us to look for food and to eat. When you feel hungry, your stomach makes noises. However, hunger doesn't happen just in your stomach. It also happens in your blood and your brain. When the amount of sugar in your blood falls, a / an ____________ (g) goes to your brain. This is just the first step in the ____________ (h) process that leads you to your refrigerator.

Critical Thinking

In Reading 1, you learned some basic facts about the sense of taste. The author states that the senses of taste, smell, and touch all contribute to how we experience food.

PERSONALIZING

Thinking about how new information applies to your own life can help you understand the text better.

A In the chart below, each taste from the reading is given with an example of food that has that taste. Fill out the chart with two additional examples, and then answer the questions below it.

SWEET	SOUR	SALTY	BITTER	SAVORY
Ice cream	*Lemon*	*Olives*	*Coffee*	*Cheese*

1 What is your favorite taste?

2 Is there any taste that you do not like?

3 Do you like spicy food? Give an example of something spicy that you do or don't like.

B Share your chart with the rest of the class.

Research

Do your own candy experiment. Ask several friends to help you.

- Tell them to close their eyes and hold their noses.
- Give them two different flavors of candy, but don't tell them which one is which.
- Give them a drink of water between each candy.
- Ask them to guess the flavor of the candy.
- Repeat the experiment, but this time, tell them to close their eyes but not their noses.

Writing

Write a short report about your research. Did your experiments support the information in the reading?

Before You Read

Connecting to the Topic

Discuss the following questions with a partner.

1 How do you know when fruits and vegetables are ripe and ready to eat?

2 What senses do you use to decide if food is safe to eat?

3 Some foods have artificial colors, that is, color has been added to them. Why do you think this happens?

Previewing and Predicting

Remember that a good way to preview is to read the title and the first paragraph of a reading.

A Read the first paragraph of Reading 2 below and the title on page 110. Based on the paragraph below, put a check (✓) next to the things you think you might learn about in the reading.

Your first contact with a meal is not with your mouth. It is with your eyes. Your eyes send the first signal to your brain: Does this food look good to eat? Scientific studies have shown that vision has an important effect on how we respond to food, and the color of the food is a major factor.

_____ a Which colors of food look good

_____ b Why we cook our food

_____ c Scientific experiments about food and visual perception

_____ d A comparison of foods across culture

_____ e How we respond to the color of food

_____ f How food is digested

B Compare your answers with a partner's.

While You Read

As you read, stop at the end of each sentence that contains words in bold. Then follow the instructions in the box in the margin.

Taste and Color

1 Your first contact with a meal is not with your mouth. It is with your eyes. Your eyes send the first signal to your brain: Does this food look good to eat? Scientific studies have shown that vision has an important effect on how we respond to food, and the color of the food is a major factor.

2 How would you respond to blue chicken or black apples? You probably would not want to eat these foods. It is likely that in nature, these colors are warnings that you should stay away. They suggest that the food is not good to eat or might be dangerous or rotten. We also use color to determine if a food is ready to eat. We look for oranges that are orange. The color means they are ripe. We don't eat them when they are still green. These reactions to color may have helped humans survive in the **past**.

WHILE YOU READ 1

What is the main idea of paragraph 2? Highlight the sentence that shows the main idea.

3 Today we still respond to the color of food. In general, we reject blue and purple food. Red and yellow, in contrast, may even increase our appetite, according to research studies. Experience has also given us clear expectations about how food should look. Sometimes our reaction to color is more powerful than our sense of taste. For example, in one experiment, people drank **flavored** drinks of different colors. When a lemon-flavored drink was red, people did not taste lemon. They said that the flavor was cherry – a red fruit. In another experiment, scientists served people blue steak and green potatoes. However, special lights made the food look normal. Everyone was enjoying the meal. Then the special lights were turned off, revealing the strange colors of the food. Suddenly, everyone stopped eating. No one was hungry anymore, and some people even became sick.

WHILE YOU READ 2

Read the next two sentences to find clues to the meaning of *flavored*. Highlight the words that help you understand the meaning.

Would you eat blue chicken?

4 We also respond to the strength of a color. For example, people think that drinks that are a darker color are sweeter or stronger in flavor. One study showed that the same cheese got very different reactions when the colors were different. If the cheese was very light yellow or white, people found it **tasteless**. In contrast, if it was a dark yellow or orange, they said it had much more flavor.

WHILE YOU READ 3

Find a phrase in the next sentence that signals a contrast with the word *tasteless*. Highlight the phrase and the words that are the opposite of *tasteless*.

5 Businesses that produce and serve food know about the power of color. A lot of the food we eat contains coloring to make it more attractive. For example, without coloring, much of the meat in stores would be gray. As a result, in some countries, producers add red color to meat, or they display it under red lights. Even the color of packaging and plates makes a difference in our opinions. In a study of restaurant food, customers said the same food tasted better on white plates than on black plates.

6 Although it is likely the connection between color and taste goes back thousands, or perhaps millions, of years, it remains an important part of our modern world. It continues to influence decisions in the food industry and in our kitchens.

Main Idea Check

Match the main ideas below to paragraphs 2–5 in Reading 2. Write the number of the paragraph on the blank line.

______ A Humans still have a strong reaction to the color of foods.

______ B Restaurants and stores often use color to make food attractive.

______ C The color of some foods warns humans to stay away.

______ D We associate the strength of color with taste.

A Closer Look

Look back at Reading 2 to answer the following questions.

1 Which food colors could be warnings? Choose three answers. (Par. 2)

a Orange
b Black
c Blue
d Green

2 Visual perception is sometimes more powerful than our sense of taste in how we think things taste. **True or False?** (Par. 3)

3 In the experiment described in the reading, why did some people become sick? (Par. 3)

a The light made them sick.
b They saw the color of the food.
c Suddenly, they could smell that the food was bad.
d They realized that the food was not real.

4 In an experiment in which people had to judge the flavor of different colors of the same fruit by looking at them instead of tasting them, which one might be judged as tasteless? (Par. 4)

a A white one
b An orange one
c A red one
d A yellow one

5 Why do some stores use red lights over their meat? (Par. 5)

a In many countries, the red lights are required.
b Meat stays fresher when it is stored under red lights.
c Studies have shown that red light makes meat taste better.
d Some customers don't think the natural color of meat is attractive.

Skill Review

In Skills and Strategies 7, you learned that you can sometimes use context and your general knowledge of the world to guess the meanings of words you do not know.

A Find the sentences below in Reading 2. Use context and your knowledge of the world in general to figure out the meanings of the words in bold. Choose the word that best fits the meaning of the word in bold.

1 Your first **contact** with a meal is not with your mouth. It is with your eyes. (Par.1)

a connection b evaluation

2 How would you **respond** to blue chicken or black apples? You probably would not want to eat these foods. (Par. 2)

a understand the importance of b act when you see or hear something

3 It is likely that in nature, these colors are **warnings** that you should stay away. (Par. 2)

a symbols b messages of danger

4 We look for oranges that are orange. The color means they are **ripe**. We don't eat them when they are still green. (Par. 2)

a ready to eat b delicious

5 For example, in one experiment, people drank **flavored** drinks of different colors. When a lemon-flavored drink was red, people did not taste lemon. They said that the flavor was cherry – a red fruit. (Par. 3)

a having a taste that comes from another food b with extra sugar for energy

B Read the sentences below. They contain words that you learned in earlier readings. Use context to choose the word in bold that best fits the meaning of the sentence.

1 There was a large **mob** / **gallery** outside of the building. I could not believe there were so many people.

2 She **crossed out** / **gave away** the names at the top of the list so that no one would be able to read them.

3 Today was an **essential** / **emotional** day for everyone, so everyone should stay home tomorrow and spend time with friends and family.

4 We need to decide on a new **role** / **strategy** to increase our sales because what we are doing now is not working.

Vocabulary Development

Definitions

Find the words in Reading 2 that complete the following definitions.

1 __________ is the ability to see. (*n*) Par. 1, last sentence

2 Something that is __________ is more important than other things of the same type. (*adj*) Par. 1, last sentence

3 Something that is __________ is old and no longer good. This food may look or smell bad. (*adj*) Par. 2, sentence 4

4 __________ are feelings or actions that are a result of something else. (*n pl*) Par. 2, last sentence

5 Your __________ is your desire to eat food. (*n*) Par. 3, sentence 3

6 Something that is __________ is usual and expected. (*adj*) Par. 3, sentence 10

7 Something that is __________ is pleasant and nice to look at. (*adj*) Par. 5, sentence 2

8 __________ is the covering for products, for example, paper or plastic. (*n*) Par. 5, sentence 5

Word Families

A The words in bold in the chart are from Reading 2. The words next to them are from the same word family. Study and learn these words.

NOUN	VERB
determination	***determine*** (Par. 2)
display	***display*** (Par. 5)
expectation (Par. 3)	*expect*
rejection	***reject*** (Par. 3)
response	***respond*** (Par. 1)

B Choose the correct form of the words from the chart to complete the following sentences.

1 Many people __________ new ideas because they don't understand them.

2 The police used special equipment to __________ where the car was.

3 There was a beautiful __________ of flowers in the market.

4 When children are afraid of their teachers, they will not __________ to questions.

5 People in the country have suffered for a long time, and they have no __________ that things will change in the future.

6 The children will display their art projects at the front of the classroom tomorrow.

7 He is very disappointed about the rejection of his application for college. Now he has to wait another year.

8 We are waiting for a confirmation of the identity of the man in the picture.

9 We expect bad weather in the next few days.

10 There was an immediate and positive reaction to the announcement of the new plan. Everyone really liked it.

Critical Thinking

In Reading 2, you learned about the relationship between color and taste perception.

> **APPLYING INFORMATION**
>
> You use critical thinking skills when you apply information you have just learned to new situations.

A Some people have difficulty seeing specific colors. We call this color blindness. There are different types of color blindness. In the most common form, people have trouble seeing the difference between red and green. Below is a picture of what meat might look like to someone who is colorblind.

Discuss the following questions with a partner or small group of classmates.

1 What kinds of difficulties do you think colorblind people have when they shop for food?
2 What kinds of strategies could they use to make good food choices?
3 Do you rely on color when you choose food?

B Share your answers and examples with the rest of the class.

Research

Do some research on blue food.

- Write down all of the naturally blue kinds of food that you can think of.
- Find a picture of a blue food that is not normally blue, like the ones in the reading.
- Show it to several people.
- Describe their reactions.
- Ask them to explain their responses.

Writing

Write a short summary of what you found out. First, describe the picture you showed them. Then describe their responses. Include the picture in your report.

Finding Supporting Details: Facts and Examples

In Skills and Strategies 4 on page 51, you learned tha[illegible] a main idea. Paragraphs also have supporting details [illegible] specific pieces of information that strengthen the ma[illegible] supporting details are facts and examples.

Examples & Explanations

①Cilantro is a green plant whose leaves are used to add flavor to food. ②However, cilantro does not taste the same to every person. ③For example, some people think it tastes sweet; others think it tastes like soap. ④Opinions on cilantro vary from place to place. ⑤Scientists say that about 17 percent of Europeans dislike the taste of cilantro. ⑥However, just 3 to 7 percent of Latin Americans and South Asians dislike it. ⑦That is why many Latin American and South Asian dishes use cilantro.

Sentence [illegible] paragraph[illegible]

Sentence [illegible] *not taste t[illegible]*

In sentence 3, the writer gives an example to support the main idea, that *some people think it tastes sweet; others think it tastes like soap.* The writer introduces this example with a signal, *for example.* Writers also use the signal *for instance* to introduce examples.

In sentences 5 and 6, the writer also gives facts to support the main idea, that *17 percent of Europeans dislike the taste of cilantro* and *3 to 7 percent of Latin Americans and South Asians dislike it.* The writer uses a signal, *scientists say,* to introduce these facts. Writers often mention scientific research when they introduce facts, using phrases like *research shows* or *studies show.*

The Language of Supporting Details

Here are some common words and phrases that signal supporting details.

WORDS AND PHRASES THAT SIGNAL EXAMPLES			
for example	*for instance*	*one example*	*another example*

WORDS AND PHRASES THAT SIGNAL FACTS			
in fact	*scientists say*	*research shows*	*studies show*

Strategies

These strategies will help you find the supporting details in paragraphs.

- As you read, ask yourself: *What is the main idea of this paragraph? How does the author strengthen the main idea?*
- Pay attention to the middle sentences of a paragraph. Look for specific pieces of information, like a number or the name of a person, place, or specific object.
- Look for signals that writers use to introduce supporting details. Study and learn the signals in the charts above.

Skill Practice 1

Read the following pairs of sentences. Write *M* next to the sentence in each pair that is a main idea. Write *S* next to the sentence that is a supporting detail.

1 ____ **A** Many chefs have an unusually strong sense of taste, and this helps them learn how to cook.
____ **B** For example, chefs can taste a dish and know exactly what is in it.

2 ____ **A** They make mistakes such as putting too much spice in a dish.
____ **B** People with a weak sense of taste may not cook very well.

3 ____ **A** Certain taste preferences can lead to health problems.
____ **B** Some people eat too much salt and sugar because they are trying to hide bitter tastes.

4 ____ **A** More and more people are starting to enjoy spicy food.
____ **B** Sales of hot chili peppers have increased at supermarkets, according to one study.

5 ____ **A** Chinese food is usually very healthy.
____ **B** Most dishes contain little fat and lots of vegetables.

6 ____ **A** In Ethiopia, it is common to eat food using only your hands.
____ **B** The way people eat varies from place to place.

Skill Practice 2

Read the following paragraphs. Then answer the questions below. Answer the question "How do you know?" by writing down examples and facts from the paragraphs. The first one is an example.

1 Not all animals taste food the same way as humans do. For example, some insects such as flies taste with their feet. Fish can taste with their skin. This helps them find food in the dark. Whales taste food with their mouths, like humans, but their sense of taste works differently. They can only taste salty flavors and not sweet or bitter ones.

a Do all animals taste food the same way as humans? *No*

b How do you know?

Example 1 *flies taste with their feet*

Example 2 ____________________

Example 3 ____________________

2 Dogs do not have a very strong sense of taste. Studies show that most humans' ability to taste is five times stronger than that of dogs. However, dogs have a super sense of smell. Dogs get much more information from their sense of smell than from their sense of taste, scientists say. In fact, dogs' sense of smell is a thousand times stronger than that of humans.

a Do dogs have a strong sense of taste? ____

b How do you know?

Fact 1 ____________________

Fact 2 ____________________

Fact 3 ____________________

3 Animals that eat plants usually have a very selective sense of taste. One example is that cows are very careful about which plants they eat. The fields where they eat contain many types of plants, and cows have to avoid the harmful ones. The koala, a furry Australian animal that lives in trees, has precise senses of smell and taste. A koala can detect different chemicals in different trees. It eats only leaves of eucalyptus trees, but it also eats only from certain individual trees. Because humans eat both plants and meat, our sense of taste is somewhat selective, but not as much as that of animals that eat only plants.

a Do animals that eat plants often have a selective sense of taste? ____

b How do you know?

Example 1 ____________________

Fact with example 1 ____________________

Example 2 ____________________

Fact with example 2 ____________________

Example 3 ____________________

Fact with example 3 ____________________

Before You Read

Connecting to the Topic

Discuss the following questions with a partner.

1 Are there some foods that you really hate? Which ones? Why?

2 Do you have a good sense of taste? In other words, are you sensitive to the different flavors in foods? Explain your answer.

3 Do you think your food preferences have changed as you have grown older? Explain your answer.

Previewing and Predicting

Remember that a good way to preview is to read the title and the first paragraph of a reading. In longer readings, you should also look at headings of sections.

A **Read the first paragraph of Reading 3 below and the title on page 121. Then read the headings of each section. Decide what topics you think will be in each section. Then write the number of the sections (*I*, *II*) next to the topics that you think will be in those sections.**

Not everyone responds the same way to certain tastes. Some people love broccoli, but others find it too bitter. Some people have a "sweet tooth," that is, they love to eat ice cream, cake, and other sweet food. Others prefer salty or spicy foods. What is responsible for these differences in taste preferences?

SECTION	TOPIC
	Age as an explanation for differences in our sense of taste
	Biology as an explanation for differences in our sense of taste
	The kinds of food that competitive people prefer
	Experience as an explanation for differences in our sense of taste
	The kinds of food that energetic people prefer

B **Compare your answers with a partner's.**

While You Read

As you read, stop at the end of each sentence that contains words in bold. Then follow the instructions in the box in the margin.

READING 3

Why Do Some People Hate Broccoli?

1 Not everyone responds the same way to certain tastes. Some people love broccoli, but others find it too bitter. Some people have a "**sweet tooth**," that is, they love to eat ice cream, cake, and other sweet food. Others prefer salty or spicy foods. What is responsible for these differences in taste preferences?

WHILE YOU READ 1

Find a phrase in this sentence that signals a definition of *sweet tooth*. Highlight the phrase and definition.

I. Factors in Taste Preferences

2 Experts say a combination of factors is responsible for taste preferences, but one of the most important is our **genes**. This explanation is particularly clear in the taste for bitter and sweet foods. There is a specific gene that allows us to taste some bitter foods. People without the gene cannot detect the bitterness. Scientists are not sure about the reason behind this genetic variation. On the one hand, the ability to taste bitter food could be a form of protection. Many bitter things are poisonous. On the other hand, many bitter foods are very healthy because they are full of important vitamins and minerals. So the bitterness gene may prevent some people from eating healthy foods. A sweet tooth may also be partly genetic. One gene allows some people to taste sweetness in foods with just a little bit of sugar in them. People without this gene require more sugar in their food to taste sweetness. As a result, they may eat too much sugar, which can cause health problems.

WHILE YOU READ 2

This sentence contains the main idea of the paragraph. Read the rest of the paragraph to find two examples that support this main idea. Highlight the two sentences with the supporting examples.

3 Genes are not the only factor in human food preferences. Experience is also important. This experience begins even before a baby is born. The food that a mother eats while she is pregnant may influence what her baby will like to eat. Experiments show, for example, that the babies of women who eat a lot of carrots while they are pregnant like the flavor of carrots. These preferences may continue when that baby becomes an adult. In addition, many studies have shown that childhood **exposure** to different kinds of food is an important factor in taste preferences. If there are not many vegetables at meals, for example, children will not learn to like their taste.

WHILE YOU READ 3

Read the rest of the paragraph to find the clues to the meaning of *exposure*. Highlight a sentence that helps you understand the meaning.

4 Some people can taste very small differences. Scientists call them "supertasters." Supertasters have more taste buds than the rest of the population. Scientists are not sure why. Women are more likely to be supertasters than men. Africans and Asians are more likely to be supertasters than Europeans. Others are especially bad at tasting differences. They are "non-tasters." They may not have the genes for specific tastes, especially bitter ones. Most of us, however, are just regular "tasters." (See Figure 4.1.)

Figure 4.1 Taste in the Population

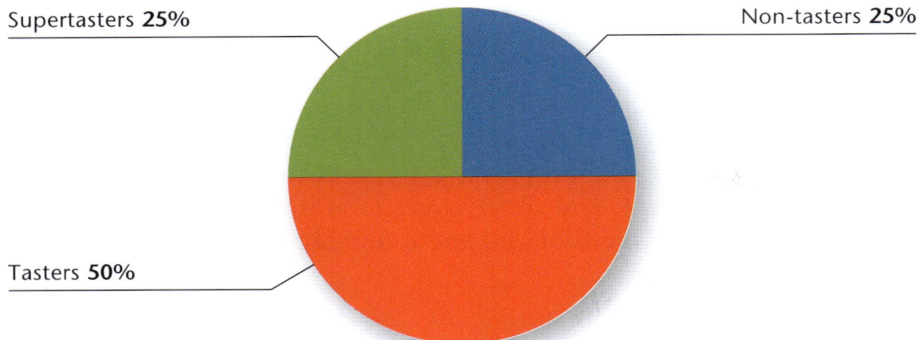

5 The ability to taste also changes during our **lives**. Children are generally very sensitive to strong tastes, especially foods that are bitter. As we age, we are more likely to accept and even enjoy these strong flavors. When women are pregnant, their taste sensitivity often increases. Many women who like strong flavors may reject them while they are pregnant. And for most of us, the ability to taste decreases with age. Some older people completely lose their ability to taste. However, this is actually because their ability to smell begins to decline, not because their sense of taste no longer functions.

WHILE YOU READ 4

This sentence contains the main idea of the paragraph. Read the rest of the paragraph to find two examples that support this main idea. Highlight the sentences with the two supporting examples you found.

II. Taste Preferences and Personality

6 Preferences in food vary across individuals. Dr. Alan Hirsch, a taste researcher, says these preferences suggest something about our personalities. He has studied more than 20,000 people. He gave them personality tests and then asked them about their taste preferences. His results revealed some consistent connections between them. For example, people who like spicy foods generally like new and exciting experiences. They take risks and welcome changes in their lives. He found that people who prefer salty foods are competitive and want to accomplish things quickly. Some people like a diet of starchy foods that don't have strong flavors, such as bread, noodles, and pasta. According to Hirsch, these people are cautious, and they don't like change. People who like to eat sour foods are more likely to criticize other people. Of course, these are only generalizations, and not everyone who likes specific foods will have the same personality.

7 Taste is the least researched and least well understood of all of our senses. The ability to distinguish among tastes and individual preferences for different tastes are complex. Scientists will continue to study them. Understanding taste and taste preferences may help them solve health problems related to the food that we eat.

Main Idea Check

Match the main ideas below to paragraphs 2–6 in Reading 3. Write the number of the paragraph on the blank line.

_____ A Our ability to taste changes as we grow older.
_____ B The ability to taste varies across the population.
_____ C Our genes explain some of our taste preferences and abilities.
_____ D Taste preferences may be related to personality.
_____ E Early experience contributes to taste preferences.

A Closer Look

Look back at Reading 3 to answer the following questions.

1 For which two taste preferences and abilities are genes important? (Par. 2)
   a Sweet
   b Sour
   c Salty
   d Bitter

2 What are two reasons why the ability to taste bitter foods is important? (Par. 2)
   a Many people dislike bitter foods.
   b Bitter things are sometimes dangerous.
   c Bitter foods are often very healthy.
   d Genes may be responsible for the ability to taste bitter foods.

3 People who can taste even a small amount of sugar in food are more likely to become too fat. **True or False?** (Par. 2)

4 If a mother wants her child to like vegetables, what are two things she should do? (Par. 3)
   a Use a little bit of sugar in all of the vegetables.
   b Eat a lot of vegetables while she is pregnant.
   c Show her child that she likes vegetables a lot.
   d Serve a lot of vegetables when her child is very young.

5 Women are more likely than men to be supertasters. **True or False?** (Par. 4)

6 Identify which groups are likely to be especially sensitive to strong flavors (*S*), not sensitive to strong flavors (*N*), or neither (*X*)? (Par. 5)

_____ a Babies and young children
_____ b People older than 75
_____ c Men in their 40s
_____ d Pregnant women

7 Match the food preferences to personality types, according to Dr. Alan Hirsch. (Par. 6)

	Food	Personality type
_____	1 spaghetti	a likes danger and risk
_____	2 chilies	b competitive
_____	3 potato chips and other salty snacks	c careful, doesn't like risks
_____	4 pickles	d critical

Skill Review

In Skills and Strategies 8, you learned that writers support the main ideas of paragraphs with supporting details. They use facts and examples to strengthen the main idea.

A The main ideas of some of the paragraphs from Reading 3 are listed below. Find supporting details for each of these paragraphs. Write a sentence on each blank line.

1 Main idea of paragraph 2: Genes contribute to our taste preferences and abilities.

a ______________________________

b ______________________________

2 Main idea of paragraph 3: Experience and exposure influence our taste preferences.

a ______________________________

b ______________________________

3 Main idea of paragraph 5: Our sense of taste changes throughout our lives.

a ______________________________

b ______________________________

c ______________________________

B Compare your answers with a partner's.

Definitions

Find the words in Reading 3 that complete the following definitions.

1 If something is ________________, it is related to just one thing but not others. (*adj*) Par. 2, sentence 3

2 ________________ is a difference among similar things. (*n*) Par. 2, sentence 5

3 A woman who is ________________ is expecting a baby. (*adj*) Par. 3, sentence 4

4 A / An ________________ is a person who is fully grown. (*n*) Par. 3, sentence 6

5 Someone who is ________________ is easily affected by things in the environment. (*adj*) Par. 5, sentence 2

6 To ________________ is to go down; to decrease. (*v*) Par. 5, last sentence

7 If something is ________________, it always behaves in the same way. (*adj*) Par. 6, sentence 5

8 To ________________ is to express disapproval or to find faults. (*v*) Par. 6, sentence 11

Words in Context

Complete the sentences with words from Reading 3 in the box below.

cautious	competitive	individuals	requires
combination	genes	personality	risk

1 The two brothers were very ________________. Each of them always wanted to be better than the other.

2 She has a very relaxed ________________. She never gets worried or upset about things.

3 We get a set of ________________ from each of our parents. They are an important factor in how we look and act.

4 There are different prices for groups and ________________.

5 If you smoke, your ________________ of having a heart attack is much higher.

6 My math course ________________ a lot of time and hard work.

7 You should be ________________ when you talk to strangers. Don't give them private information.

8 The menu at the new restaurant is a ________________ of French and Mexican food.

Academic Word List

The following are Academic Word List words from all the readings in Unit 4. Use these words to complete the sentences. (If necessary, review the AWL words in Key Vocabulary on pages 257–267.)

adults (*n*)	consistent (*adj*)	normal (*adj*)	specific (*adj*)	variation (*n*)
complex (*adj*)	major (*adj*)	response (*n*)	survival (*n*)	vision (*n*)

1 In most countries, only ________________ are allowed to vote, usually at the age of 18 or older.

2 For many wild animals, ________________ depends on their ability to run, fly, or swim quickly away from danger.

3 I am shopping for a ________________ kind of cheese. It is the only kind I use.

4 Predicting the weather is a very ________________ process that requires several computers.

5 There is not very much ________________ in hair color in Japan. Most people have black hair.

6 His ________________ is worse now that he is older. He cannot see well enough to drive.

7 There has been a very positive ________________ to the new book. A lot of people are buying it.

8 This year we have had more than the ________________ amount of rain.

9 This student's work is very ________________. He gets about 80 percent on most of his tests.

10 There is a ________________ storm coming tonight. The weather report says it may rain for two or three days.

Critical Thinking

In Reading 3, you learned about some of the factors that influence our taste preferences.

> **PERSONALIZING**
>
> Thinking about how new information applies to your own life can help you understand the text better.

A Discuss the following questions with a partner.

1 The reading discusses the influence of genes. Do other people in your family have taste preferences that are similar to yours?

2 The reading also discusses the effect of the environment, that is, exposure. Do you think this is true for you? Do you still eat and like the foods that you ate when you were growing up? If you have brothers or sisters, do they have similar preferences? Explain your answer.

3 In what ways have your taste preferences changed since you were a child?

4 Do you think you are a supertaster, a non-taster, or just a taster? Explain your answer.

5 Do any of the personality characteristics in the reading describe you? Do you have the taste preferences that the reading predicts?

B Share your answers with the rest of the class.

Research

Food that seems unusual in one culture is normal in another. For example, insects are not considered food in some cultures. Interview ten classmates or friends on their food experiences and preferences. Find out the answers to these questions.

1 What is the most unusual food you have ever eaten?

2 Where did you eat it?

3 Can you describe the experience?

4 Did you enjoy it?

Writing

Choose the most interesting experience that you heard about during your research. Write a short report about what happened and what the person ate.

Improving Your Reading Speed

Good readers read quickly and still understand most of what they read.

A Read the instructions and strategies for Improving Your Reading Speed in Appendix 3 on page 270.

B Choose one of the readings in this unit. Read it without stopping. Time how long it takes you to finish the text in minutes and seconds. Enter the time in the chart on page 271. Then calculate your reading speed in number of words per minute.

MAKING CONNECTIONS

ADDITIONAL INFORMATION CONNECTORS

Writers often add to information about an idea, person, or thing that they have already written about. Some words that signal this addition are *another*, *other*, *too*, and *also*. When you see these words, look back to see what information the writer is adding to, and look forward to see what the new information is.

In the following example, the word that signals additional information is in bold. The earlier idea, person, or thing is underlined. The additional information is also underlined. The arrow shows the connection.

> Taste buds all over the tongue and mouth tell us how things taste. Our sense of smell contributes to taste, **too**.

Exercise 1

Read the following groups of sentences. Highlight the word that signals additional information. Underline the original idea, person, or thing in the first sentence. Underline the additional information. Draw arrows from the highlighted word to the underlined items. The first one is an example.

1 Humans have a good sense of smell. However, our other senses are stronger.

2 Humans have a good sense of smell. However, many other animals have a much better sense of smell.

3 One animal with a good sense of smell is the rabbit. Dogs also have a very good sense of smell.

4 Age is one factor that may affect your sense of smell. Smoking is another factor.

5 Our sense of smell gets weaker with smoking. However, it can also get stronger with practice.

6 Some people lose their sense of smell. When that happens, they usually lose their sense of taste, too.

Exercise 2

Make a clear paragraph by putting sentences A, B, and C into the best order after the numbered sentence. Look for pronouns, category words, and words that signal addition to help you. Write the letters in the correct order on the blank lines.

1 Carol has no sense of smell. _A_ _B_ _C_

- **A** The fruit in her refrigerator is often old and soft, and it smells bad.
- **B** Her milk is often too old, too, but she doesn't know it.
- **C** This can be a dangerous problem.

2 You could lose your sense of smell even when you are still young. _C_ _B_ _A_

- **A** It could also hurt your nose.
- **B** Its impact could damage nerves in your brain that help you smell.
- **C** This could happen as a result of a car accident.

3 You should always drink enough water. _B_ _A_ _C_

- **A** Exercise is another way to keep it sharp.
- **B** This can keep your sense of smell sharp.
- **C** Both of these steps are also useful for your general health.

4 It is sad when people lose their sense of smell. _A_ _B_ _C_

- **A** Fortunately, they can usually still taste spicy things.
- **B** These spicy foods include chilies and pepper.
- **C** People with no sense of smell can often taste other strong flavors, like raw onions.

5 A smell can bring back an old memory. _C_ _A_ _B_

- **A** It could also be of a person, for example, your grandmother.
- **B** For example, it could be a memory of her delicious food.
- **C** This could be of an event that occurred when you were a child.

5
OCEANS
SKILLS AND STRATEGIES
• Finding the Meanings of Words: Learner Dictionaries
• Finding Steps in a Process

Finding the Meanings of Words: Learner Dictionaries

You have learned that good readers look for definitions, examples, contrasts, and other clues to understand difficult words. However, if a word is very important and you cannot understand its meaning from the context, you might use a learner dictionary to find its definition. Learner dictionaries give definitions that are clear and easy to understand. If a word has several definitions, a learner dictionary will help you choose which definition best fits the context of the reading.

Examples & Explanations

The boat was far away from the **shore**.

If the meaning of *shore* is not clear from the information in the sentence, you can find the definition in a learner dictionary: *the land next to the edge of an ocean or a lake.* A learner dictionary will also usually include a sample sentence. This sample sentence can help you understand the meaning of the word.

shore /ʃɔʊr/ *n* the land next to the edge of the ocean or a lake

On March 19, we arrived in the **port** of Vancouver.

The dictionary gives three definitions for the noun *port*. Which one is the best choice? The information in the sentence shows that it is probably "a town or area in a town next to water where boats arrive and leave from."

port /pɔʊrt/ *n* a town or area in a town next to water where boats arrive and leave from
port /pɔʊrt/ *n* a part of a computer where you can connect another piece of equipment
port /pɔʊrt/ *n* a strong red wine made in the country of Portugal

Some companies **ship** their products to countries around the world.

Ship can be a noun or a verb. Knowing the part of speech the writer is using in the sentence can help you choose the correct definition. In this example, the writer uses *ship* as a verb. The correct definition is "to send things from one place to another on a boat, truck, train, or plane."

ship /ʃɪp/ *n* a large boat used for carrying people and things across the sea
ship /ʃɪp/ *v* to send things from one place to another on a boat, truck, train, or plane

Strategies

These strategies will help you use learner dictionaries to understand unknown words.

- If you cannot find the meaning of an important word in a reading, look up the word in a learner dictionary. This kind of dictionary gives definitions that are clear and easy to understand.
- If your learner dictionary gives several definitions for one word, decide which one best fits the reading. The meaning of the context is one clue; the part of speech is another.
- If your learner dictionary gives a sample sentence for the word, use the sample sentence to help you understand the meaning of the word.

Skill Practice 1

Read the following sentences. Highlight the definition that best fits the sentence. The first one is an example.

1 Fish is an important part of the **diet** of people who live near the shore.

diet /ˈdɑɪ·ɪt/ *n* the food that someone usually eats

diet /ˈdɑɪ·ɪt/ *v* to eat less food so you become thinner

2 Fish is the biggest **export** of the country of Iceland.

export /ˈɛk·spɔrt/ *n* a product that you sell in another country

export /ɛkˈspɔrt/ *v* to send goods to another country so you can sell them there

3 There are very few farms in Iceland, so much of the **produce** that people eat is shipped from other countries.

produce /ˈproʊ·dus/ *n* food that is grown in large amounts in order to be sold, such as the food that farmers grow

produce /prəˈdus/ *v* to make or grow something

4 Many people who live on islands learn how to **sail**.

sail /seɪl/ *n* a large piece of material that catches air and makes a boat move

sail /seɪl/ *v* to travel from place to place by boat

5 The captain stood at the **bow** of the ship.

bow /bɑʊ/ *n* the act of bending the top part of your body forward to show respect for others

bow /bɑʊ/ *n* the front part of a ship

6 Passengers on a ship can **trip** and fall into the water if they are not careful.

trip /trɪp/ *n* a journey in which you visit a place for a short time and then return home

trip /trɪp/ *v* to fall or almost fall because you hit your foot on something while you are walking or running

7 The captain entered today's date in the ship's **log**.

log /lɔg/ *n* a thick piece of wood from a tree

log /lɔg/ *n* an official record of events in a journey

8 We can put the meat, fruit, and vegetables in the refrigerator, and **store** the rest of the food in the back of the ship.

store /stɔr/ *n* a shop or place where you can buy things

store /stɔr/ *v* to put something somewhere and not use it until you need it

Skill Practice 2

Read the following sentences, and notice the words in bold. Look these words up in a learner dictionary, and decide which definition best fits each sentence. Write the definitions on the blank lines. Use the word's part of speech and the context to help you choose the best definition. The first one is an example.

1 When the storm began, the captain came out of his **cabin**.

cabin = *a small room to sleep in on a ship*

2 The captain studied the **chart** to find the nearest port.

chart = ______________________________

3 The captain kept a **record** of every storm that he experienced.

record = ______________________________

4 The sailors were able to **net** several fish, and they ate well that night.

net = ______________________________

5 When the ship reached the port, the captain invited a few townspeople to **board** the ship.

board = ______________________________

6 The sailors **exchanged** the fish that they had caught for fresh fruit.

exchange = ______________________________

7 The port was full, so the ship had to **anchor** off the shore.

anchor = ______________________________

8 **Wind** started to fill the sails, so the sailors raised the anchor and left.

wind = ______________________________

Before You Read

Connecting to the Topic

Discuss the following questions with a partner.

1 Today we travel quickly by car and airplane. We move things by train and truck. How important do you think oceans are for travel and trade today? Explain your answer.

2 Do people in your community eat a lot of ocean fish? Do you? Does fish cost a lot or only a little?

3 In what parts of the world is fishing important?

Previewing and Predicting

Previewing a reading's title – as well as charts, maps, and diagrams – can help you predict what the reading will be about.

A **Read the title of Reading 1, and look at Figures 5.1 and 5.2 on pages 136 and 137. Then write *T* on the blank lines if the following statements are true and *F* if they are false.**

_____ a The ocean fish population is very healthy.
_____ b The fish population is decreasing.
_____ c Silk and spices came from Indonesia.
_____ d Coffee and silver came from Mexico.

B **What do you think this reading will be about? Put a check (✓) next to the topic or topics that you think will be included in the reading.**

_____ a Oceans and global warming
_____ b Changes in fish populations
_____ c Ships and trade in history
_____ d Good places to fish around the world
_____ e The importance of oceans
_____ f Fishing as a hobby

C **Compare your answers with a partner's.**

While You Read

As you read, stop at the end of each sentence that contains words in bold. Then follow the instructions in the box in the margin.

READING 1

Oceans – An Economic Resource

1 Oceans cover almost three quarters of the earth's surface. They are a very important natural resource. More than half of our oxygen comes from small ocean plants. About 90 percent of the world's water originates in the oceans. However, oceans provide more than basic necessities like air and water. They are also a significant economic resource, especially for food, transportation, and **trade**.

> **WHILE YOU READ 1**
> Which sentence gives the main idea of the whole reading?
> a) The same sentence
> b) The sentence before
> c) The sentence after

2 Fish are one of the most important ocean resources. Throughout history, people have depended on fish from the oceans. Historians can trace fishing back more than 40,000 years. However, ocean fishing from large boats probably began only in about the ninth century. Since then, fish have become a major form of protein in our diet. Today, about 17 percent of the animal protein that humans eat comes from fish.

3 Unfortunately, the number of fish in the oceans has decreased dramatically in the last 50 years, mostly as a result of overfishing. Overfishing refers to the practice of taking too many fish. This is especially true for large species. Fishermen begin by selecting only the older, adult fish. After these are gone, they begin to take younger fish. When this happens, many fish do not live long enough to breed. As a result, the population begins to decline rapidly. This has already happened to many **species** of large fish. Bluefin tuna, for example, are one of the most popular fish for sushi. They once grew to more than 1,000 pounds (453.5 kilograms). Tuna of this size have almost disappeared. They are not the only species in danger, however. The populations of many species of large fish have declined by 90 percent. A 2006 study looked at the populations of 7,800 different species of fish and made some frightening predictions. If overfishing continues, by 2048, most of these species will disappear. Since that study, some governments have

> **WHILE YOU READ 2**
> Look for an example of a species of fish in the next sentence. Highlight it.

Figure 5.1 Global Loss of Seafood Species

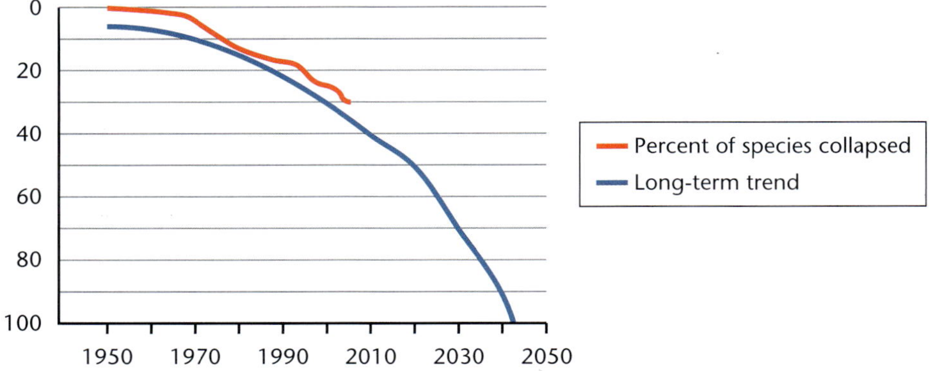

increased their efforts to control overfishing. Some fish, including some species of salmon, are beginning to recover, but many are still in danger.

4 Another reason why the ocean is a great economic resource is that it provides an open **route** for maritime travel. Ocean travel allows people to move across long distances to places that are difficult or impossible to reach by land. More important, maritime travel allows people to trade even when they live far apart. Almost since the beginning of civilization, maritime travel has had a significant role in trade. However, the greatest growth in maritime travel and trade occurred in a period called "The Age of Exploration." This period lasted from the fifteenth though the eighteenth centuries. New technology allowed larger ships to take longer voyages across oceans. During this time, many European countries sent ships all over the world, to Africa, Asia, Australia, and North and South America. These ships began to bring back many valuable goods. Most of all, Europe wanted gold and silver. Later, Europeans began to farm in these distant places. They brought back sugar, cotton, and coffee as well as new products. (See Figure 5.2.) Maritime trade resulted in enormous economic growth in Europe during this period.

WHILE YOU READ 3

Which definition of *route* is the writer using?
a) A path
b) A way to achieve something

5 The exchange also went in the other direction. It brought new and unfamiliar European items to other parts of the world. For example, Europeans **introduced** some species of horses, pigs, sheep, and cows to North and South America. This massive exchange of goods was only possible as a result of maritime travel. It could not have happened over land. The significance of maritime trade did not end with the Age of Exploration. It remains very important today. Ninety percent of all trade between countries still travels by ship across the oceans.

WHILE YOU READ 4

Which definition of *introduce* is the writer using?
a) Tell someone another person's name
b) Cause something to be used for the first time

Figure 5.2 Goods Shipped to Europe During the Age of Exploration

Main Idea Check

Match the main ideas below to paragraphs 2–5 in Reading 1. Write the number of the paragraph on the blank line.

_____ A Oceans allow people to travel from place to place.
_____ B Humans depend on fish as a source of food.
_____ C Ocean travel brought many European goods to other parts of the world.
_____ D Recently, overfishing has become a serious problem.

A Closer Look

Look back at Reading 1 to answer the following questions.

1 Fishing has a long history. **True or False?** (Par. 2)

2 Humans have always used large boats to catch fish. **True or False?** (Par. 2)

3 How does overfishing happen? Put the events (A–F) in the order that they happen. Write the correct letter in each box. (Par. 3)

A Governments try to protect the species of fish.
B Fishermen catch big, adult fish.
C Small fish cannot grow big enough to breed.
D Fishermen catch small, young fish.
E A species of fish starts disappearing quickly.
F The big, adult fish disappear.

4 What were Europeans trying to find during the Age of Exploration? (Par. 4)

a New farmland
b Valuable resources
c Other civilizations
d Maritime technology

5 The Age of Exploration changed Europe, but not North and South America. **True or False?** (Par. 5)

6 The ocean is the most important route for international trade. **True or False?** (Par. 5)

Skill Review

In Skills and Strategies 9, you learned that learner dictionaries sometimes give several definitions for one word. To use the dictionary well, you have to choose the definition that best fits the context. Knowing the word's part of speech in the reading can help you choose the best definition.

A Look at the sentences from Reading 1. Are the words in bold nouns or verbs? Write *N* (noun) or *V* (verb) on the blank lines.

_____ 1 Historians can **trace** fishing back more than 40,000 years.

_____ 2 Overfishing refers to the **practice** of taking too many fish.

_____ 3 When this happens, many fish do not live long enough to **breed**.

_____ 4 Ocean travel allows people to move across long distances to places that are difficult or impossible to **reach** by land.

_____ 5 Later, Europeans began to **farm** in these distant places.

_____ 6 The **exchange** also went in the other direction.

B In a learner dictionary, look up the words in bold from A. Which definition best fits the meaning in the sentence? Write the definitions on the blank lines.

1 **trace** ________________________________

2 **practice** ________________________________

3 **breed** ________________________________

4 **reach** ________________________________

5 **farm** ________________________________

6 **exchange** ________________________________

C Compare your answers with a partner's.

Vocabulary Development

Definitions

Find the words in Reading 1 that complete the following definitions.

1 A / An ________________ is something that a country or person has and can use. (*n*) Par. 1, sentence 2

2 ________________ is a gas in the air that humans and other animals need to live. (*n*) Par. 1, sentence 3

3 A / An ________________ is a group of animals or plants that share characteristics. (*n*) Par. 3, sentence 3

4 If something is happening ________________, it is happening very quickly. (*adv*) Par. 3, sentence 7

5 In ________________ travel, someone goes by ship across a sea. (*adj*) Par. 4, sentence 1

6 ________________ is human society and all its social organizations. (*n*) Par. 4, sentence 4

7 A / An ________________ is a length of time. (*n*) Par. 4, sentence 5

8 A / An ________________ thing is very big. (*adj*) Par. 5, sentence 4

Words in Context

Complete the sentences with words from Reading 1 in the box below.

apart	cotton	goods	quarter
century	dramatically	necessities	recover

1 We live in the twenty-first ________________.

2 Only one ________________ of our planet consists of dry land.

3 The ocean is an important source of food, oxygen, and other ________________ for human life.

4 Many of the ________________ we buy, such as televisions and clothing, are shipped by sea.

5 Singapore and Panama City are 11,700 miles ________________, separated by the Pacific Ocean.

6 The price of bluefin tuna is increasing ________________; it went up 50 percent in just one month.

7 When governments make laws against overfishing, fish populations start to ________________.

8 Much of our clothing is made from ________________, a type of plant.

Critical Thinking

In Reading 1, you learned how oceans are an important resource for both food and trade.

PERSONALIZING

Thinking about how new information applies to your own life can help you understand the text better.

A **Discuss the questions below with a small group.**

1 How much fish do people in your home country eat?

2 Are there any traditional dishes in your home country that involve fish?

3 Is fishing an important business in some parts of your home country? Explain.

4 Would you like to work on a fishing boat? Why or why not?

5 What can people do to stop the problem of overfishing?

B **Share one idea from your discussion with the rest of the class.**

Research

Do some research about maritime shipping and ocean fishing in a country with a coast.

Writing

Write a short report about your research. What did you learn about maritime shipping and ocean fishing in the country you researched?

Before You Read

Connecting to the Topic

Discuss the following questions with a partner.

1 In your home country, does the weather change during the year, or does it stay almost the same all year? Explain your answer.

2 Do you think the weather in your home country is different now than it was when your parents or grandparents were young? Is it warmer, colder, or drier? Are there more storms? Explain your answers.

3 You have probably heard or read a lot about climate change. How do you think climate change is related to oceans?

Previewing and Predicting

Remember to preview the title, charts, maps, and diagrams that you see in a reading. They can help you predict what the reading will be about.

A Read the title of Reading 2, and look at Figures 5.3, 5.4, and 5.5 on pages 143–144. Then write *T* on the blank lines if the statements are true and *F* if they are false.

_____ 1 There was less Arctic ice in 2010 than in 1995.

_____ 2 The average temperature of the oceans' surface was higher in 1950 than in 1900.

_____ 3 The change in the temperature of the oceans' surface between 1900 and 2012 was the greatest around North America.

_____ 4 The hot and cold air move in opposite directions during the summer and the winter.

B Compare your answers with a partner's.

While You Read

As you read, stop at the end of each sentence that contains words in bold. Then follow the instructions in the box in the margin.

READING 2

The Role of Oceans in Weather and Climate

1 The oceans have a major impact on weather and climate. These two terms are related, but they are not the same. Weather refers to the conditions over a short period of time. For example, weather includes today's temperature or tomorrow's rain. Climate describes general conditions over a long period of time. For example, Dubai has a hot, dry climate; Singapore has a hot, wet climate. How are climates related to oceans? Energy is a major factor in both weather and climate, and oceans play an important role in the control and distribution of global energy.

2 Oceans absorb most of the solar energy that reaches Earth's surface. Oceans store this energy and then transport it around the world. This distribution occurs in several ways. First, it occurs through the movement of the water. The flow of water in the oceans is called a current. The movement of water in the oceans' currents is predictable; in other words, it happens in a consistent way that scientists understand. The wind drives currents that are on the surface of the water. These currents have a major influence on weather **patterns**. When the water at the surface is warm, the result may just be some rain. If the surface is a lot warmer, the result may be strong storms. The most violent storms, called hurricanes or typhoons, develop only when the water at the ocean's surface is very warm – usually about 80 degrees Fahrenheit (27 degrees Celsius).

WHILE YOU READ 1

Which definition of *patterns* is the writer using?

a) The way something is repeated

b) A design of lines, shapes, and colors

3 Another energy distribution cycle occurs in the air above the ocean. Water from the ocean evaporates. This means it becomes a gas (called *vapor*) and rises into the air. The vapor traps heat energy from the oceans. Wind moves the vapor, sometimes for thousands of miles. When the warm vapor in the air hits a cool spot, its temperature drops. At that point, the vapor turns into a liquid or solid, in the form of rain or snow. When this happens, it releases the heat again. This completes the energy cycle.

4 Finally, energy moves around the world as a result of differences in temperature on land and in the oceans. Warm air rises, and cold air sinks. When this occurs, the cold air and hot air begin to move in a circle. (See Figure 5.3.) In winter, when the ocean is warmer than the land, the warmer air over the ocean rises. The colder air that was over the land is pulled into the space that the warm air left behind. The opposite happens in summer. This creates a cycle that moves energy around the world in the form of hot and cold air.

Figure 5.3

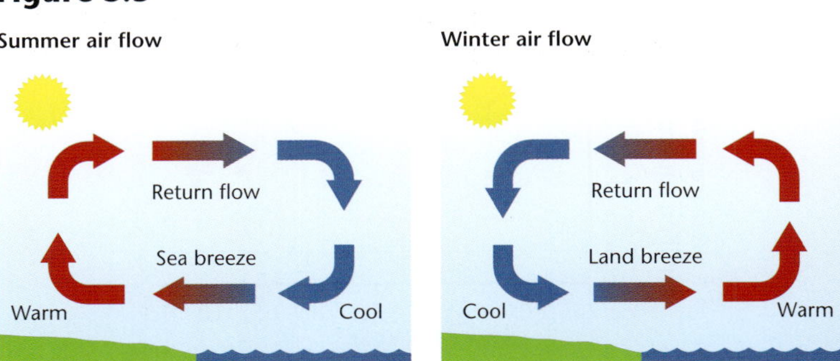

Figure 5.4 Average Global Sea Surface Temperature, 1880–2013

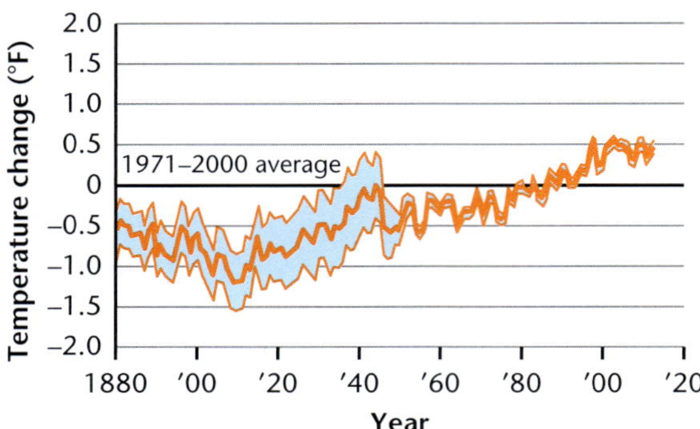

5 All of these processes are important factors in weather. They change constantly – every day, week, or month. Sometimes, however, changes become permanent. When this happens, we describe them as changes in climate. Most scientists believe that the world is experiencing a change in climate. The temperature on land is increasing. The temperature of the oceans is also increasing, just a little more slowly. (See Figure 5.4.) The ocean temperature has risen about a half a degree Fahrenheit (0.3°C) in the last hundred years. This increase has occurred partly because of the increase in carbon dioxide (CO_2) in the atmosphere. The higher levels of CO_2 are mostly from cars and factories that burn **fossil fuels**, like oil, gas, and coal.

WHILE YOU READ 2

Look for three examples of fossil fuels in this sentence. Highlight them.

6 The rise in temperature is important – and **dangerous** – for two reasons. First, although this increase is small, it is melting ice in the Arctic and Antarctic. (See Figure 5.5.) As the ice melts, the level of the oceans rises. Scientists say that the water level is rising about 0.13 inches (0.33 centimeters) every year. This means more floods for people who live near an ocean, especially during storms. Second, warmer oceans mean more frequent and more serious storms. Most scientists believe that these changes in ocean temperature are permanent. They say there is no way to reverse the process, so it is likely we will continue to live with its consequences.

WHILE YOU READ 3

Look for two examples of dangerous weather events in this paragraph. Highlight them.

Figure 5.5 September Monthly Average Arctic Sea Ice Extent, 1979–2013

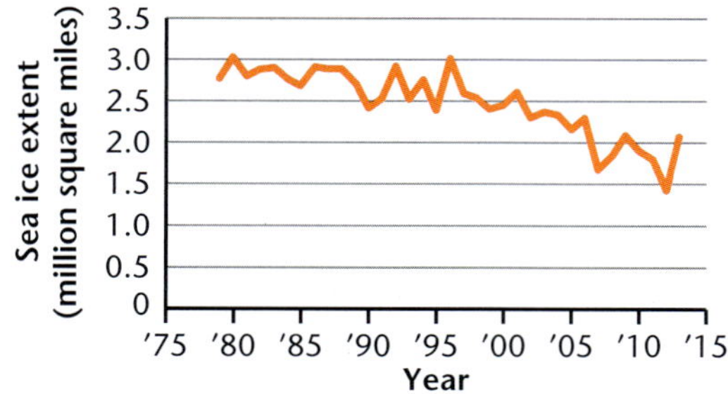

Main Idea Check

Match the main ideas below to paragraphs 2–6 in Reading 2. Write the number of the paragraph on the blank line.

_____ **A** A permanent climate change is happening.
_____ **B** The rise in temperature leads to higher sea levels and stronger storms.
_____ **C** Oceans release energy into the air, which can lead to rain and snow.
_____ **D** Temperature differences between land and sea create seasonal weather.
_____ **E** Oceans collect energy from the sun and send that energy to other places.

A Closer Look

Look back at Reading 2 to answer the following questions.

1 Do these phrases describe weather or climate? Write *W* or *C* on the blank lines. (Par. 1)

_____ **a** A rainy day
_____ **b** Dry summers
_____ **c** A cloudy sky
_____ **d** A lot of snow every January
_____ **e** 75°F (24°C) and sunny

2 Which of the following distribute energy from the ocean? Choose two answers. (Pars. 2 and 3)

a Currents
b Wind
c Climate
d Fossil fuels

3 How does energy get distributed through the movement of water vapor? Put the events (A–E) in the order that they happen. Write the correct letter in each box. (Par. 3)

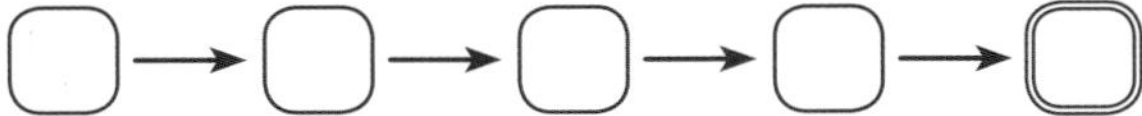

A The vapor turns to a liquid or solid that may fall as rain or snow.
B The ocean releases vapor into the air.
C Winds move ocean vapor from place to place.
D Energy from the sun enters the ocean.
E Air full of water vapor enters a cooler area.

4 Climates are changing because of human activity. **True or False?** (Par. 5)

5 Which of the following could be a result of rising ocean temperatures? (Par. 6)

a More hurricanes and typhoons
b More ice in the Antarctic and Arctic
c Less energy from the sun
d Less water in the ocean

Skill Review

In Skills and Strategies 9, you learned that learner dictionaries sometimes give several definitions for one word. Dictionaries can help you understand the words in a reading and help you use those words correctly in the future.

A Look at the sentences from Reading 2. Highlight the definition for the word in bold that best fits the sentence.

1 How are climates **related** to oceans?
related (*adj*) connected
related (*adj*) belonging to the same family

2 The vapor **traps** heat energy from the oceans.
traps (*n*) pieces of equipment for catching animals
traps (*v*) prevents something from leaving

3 At that point, the vapor **turns** into a liquid or solid, in the form of rain or snow.
turns (*v*) moves and faces a different direction
turns (*v*) becomes

4 The wind **drives** currents that are on the surface of the water.
drives (*v*) makes a car, bus, truck, etc., move along
drives (*v*) provides the power to move something

5 When the vapor air hits a cool **spot**, its temperature drops.
spot (*n*) a particular place or area
spot (*n*) a small round area on a surface that is a different color

6 When this happens, it **releases** the heat again.
releases (*v*) lets someone go free after having kept them somewhere
releases (*v*) lets a gas or liquid flow out

7 As the ice melts, the **level** of the oceans rises.
level (*n*) the amount or degree of something
level (*n*) the height of something in relation to the ground

B **Complete each sentence with a word from A. Use the definitions that you did not highlight in A.**

1 The professor spilled some coffee, and now he has a brown ________________ on his sweater.

2 When the weather becomes dangerous, the captain always ________________ the ship around and returns home.

3 We put ________________ in the basement to catch the mice.

4 At the end of the story, the king finally ________________ the prisoner.

5 My brother ________________ a taxi on the weekend.

6 The students have the same last name, but they are not ________________.

7 The students' ________________ of interest in the class increased after the teacher started showing movies.

C **Compare your answers with a partner's.**

Vocabulary Development

Definitions

Find the words in Reading 2 that complete the following definitions.

1 A / An ________________ issue is one that relates to the whole world. (*adj*) Par. 1, last sentence

2 ________________ energy is energy that comes from the sun. (*adj*) Par. 2, sentence 1

3 When water flows ________________, it flows all the time. (*adv*) Par. 2, sentence 6

4 If something is ________________, it is likely to hurt or kill someone else. (*adj*) Par. 2, last sentence

5 A / An ________________ is a process that happens over and over, starting again as soon as it finishes. (*n*) Par. 3, sentence 1

6 If something is ________________, it will continue without changing. (*adj*) Par. 5, sentence 3

7 ________________ are large amounts of water covering areas that are usually dry. (*n pl*) Par. 6, sentence 5

8 ________________ are the results of an action or situation, especially bad results. (*n pl*). Par. 6, last sentence

Word Families

A **The words in bold in the chart are from Reading 2. The words next to them are from the same word family. Study and learn these words.**

NOUN	VERB
absorption	***absorb*** (Par. 2)
distribution (Par. 1)	*distribute*
energy (Par. 1)	*energize*
evaporation	***evaporate*** (Par. 3)
reversal	***reverse*** (Par. 6)

B **Choose the correct form of the words from the chart to complete the following sentences.**

1 The floor was very wet, so we used towels to ________________ the water.

2 When it is hot and sunny, the water on the ground will ________________ quickly.

3 Some water pollution is caused by the ________________ of chemicals from factories into the oceans.

4 The captain will ________________ supplies to all the people on the ship.

5 Much of the ________________ that powers our cars comes from burning fossil fuels.

6 After many years without enough rain, some lakes might disappear because of ________________.

7 We do not like the decision, and we hope there is a ________________ of it.

8 The train system is important in the ________________ of newly made cars to salesrooms throughout the country.

9 Coffee and tea ________________ your body and make you feel more awake.

10 Usually the students study math first and then science, but sometimes they ________________ the order.

Beyond the Reading

Critical Thinking

In Reading 2, you learned how the oceans help create climates and weather.

> **APPLYING INFORMATION**
>
> You use critical thinking skills when you apply information you have just learned to new situations.

A Discuss the following questions with a partner.

1 What do you think is the ideal climate? Describe it.

2 Which adjectives can describe the climate of your hometown?

3 How does the weather change from season to season in your hometown?

4 Do people in your hometown have to deal with any problems related to weather or climate? Explain.

5 How would you feel if the climate in your hometown became much hotter? How would you feel if it became drier, colder, or wetter?

B Share your answers with the rest of the class.

Research

Interview someone who was alive 50 years ago and can remember the weather back then. Ask them the following questions about climate change:

- Have temperatures changed over the last 50 years? For example, are summers getting hotter, or are winters getting colder?
- Has the climate become wetter or drier over the last 50 years? For example, does it rain more often or less often than it did in the past?
- Have storms become stronger or more frequent?
- Have you noticed any other changes in the local climate?
- Are you worried about climate change? Why or why not?

Writing

Write a brief summary of your research. What changes did you learn about?

Finding Steps in a Process

Sometimes writers explain a process. A process is how something works or happens. When writers explain the steps in a process, they tell what happens, one thing after another. Writers often use time sequence words to signal these steps.

Examples & Explanations

Scientists say the sea level is rising. As humans produce more and more carbon dioxide (CO_2), the world becomes warmer, including ocean water. When water becomes warmer, it expands (gets bigger). Sea ice also starts to melt. This adds more water to the ocean. Over time, the sea level becomes higher and higher.

In this paragraph, the main idea is *the sea level is rising*. To explain the process of rising sea levels, the writer gives the steps. First, the water becomes warmer, then it expands and ice starts to melt, and finally, sea levels rise. The steps follow a time order.

To protect themselves from rising sea levels, some cities build seawalls. First, experts choose the best location for the seawall. To do this, they have to study water levels over a long period of time. Next, construction of the wall begins. The seawall is built near the shore, with heavy materials like metal and concrete. The completed seawall then keeps ocean water from damaging buildings and land near the shore during storms. The biggest seawall in the world is near Gunsan, South Korea. It was completed in 2006 and is 21 miles (33 kilometers) long.

The writer explains a process: how cities build seawalls. Writers usually introduce the process before they give the steps. This writer introduces the process in the first sentence. He gives the steps in the middle sentences. The writer uses the signals *first*, *next*, and *then* to introduce each step of the process. Writers often use time sequence words like these to signal the steps in a process.

The Language of Steps in a Process

Here are some common words and phrases that signal time sequence.

BEGINNING	MIDDLE	END
first, start, begin, in the beginning	*next, then, after that, when, over time*	*finally, last, in the end*

Strategies

These strategies will help you find the steps in a process while you read.

- Look for paragraphs that explain a process. Ask yourself: *Does the writer explain how something works or happens? Does the paragraph follow a time order?*
- Remember that writers usually introduce the process in the beginning of the paragraph and then give the steps in the following sentences.
- Look for time sequence words. Writers often use these signals to introduce the steps in a process.

Skill Practice 1

Read the following paragraphs. Highlight four time sequence signals in each paragraph. The first two are examples.

1 How do you get from place to place in a city whose streets are made of water? In Venice, Italy, on the Adriatic Sea, you can take a *vaporetto*. It is like a bus on the water. First, you have to decide which vaporetto to take. There are many different routes, so you may want to look at a map. After that, you must buy a ticket from a ticket office. Then, you need to put the ticket into a special machine. The machine writes the date and time on your ticket. You are finally ready to go to the station to wait for the next vaporetto.

2 Venice's streets of water are very beautiful. However, the city is in danger because the water is getting too high. How did this happen? First, the city was built on very soft ground. Over time, the weight of the city pushed down on the ground. This caused the city to sink. Then, sea levels started rising because of changes in the environment. Finally, water started to enter homes and businesses in Venice. Today, if there is a strong storm, up to 50 percent of the city can be covered in water.

3 One group of scientists has an interesting solution to Venice's problem: to fight water with more water. To start, the scientists will build 12 large pipes. Next, they will use the pipes to push water deep into the sand under the city. This will cause the area of sand under the city to expand. Over time, Venice will rise by as much as 12 inches (30 centimeters). In the end, the city will be safe from storms and flooding. The scientists say their plan will be cheap and effective, but other scientists are not so sure.

Skill Practice 2

Read the paragraphs in Skill Practice 1 again. Write the steps in each process on the lines below. Use the time sequence signals you circled to help you identify the steps. The first two are examples.

Paragraph 1

Process: In Venice, Italy, on the Adriatic Sea, you can take a *vaporetto*.

Step 1: *You have to decide which vaporetto to take.*

Step 2: *You must buy a ticket from a ticket office.*

Step 3: ______

Step 4: ______

Paragraph 2

Process: Venice is in danger because the water is getting too high.

Step 1: ______

Step 2: ______

Step 3: ______

Step 4: ______

Paragraph 3

Process: One group of scientists has an interesting solution to Venice's problem: to fight water with more water.

Step 1: ______

Step 2: ______

Step 3: ______

Step 4: ______

Before You Read

Connecting to the Topic

Look at the pictures of the ocean, and discuss the following questions with your partner.

1 Have you ever seen a part of the ocean that looks like either of these pictures? Explain your answer.

2 Which one do you think is more common? Why do you think so?

Previewing and Predicting

Previewing images such as charts, maps, and diagrams can help you predict what the reading will be about. It is also important to preview the section headings in a longer reading.

A Read the section headings in Reading 3. Look at any graphs, pictures, and maps. Decide what you will read about in each section. Then write the number of the section (*I–III*) next to each topic to show where it might appear.

SECTION	TOPIC
	The effect of noise on ocean animals
	The kinds of pollution in the oceans
	Acid levels in the ocean
	Where ocean garbage is located
	The impact of acid in the oceans

B Compare your answers with a partner's.

While You Read

As you read, stop at the end of each sentence that contains words in bold. Then follow the instructions in the box in the margin.

The Health of Our Oceans

1 The oceans provide water, oxygen, food, and economic opportunities. For these and other reasons, the health of our oceans is very important. When the health of our oceans is in danger, so is the health of the human race. Some scientists are worried that, unfortunately, our oceans are sick and they are getting **sicker**.

WHILE YOU READ 1

Look for the word in this sentence that tells the topic of the reading. Highlight it.

I. Acidity Levels

2 Global warming is affecting the oceans in many ways: higher temperatures, rising sea levels, and also, increasing acidity. Acids are chemicals that can harm the ocean environment. How is the acidity of the oceans increasing? First, humans burn fossil fuels, which releases carbon dioxide (CO_2). Then, oceans absorb much of the CO_2 – about 22 million tons a day. Over time, the CO_2 level of the oceans increases. In the end, the CO_2 combines with other chemicals in the water to create large amounts of acid. Scientists estimate that ocean acidity has increased 25 to 30 percent since the beginning of the eighteenth century. They predict that by 2100, that figure will be 100 to 150 percent. (See Figure 5.6.)

3 The increase in acidity has serious consequences. It can disrupt the life of the plants and animals that live in the ocean. The disruption begins with the smallest forms of **life**. There are millions of tiny plants in the oceans that produce much of the oxygen in the air. When the acidity level in the oceans rises, these plants begin to die. The number of these plants has already decreased by one percent in just 15 years. When they die, we lose an important source of oxygen. The higher level of acidity affects other organisms in the ocean too. For example, it can dissolve the shells of snails and slow the growth of clams. Over time, the damage to these plants and animals means less food for the larger fish, like salmon, and shellfish, like shrimp and lobster, that eat **them**.

WHILE YOU READ 2

Look for a time sequence signal in this sentence. Highlight it.

WHILE YOU READ 3

Look for a time sequence signal in this sentence. Highlight it.

II. The Noisy Ocean

4 The oceans are noisy. In recent years, they have become much noisier. Experts estimate that in some busy areas, it is one hundred times louder than in the past. This new noise comes from ships, construction, and

Figure 5.6 Historical and Projected pH and Dissolved CO_2

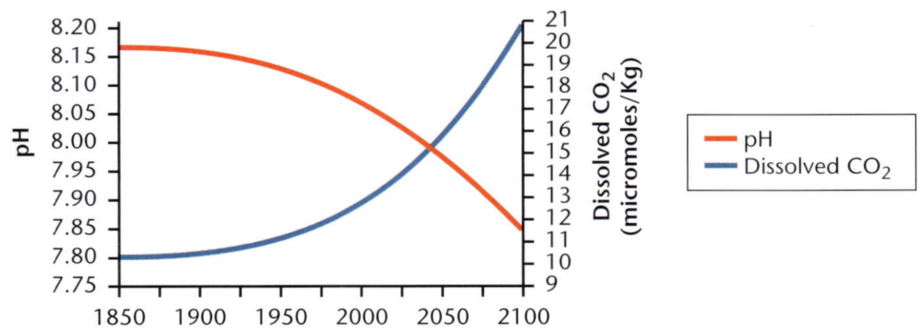

industry. There is not yet very much scientific research on the effects of this noise, but some experts believe that it is causing problems for sea animals.

5 You may know that whales and dolphins make sounds, but fish do, too. Many sea animals use these sounds to communicate with others. They send and receive warnings, as well as signals about food and safe places to rest. These sounds are essential for their health and safety. In a noisy ocean, animals may not be able to hear them. It is especially important for baby sea animals to learn about these sounds. The noise of human activity can disrupt this learning process. As a result, the young animals may begin to respond to the sounds made by humans instead of other sea animals. A noisy ocean can become a dangerous place.

III. Liquid and Solid Pollution

6 Acidity and noise are forms of pollution. Other forms of pollution can also be dangerous to sea life. The huge volume of water in the ocean acts like a **filter**. It can clean out some of the toxic material that people put into it. However, scientists believe that the oceans are reaching the limit of their ability to do this. Some of these toxic materials are liquid chemicals, which mix easily into seawater. These toxic chemicals can be dangerous to both sea life and humans. First, the chemicals kill some small plants and animals. Then, the chemicals start to affect fish. The chemicals enter the fish with the ocean water and are stored in their bodies. Over time, the chemicals are passed on to bigger fish that eat the small fish. The levels of some chemicals in certain fish like tuna can be a thousand times higher than the levels in the ocean. Finally, if we eat those bigger fish, the toxic chemicals enter our bodies. (See Figure 5.7.) As a result, some governments have warned that we should not eat too much fish.

WHILE YOU READ 4

What part of speech is *filter* in this sentence?
a) Noun
b) Verb

7 Solid waste, especially plastic, is also a big problem. Eating plastic can kill birds, fish, and sea mammals. Unfortunately, plastic objects sometimes look like food. For example, plastic bags look very much like jellyfish. Plastic in the ocean lasts for a very long time. The ocean currents have pushed piles of these plastic objects together. Some of these piles are as big as small islands. One of the largest ones is in the Pacific Ocean between Hawaii and California. It covers thousands of square miles. It is not the only one, however. There are several other "garbage islands," and more are forming all the time.

8 Although the health of our oceans is clearly in danger, there is some good news. Experts believe that a lot of the damage caused by high acidity, noise, and other forms of pollution is not permanent. We can reverse much of the damage if we change our destructive behavior and work together to support the health of our oceans.

Figure 5.7 Cycle of Pollution from Sea Plants to Humans

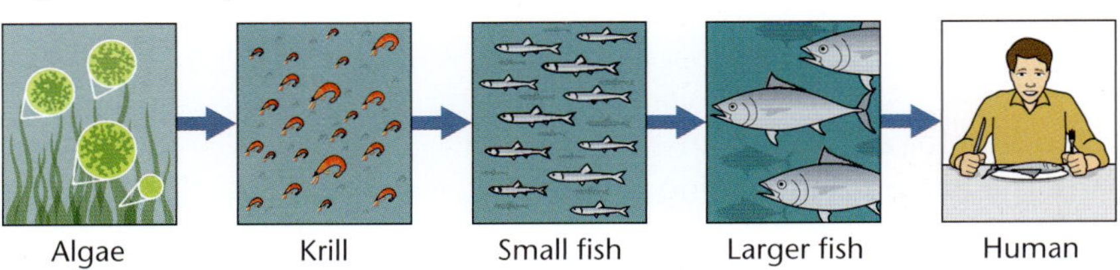

Main Idea Check

Match the main ideas below to paragraphs 2–8 in Reading 3. Write the number of the paragraph on the blank line.

_____ A The oceans are becoming noisier because of human activity.

_____ B Toxic chemicals are another form of ocean pollution.

_____ C Global warming is increasing the acidity of the oceans.

_____ D The increase in noise is dangerous for some sea animals.

_____ E Solid materials are one of the most serious forms of pollution.

_____ F The increase in acidity has harmful results.

_____ G Humans can stop polluting the oceans, but it will not be easy.

A Closer Look

Look back at Reading 3 to answer the following questions.

1 Why should people care about the health of the oceans? (Par. 1)
  a The oceans are beautiful.
  b Humans depend on the oceans.
  c Scientists are still learning about the oceans.
  d Many people travel across the oceans.

2 What is the cause of increasing ocean acidity? (Par. 2)
  a Overfishing
  b Increasing temperatures
  c Rising sea levels
  d Burning fossil fuels

3 What is a result of increasing ocean acidity? (Par. 3)
  a Strong shellfish
  b Less oxygen
  c Unsafe swimming
  d More plant life

4 Sea animals use sounds to communicate with each other. **True or False?** (Par. 5)

5 Ocean pollution may make some types of fish unsafe to eat. **True or False?** (Par. 6)

6 Which of the following are reasons for the formation of garbage islands? Choose three answers. (Par. 7)
  a Carbon dioxide
  b Pollution
  c Shellfish
  d Currents
  e Plastic stays in the ocean for a long time.
  f The temperature of the oceans is increasing.

Skill Review

In Skills and Strategies 10, you learned how writers give the steps in a process. You learned that writers often use time sequence signals to introduce the steps.

A Many of the paragraphs in Reading 3 explain a process. These processes are listed below. Write the steps in each process. Use the time sequence signals in the reading to help you. The first one is an example.

1 Process in paragraph 2: The oceans are becoming more acidic.

a *People burn fossil fuels and create more CO_2.*

b __________

c __________

d __________

2 Process in paragraph 6: Toxic chemicals can be dangerous to both sea life and humans.

a __________

b __________

c __________

d __________

B Read the following sentences about a process that is explained in paragraphs 4 and 5. They give steps in the process. Then write the name of the process on the blank line.

1 New noise comes from ships, construction, and industry.

2 Animals may not be able to hear each other's messages about food and safety.

3 Baby sea animals do not learn about important animal sounds.

4 They begin to respond to the sounds made by humans instead of other sea animals.

5 A noisy ocean can become a dangerous place.

Process in paragraphs 4 and 5: __________

C Compare your answers to exercises A and B with a partner's.

Vocabulary Development

Definitions

Find the words in Reading 3 that complete the following definitions.

1 ________________ is the amount of acid in a substance. (*n*) Par. 2, sentence 1

2 To ________________ is to guess the amount or size of something. (*v*) Par. 2, sentence 8

3 To ________________ something is to stop it from continuing in its usual way. (*v*) Par. 3, sentence 2

4 A ________________ is where something comes from. (*n*) Par. 3, sentence 7

5 ________________ is damage caused to air, water, etc., by harmful substances and waste. (*n*) Par. 6, sentence 1

6 The ________________ is the amount of something, especially when the amount is large. (*n*) Par. 6, sentence 3

7 If something is ________________, it contains harmful chemicals. (*adj*) Par. 6, sentence 4

8 If something is ________________, it causes a lot of damage. (*adj*) Par. 8, last sentence

Words in Context

A Match the first part of each sentence with the letter that best completes it. Each completion should fit with the meaning of the words in bold.

_____ 1 The blue **whale**
_____ 2 Some types of **jellyfish**
_____ 3 Examples of **shellfish**
_____ 4 **Lobsters** are much bigger
_____ 5 It takes a lot of **shrimp**
_____ 6 Examples of **mammals**
_____ 7 A **dolphin** is about
_____ 8 The smallest **organisms** in the ocean

a are poisonous to humans.
b are whales, dolphins, and humans.
c are shrimp and lobsters.
d are tiny plants.
e is the largest animal in the ocean.
f to feed a hungry person.
g than shrimp.
h the same size as a human.

B Compare your answers with a partner's.

Academic Word List

The following are Academic Word List words from all the readings in Unit 5. Use these words to complete the sentences. (If necessary, review the AWL words in Key Vocabulary on pages 257–267.)

consequences (*n*)	cycle (*n*)	dramatically (*adv*)	period (*n*)	source (*n*)
constantly (*adv*)	distribution (*n*)	estimate (*v*)	recover (*v*)	volume (*n*)

1 The earth's population has tripled in the last 60 years; how did it increase so ________________?

2 Scientists ________________ there will be about 10 billion people on Earth in the year 2050.

3 Overpopulation can lead to serious ________________ such as a lack of food and water.

4 If humans stop cutting down trees, the forest will ________________ over time.

5 The ocean is an important ________________ of food for many people.

6 The ________________ of work was fair; every team member had the same amount to do.

7 Last year the ________________ of the company's sales was very high; more than five million computers were sold.

8 Every butterfly goes through the same three stages during its life ________________.

9 Childhood is the most important ________________ in life for language learning.

10 Because people invent new words every year, the English language is ________________ changing.

Critical Thinking

In Reading 3, you learned about some forms of pollution that are affecting oceans.

> **CLARIFYING CONCEPTS**
>
> Critical thinking includes exploring an idea in a text by thinking about how it would fit in a different context.

A Imagine you work for an organization whose goal is to protect the oceans. How can your organization make people more aware of the following problems? Make a list of your ideas. Work in a small group.

- Increasing acidity in the oceans
- Noise pollution in the oceans
- Chemical pollution in the oceans
- Solid waste pollution in the oceans

B Share one of your group's ideas with the rest of the class.

Research

Do some research about organizations whose goal is to protect the oceans. How are they making people more aware of the following problems?

- Increasing acidity in the oceans
- Noise pollution in the oceans
- Chemical pollution in the oceans
- Solid waste pollution in the oceans

Writing

Write a short report about the results of your research. How are organizations making people aware of pollution in the oceans?

Improving Your Reading Speed

Good readers read quickly and still understand most of what they read.

A Read the instructions and strategies for Improving Your Reading Speed in Appendix 3 on page 270.

B Choose one of the readings in this unit. Read it without stopping. Time how long it takes you to finish the text in minutes and seconds. Enter the time in the chart on page 272. Then calculate your reading speed in number of words per minute.

TIME SEQUENCE CONNECTORS

When writers give steps in a process or a sequence of events, they often use words or phrases to make the time sequence clear. They use words and phrases such as *first*, *then*, *after*, and *finally* to show how one step or event connects to another. You also learned time sequence words and phrases in Skills and Strategies 10 on page 150.

Exercise 1

Read the following sentences. Highlight any time sequence words or phrases. Write *1* over the part of the sentence that tells the first step, and *2* over the part of the sentence that tells the second step. The first one is an example.

1 The ship hit a large rock, and then it started to sink. (*1* over "hit"; *2* over "it")

2 A large amount of oil spilled into the ocean after the ship sank.

3 The oil first covered the surface of the water; next, it reached the beach.

4 Many animals became sick after they came into contact with the oil.

5 The TV news reported the oil spill, and then everyone started talking about it.

6 Many people went to the beach to help clean up when they heard about the oil spill.

7 The volunteers helped clean the beach, and over time, the area recovered.

8 Oil spills may finally become less common, but right now they are a serious problem.

Exercise 2

Make a clear paragraph by putting sentences A, B, and C into the best order after the numbered sentence. Look for pronouns, category words, and time sequence connectors to help you. Write the letters in the correct order on the blank lines.

1 At one time, there were plenty of whales in the ocean. ___ ___ ___

A	B	C
These boats helped people catch many whales in a short period of time.	However, in the nineteenth century, humans began using large boats to catch whales.	By the 1930s, humans were catching over 50,000 whales per year.

2 Whale populations declined dramatically. ___ ___ ___

A	B	C
However, these actions were not very effective.	In the 1940s, some countries created laws to protect whales.	Governments started to worry that whales could disappear.

3 In the 1960s, scientists made important discoveries about whales. ___ ___ ___

A	B	C
First, they discovered that whales could communicate and solve problems.	These discoveries changed the way people thought about whales.	Then, in 1967, a scientist discovered that some species of whales can sing.

4 Around the world, people became interested in protecting whales. ___ ___ ___

A	B	C
The shirts became very popular, and Maris used the money she earned to educate people about whales.	She started making T-shirts with a picture of a blue whale and the words "Save the Whales."	One such person was a 14-year-old girl named Maris Sidenstecker from Los Angeles.

5 Today, many species of whales have recovered. ___ ___ ___

A	B	C
The Pacific gray whale is one example.	If humans keep working to protect whales, other species may recover in the future.	The blue whale is another species whose numbers are increasing.

6 COMMUNICATION

SKILLS AND STRATEGIES

- Noticing Parts of Words: Noun Suffixes
- Finding Advantages and Disadvantages

Skill Practice 2

Write the words you highlighted in Skill Practice 1 on the blank lines. Then write simple definitions for each word. Use your knowledge of noun suffixes to help you. The first one is an example.

1 *owner* = *a person who owns something*

2 ________ = ________________________________

3 ________ = ________________________________

4 ________ = ________________________________

5 ________ = ________________________________

6 ________ = ________________________________

7 ________ = ________________________________

8 ________ = ________________________________

9 ________ = ________________________________

10 ________ = ________________________________

Before You Read

Connecting to the Topic

Look at the drawing and discuss the following questions with a partner.

1 What do you think the man in this picture is doing?
2 When do you think the man lived?
3 How has the act of writing changed since then?
4 What kinds of things do you write most often?
5 Do you ever write personal letters to family or friends?

Previewing and Predicting

Remember that reading the title and the first few sentences in each paragraph can help you to predict what the reading will be about.

A Read the title of Reading 1 and the first few sentences of each paragraph. Then, put a check (✓) next to the topic or topics you think might be in the reading.

_____ a Why people write letters
_____ b The importance of education
_____ c The history of Egypt
_____ d Personal stories about immigrants
_____ e The loss of writing skills
_____ f Writing and technology
_____ g Changes in writing traditions

B Compare your answers with a partner's.

While You Read

As you read, stop at the end of each sentence that contains words in bold. Then follow the instructions in the box in the margin.

READING 1

Scribes – A Tradition

1 Wong Chong Mun left China in 1899 and went to San Francisco. He was a teacher in China, but there were not many good jobs for Chinese people in the United States at that **time**. He took other jobs: a cook, a dishwasher. But as the Chinese community in San Francisco grew, he found a different job, as a **scribe**. A scribe is a person who reads and writes for people who cannot. Wong was one of the few Chinese immigrants in his community who could read and write. So, when other Chinese immigrants wanted to write home to their families, they went to Wong for help. Wong also read letters for them when their families wrote back.

WHILE YOU READ 1

Look for a word with a noun suffix in this sentence. Highlight it.

WHILE YOU READ 2

Which sentence gives the meaning of *scribe*?

a) The same sentence
b) The sentence before
c) The sentence after

2 The scribe tradition goes back thousands of years to ancient Egypt. Scribes wrote and copied business, religious, and government records. Later, as mechanical printing became more widespread, scribes began to perform new functions. They helped people understand and fill out government documents. This was especially important for people who did not have much education. In many countries all over the world, scribes still perform this function today.

3 However, writing letters has always been an important job for scribes, too. It is a valuable service, especially important for people who have left their families and moved to another city or country. G. P. Sawant is a scribe who started working in Mumbai, India, in 1982. His most frequent customers are young women who have come to Mumbai to find work. They want to write to their families and send them money, but many of them cannot read or write. In 2007, Sawant said he had written more than 10,000 letters during his career.

A scribe in Kolkata, India

4 Today, however, there is less need for scribes like Sawant. One reason is the increase in **literacy** (the ability to read and write). Another reason is new technology. People don't write many letters anymore. They speak by telephone, or they send a text message. In many countries, scribes have already disappeared. Almost 50 years ago, a story in a Saudi Arabian newspaper described the decline of the profession. Rashid as-Salih had been a scribe in a Saudi town for many years. He had helped many people fill out government documents, but he understood that his job would soon disappear. In the article, he sadly describes his situation: "Today, everybody can write. Today there is little need for a scribe, and tomorrow there will be no need at all."

WHILE YOU READ 3

Which sentence gives the meaning of *literacy*?
a) The same sentence
b) the sentence before
c) the sentence after

5 In some parts of the world, however, the tradition remains alive – at least once a year. Alassane Maiga has been a scribe in Bamako, Mali, for 15 years. On most days, he sits at his table outside the post office. He sometimes writes letters for other people, but mostly, he helps people with government documents. On one day every year, however, he doesn't work on documents. He just writes lots of letters – love letters. Valentine's Day is Maiga's busiest day of the year. He and the other scribes are so busy that they work all day. Sometimes they even work all night. Each love letter Maiga writes is different. He tries to understand what the sender wants to express: does he feel sadness, loneliness, or just **happiness**? He also thinks about the person who will receive the letter. What would that person like to hear? He may even add some decorations to the letter. For all that work, he charges extra. On Valentine's Day, a letter costs about four times more than on any other day.

WHILE YOU READ 4

Look for four words with noun suffixes in this sentence. Highlight them.

Main Idea Check

Match the main ideas below to paragraphs 2–5 in Reading 1. Write the number of the paragraph on the blank line.

_____ A Scribes also help people send messages to friends and family.

_____ B In some places, the scribe tradition continues.

_____ C The scribe tradition is coming to an end in many places.

_____ D There is a long history of scribes helping people with documents.

A Closer Look

Look back at Reading 1 to answer the following questions.

1 Wong Chong Mun wrote letters only in English. **True or False?** (Par. 1)

2 According to paragraph 2, the scribe tradition began in which country?
- a Egypt
- b India
- c Mali
- d Saudi Arabia

3 How did most scribes help people with documents in the past? (Par. 2)
- a Sending them
- b Copying them
- c Filling them out
- d Printing them

4 How do most scribes help people with documents today? (Par. 2)
- a Sending them
- b Copying them
- c Filling them out
- d Printing them

5 Match the beginning of a sentence in Column A with its correct ending in Column B.

	Column A	Column B
_____	1 Wong Chong Mun	a is busy on Valentine's Day.
_____	2 Scribes in ancient Egypt	b charge extra.
_____	3 G. P. Sawant	c has been a scribe since 1982.
_____	4 Many young Indian women	d was a Chinese immigrant.
_____	5 Rashid as-Salih	e worked as a scribe in Saudi Arabia.
_____	6 A newspaper in Saudi Arabia	f come to Mumbai to find work.
_____	7 Alassane Maiga	g copied documents by hand.
_____	8 Scribes who send Valentine's Day letters	h explained how scribes are becoming less common.

6 Why are scribes disappearing? Choose three answers.

a Newspapers write negative things about scribes.
b Many people use mechanical printing.
c People can communicate with cell phones.
d Literacy is increasing.
e People have to fill out complicated government documents.

Skill Review

In Skills and Strategies 11, you learned about the suffixes *-er*, *-or*, *-ment*, *-ness*, and *-tion*. These suffixes can help you identify nouns and understand the meaning of those nouns.

A Look back at Reading 1. Fill in the blanks below with the correct words that have noun suffixes.

1 Before he became a scribe, Wong Chong Mun worked as a ________________ in China and as a ________________ in San Francisco. (Par. 1)

2 Scribes help people who do not have much ________________. (Par. 2)

3 Rashid as-Salih helps people fill out ________________ documents. (Par. 4)

4 If a person is happy, Alassane Maiga tries to express the feeling of ________________ when he writes a letter. (Par. 5)

5 Alassane Maiga may add some ________________ to Valentine's Day letters. (Par. 5)

B Compare your answers with a partner's.

Vocabulary Development

Definitions

Find the words in Reading 1 that complete the following definitions.

1 ________________ are people who have come from one country to live in a different country. (*n pl*) Par. 1, sentence 6

2 When people keep ________________, they keep important information on paper or on computers so they can use it again in the future. (*n pl*) Par. 2, sentence 2

3 If something is ________________, it relates to or is operated by machines. (*adj*) Par. 2, sentence 3

4 ________________ are the purposes or duties that are part of someone's job. (*n pl*) Par. 2, sentence 3

5 If something is ________________, it happens often. (*adj*) Par. 3, sentence 4

6 ________________ is the ability to read and write. (*n*) Par. 4, sentence 2

7 A / An ________________ is a written communication sent by cell phone. (*2-word n*) Par. 4, sentence 5

8 Something that is ________________ is living, not dead. (*adj*) Par. 5, sentence 1

Words in Context

Complete the sentences with words from Reading 1 in the box below.

cook	especially	post office	tradition
documents	fill out	technology	valuable

1 You have to ________________ this document with your name, address, and age.

2 My mother always makes delicious meals; she is an excellent ________________.

3 The watch is made of gold; it is very ________________.

4 Some people do not understand modern ________________ like computers and cell phones.

5 People can send letters and packages at the ________________.

6 My friend goes to the lake with his parents every year; it is a family ________________.

7 Books are expensive to print, ________________ if they have color pictures.

8 People entering a foreign country need to bring ________________ like passports and visas.

Critical Thinking

In Reading 1, you learned about the scribe tradition and why it may be disappearing.

> **EXPLORING OPINIONS**
>
> Critical readers form their own opinions about important topics in a text.

A Circle the word or phrase that you think best completes each statement below.

1 In today's society, being a scribe is a better / worse job than being a cook.

2 Scribes should feel proud of / worried about their jobs.

3 In the future, handwriting will not be necessary / still be important.

4 Most government documents are easy / difficult to fill out.

5 Emails can / cannot express the same feelings as a personal letter.

6 Men / women write the best love letters.

B Share your answers with a small group of classmates and explain your opinions.

Research

Read statements 3, 4, 5, and 6 from Critical Thinking part A above. Choose one of the statements. Talk to five people from outside your class. Ask them which word or phrase they think best completes the statement, and why. Write down each person's response and his or her age.

Writing

Write a short report about your research. Are the opinions similar or different? Why are they similar or different?

Connecting to the Topic

Discuss the following questions with a partner.

1 Have you ever experienced a really bad storm? Describe what happened.

2 You have probably read stories in the news about natural disasters, such as earthquakes and hurricanes. What are some of the biggest problems for people who live through natural disasters?

3 What would you do if you were in an earthquake or a hurricane? Do you think you would be prepared?

4 Would you be able to communicate with friends and family? How?

Previewing and Predicting

Remember that looking at the title, the first few sentences in each paragraph, and any charts or graphs can help you to predict what the reading will be about.

A Read the title and first few sentences of each paragraph in Reading 2. Look at the graph. Based on this information, put a check (✓) next to things you think might be in the reading.

_____ a The problems that people experience during natural disasters

_____ b Cell phone use during natural disasters

_____ c The number of people who die in natural disasters

_____ d What you can do to help people in natural disasters

_____ e How to prevent natural disasters

_____ f The role of technology in natural disasters

_____ g How people get information in a natural disaster

B Compare your answers with a partner's.

While You Read

As you read, stop at the end of each sentence that contains words in bold. Then follow the instructions in the box in the margin.

Communication in Natural Disasters

1 During **natural disasters**, such as storms, floods, or earthquakes, disaster victims need information quickly. Fifty years ago, people turned to the radio or television for news and information in these emergencies, or they tried to call a government office. These were not very effective forms of communication for several reasons. First, after a natural disaster, there may be no electricity or traditional telephone service. Second, the radios and televisions may be broken or lost. Finally, in some communities, many people do not own a radio or television.

2 Today, there are more effective forms of communication during **natural disasters**. Cell phones and the Internet have significantly changed how we respond in these situations. Many people do not have a radio, television, or landline telephone in their homes. However, almost everyone does have access to a cell phone. In 2014, more than 95 percent of the world's population had access to a **cell phone**. Experts estimate that there were more than 7 billion cell phones in use in 2014.

3 If there is no electricity, disaster victims and emergency workers can still use cell phones to communicate, for as long as their batteries last. Some cell phones also give them access to the Internet. Disaster victims can communicate through Internet sites such as Facebook and Twitter. For these reasons, cell phones have become the most common and effective way to communicate during and after natural disasters. During a disaster, people can use Internet sites to find and post information. They can tell their families and friends that they are safe. The government and organizations that provide aid can post information on their pages. When a major storm hit New York City in 2012, the government disaster agency

WHILE YOU READ 1

Look for three examples of natural disasters in this sentence. Highlight them.

WHILE YOU READ 2

Which sentence gives the most effective forms of communication in natural disasters?
a) The same sentence
b) The sentence before
c) The sentence after

WHILE YOU READ 3

Look for a word with a noun suffix in this sentence. Highlight it.

Figure 6.1 Cell Phone Users per 100 People

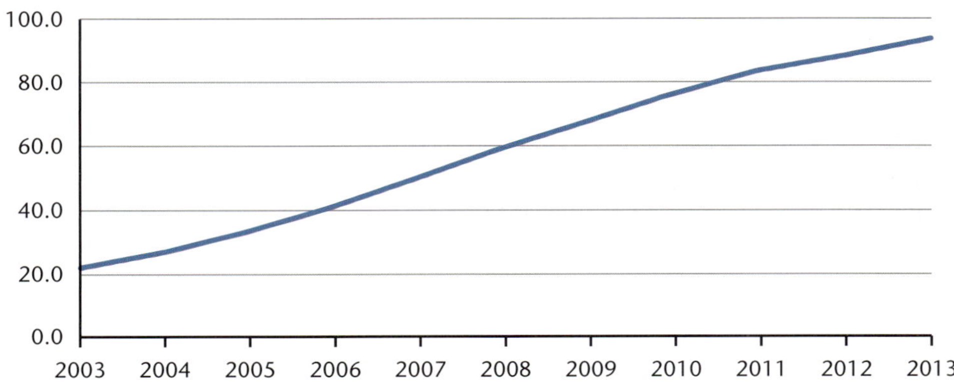

Source: International Telecommunication Union

used social media to let disaster victims know where to find food, water, and a safe place to sleep – and even where to recharge their cell phones. The agency also used its website to stop rumors. For example, a rumor that the supply of bottled water had run out caused some people to get very worried. When the agency announced online that the rumor was not true, the panic ended.

4 Disaster victims can also send or post messages for emergency workers about their community. How many people are hurt? What kind of help do they need? Are some roads closed? Are some places still dangerous? They can send or post photographs so that emergency workers know how to prepare. This information can also keep the emergency workers safe.

5 After a disaster, survivors and emergency workers often continue to use this technology in recovery efforts. At this point, they begin to communicate with the rest of the world. They can ask for money, equipment, and volunteers to help rebuild their communities. This has been a very effective way for communities to make other people aware of their needs and get help. And perhaps just as important, it is free. A survivor can send a request that reaches a million people almost instantly, and it costs nothing.

6 Recent **disasters** show the power of this technology. During and right after the Japanese earthquake and tsunami in 2011, there were 1,200 Twitter messages from Tokyo about the disaster every minute. There were 4.5 million Facebook messages worldwide with the words "earthquake" or "tsunami." After a tornado in the United States the same year, a community in Alabama posted a request for volunteers on the Internet. They needed assistance to repair the damage to their school. Eighty people arrived to help within 30 minutes. In Bangladesh, the government has started sending flood warnings to the cell phones of people who live near rivers. A 2012 study by the Red Cross suggests that, in the future, people will not be listening to the radio or watching television after a disaster. Instead, they will reach for their cell phones.

WHILE YOU READ 4

Look for an example of a recent disaster in the next sentence. Highlight it.

Main Idea Check

Match the main ideas below to paragraphs 2–6 in Reading 2. Write the number of the paragraph on the blank line.

_____ A Survivors can communicate with emergency workers.
_____ B Most people have access to a cell phone these days.
_____ C Cell phones can work when the electricity is out, and some can access important information online.
_____ D After disasters in Japan and the United States, social media were very helpful.
_____ E Communication technology is also helpful as people rebuild communities.

A Closer Look

Look back at Reading 2 to answer the following questions.

1 Do these statements describe televisions or cell phones? Write *T* (televisions) or *C* (cell phones). (Pars. 1–3)

_____ a Most people have one.
_____ b They work when the power goes out.
_____ c They are big, heavy, and often break during disasters.
_____ d They were an important source of information 50 years ago.
_____ e They are changing how people communicate during natural disasters.

2 Choose five uses of cell phones that the writer mentions. (Pars. 3–5)

a Contact family and friends
b Access social media websites
c Write important times and dates on calendars
d Get information from government agencies
e See in the dark with the light from the screen
f Learn if information is true or false
g Send pictures to emergency workers

3 Cell phones are not useful in recovery situations. **True or False?** (Par. 5)

4 Match each natural disaster with people's use of communication technology. (Pars. 3 and 6)

	Natural disaster	Use of communication technology
_____	1 A major storm in New York	a Asking for volunteers to repair a school
_____	2 A tsunami in Japan	b Stopping rumors about the water supply
_____	3 A tornado in Alabama	c Sending warnings to people near rivers
_____	4 Floods in Bangladesh	d Posting 4.5 million messages on Facebook

Skill Review

In Skills and Strategies 11, you learned about the noun suffixes *-er*, *-or*, *-ment*, *-ness*, and *-tion*. These suffixes can help you understand words. They can also increase your vocabulary.

A **The words below are from Reading 2. Add the suffix *-er*, *-or*, *-ment*, *-ness*, or *-tion* to each word to form a new noun. The first one is an example.**

1 effective *effectiveness*

2 send ______

3 announce ______

4 photograph ______

5 aware ______

6 suggest ______

B **Use the nouns you created in A to complete the sentences below.**

1 Today we read about the ______ of cell phones during natural disasters.

2 The agency posted an important ______ on its website.

3 Jerry has an expensive camera, but he is not a very good ______.

4 We received the letter by mistake, so we returned it to the ______.

5 In the past, few people knew about environmental problems, but today there is much more ______.

6 Jane's father gave her several ______ about how to get a summer job.

C **Compare your answers with a partner's.**

Vocabulary Development

Definitions

Find the words in Reading 2 that complete the following definitions.

1 A / An ______________ is a sudden, strong movement of the earth's surface. (*n*) Par. 1, sentence 1

2 ______________ are people who have suffered from a disaster or dangerous situation. (*n pl*) Par. 1, sentence 1

3 ______________ is money, food, or equipment given to help people. (*n*) Par. 3, sentence 7

4 A / An ______________ is a government organization that provides a particular service. (*n*) Par. 3, sentence 8

5 ______________ are statements that may or may not be true and are communicated quickly from person to person. (*n pl*) Par. 3, sentence 9

6 The ______________ of food is the amount of food that is available for use. (*n*) Par. 3, sentence 10

7 ______________ is a sudden strong feeling of worry that makes you unable to think clearly. (*n*) Par. 3, last sentence

8 ______________ are people who do work for no pay in order to help others. (*n pl*) Par. 5, sentence 3

Word Families

A The words in bold in the chart are from Reading 2. The words next to them are from the same word family. Study and learn these words.

NOUN	VERB
information (Par. 1)	*inform*
communication (Par. 2)	*communicate*
equipment (Par. 5)	*equip*
request (Par. 5)	*request*
damage (Par. 6)	*damage*

B Choose the correct form of the words from the chart to complete the following sentences.

1 After the tree fell on the house, there was a lot of ______________ to the roof.

2 After a natural disaster, a cell phone and a flashlight are both very useful pieces of ______________ .

3 We did not know how to prepare for a natural disaster, so we went online to find some ______________ .

4 The government disaster office decided to ______________ all its workers with a helmet and a shovel.

5 We used social media websites to ______________ more volunteers for our town.

6 We do not speak the same language, but we can still ______________ with our hands.

7 When a student stole the answers to the test, his classmates decided to ______________ the teacher.

8 In the past, parents rarely talked to teachers at the school, but recently, ______________ between them has improved.

9 Smoking can seriously ______________ your health.

10 The students made a ______________ for more time to finish their homework.

Critical Thinking

In Reading 2, you learned how cell phones and the Internet are changing the way people communicate in natural disasters.

> **APPLYING INFORMATION**
>
> You use critical thinking skills when you apply information you have just learned to new situations.

A Work in a small group. Complete the tasks.

1 Choose one type of natural disaster that is possible in the place you live.
2 Make a list of things people can do to prepare for this type of natural disaster.
3 Say which things on the list you have done and which things you have not done.
4 Decide which person in your group is best prepared for a natural disaster.

B Share your answers with the rest of the class.

Research

Think of a recent natural disaster. Go to a popular social media website like Twitter or Facebook, and search for information about the natural disaster. Then answer the questions.

1 Which of the following types of messages can you find on the website?
- People telling family and friends they are safe
- Information from emergency workers and government agencies
- Requests for aid

2 Which type of message is the most common?

Writing

Write a short report about your research. What did you learn about communication in natural disasters?

Finding Advantages and Disadvantages

Writers sometimes give advantages and disadvantages to support their main ideas. An advantage is a positive (good) detail, and a disadvantage is a negative (bad) detail. Good readers can find advantages and disadvantages. These explanations help them answer questions like "Why should people do something?" or "Why should people not do something?"

Examples & Explanations

Today, many people prefer to communicate by texting. The main advantage of texting is its convenience: texts are fast to write and easy to send. But the low cost of texting is a benefit, as well. Most cell phone users can send all the texts that they want for just a few dollars each month.

In this paragraph, the topic is texting. The writer gives advantages of texting: It is cheap and convenient. The writer introduces these details with the signal words *advantage* and *benefit*. Writers also use the word *positive* to signal an advantage.

Many teachers worry about the impact of texting on their students. One disadvantage is that students can spend too much time texting and too little time studying. Another negative aspect of texting is its effect on students' writing. Students may forget how to use correct grammar and how to spell properly.

This paragraph gives disadvantages of texting: Students spend too much time texting, and texting has an effect on students' writing. The writer uses the signals *disadvantage* and *negative* to introduce these details. Writers also use the word *problem* to signal a disadvantage.

Texting can also affect friendships. On the one hand, texts help friends share feelings, ideas, and information easily. Even short text terms such as *LOL* (laughing out loud) or *XOXO* (hugs and kisses) can show someone's feelings. On the other hand, texts can create misunderstandings. They do not show body language. As a result, it is harder to know someone's real feelings from a text than from a face-to-face conversation.

This paragraph gives both advantages and disadvantages of texting. The writer uses the phrases *on the one hand* to introduce the advantages and *on the other hand* to introduce the disadvantages. Writers often use these contrast signals when they give both positive and negative details about a topic.

The Language of Advantages and Disadvantages

Here are some common words and phrases that signal advantages and disadvantages.

WORDS THAT SIGNAL ADVANTAGES	WORDS THAT SIGNAL DISADVANTAGES
advantage	*disadvantage*
benefit	*problem*
positive	*negative*

Strategies

These strategies will help you find advantages and disadvantages while you read.

- Find the topic of the reading. Then, as you read, ask yourself questions about the topic: *Why should people do that? Why should people not do that?*
- Look quickly at the first few sentences of a paragraph. They might help you know if the paragraph gives both advantages and disadvantages, or only advantages or disadvantages.
- Look for words and phrases that signal advantages and disadvantages. Study and learn the signal words in the chart.
- If the reading has a lot of advantages and disadvantages, make a list of them as you read.

Skill Practice 1

Read the following paragraphs. Find the words that signal advantages or disadvantages. Highlight two signals in each paragraph.

1 Many scientists believe texting is improving our ability to communicate. One advantage of texting is that it makes communication more creative. People invent new words when they text and find simple ways to explain complicated ideas. Another benefit of texting is that it helps people share information quickly and easily.

2 Some scientists believe that texting is changing students' behavior. If students often text, they may have problems in school. In fact, studies show that students who often text receive lower grades. Another negative effect of texting is that it may be making students less honest. Scientists studied the ways students communicate. They found that the students lied more often in texts than face-to-face. Why is that? The scientists explained that people are more likely to lie when they do not have to worry about their body language.

3 Texting is not only affecting our communication, but also our bodies. On the one hand, some people experience physical benefits from texting. They develop stronger, faster fingers. For example, the fastest texters in the world can type more than eight characters per second with no mistakes. On the other hand, some people have physical problems from texting too much. They lose strength in their hands and find it difficult to hold heavy objects. Doctors call the condition "text thumb."

Skill Practice 2

Read the following paragraphs. Then fill in the blanks with an advantage or disadvantage from the paragraph. Use the signals you find to help you.

1 Today, texting is the most effective way to communicate. One advantage is that most people have access to text messaging on their cell phones. We can communicate with almost anyone by text. Another positive aspect is that texters can communicate with many people at the same time. For example, they can send one message or photograph to all their friends and family members.

a Advantage: ______________________________

b Advantage: ______________________________

2 For drivers, texting has both advantages and disadvantages. One the one hand, drivers can send a quick message while their car is stopped. They can let people know they have arrived safely or that they will be late. On the other hand, if people text while driving, even a short text can be dangerous. Each text takes about four to five seconds to write, and during those four or five seconds, drivers do not watch the road. As a result, some have accidents.

a Advantage: ______________________________

b Disadvantage: ______________________________

3 Texting is changing the ways doctors and patients communicate. One benefit is that doctors and patients are communicating more often. For example, many doctors have started texting patients to remind them to take their medicine. On the other hand, doctors are accidentally revealing patients' information. Sometimes the wrong person sees the patients' text message and learns about his or her medical problems.

a Advantage: ______________________________

b Disadvantage: ______________________________

Before You Read

Connecting to the Topic

Discuss the following questions with a partner.

1 Do you use a social networking site, like Facebook or Weibo?

2 If so, how often do you go online to check it or post a message or photo?

3 Do you have online friends that you never see face-to-face? If so, how are these relationships different from those with your face-to-face friends?

4 What happens if someone says something bad or posts something embarrassing about another person on one of these sites? Can you describe an example of this?

Previewing and Predicting

Previewing a reading's title and section headings can help you predict the topic and main idea of a reading.

A Read the title and the headings of the sections in Reading 3. Then decide what the topic and the main idea of the reading will be.

1 What will the topic of Reading 3 probably be?
  a Internet users
  b Social networks
  c Facebook friends
  d Online relationships

2 What will the main idea of Reading 3 probably be?
  a They all seem similar, but there are four different types.
  b They vary from country to country because of cultural differences.
  c They are popular, but they have disadvantages in addition to their advantages.
  d They do not have a long history, but they are very important to society.

B Compare your answers with a partner's.

While You Read

As you read, stop at the end of each sentence that contains words in bold. Then follow the instructions in the box in the margin.

READING 3

How Do Social Networks Affect Our Daily Lives?

I. The Rise of Social Networks

1 If you are like 750 million other people, you check your Facebook page every day. Ten years after the social networking site (SNS) Facebook began in 2004, it had more than a billion users around the **world**. In the beginning, most Facebook members lived in the United States, but recently, the biggest growth has been in other parts of the world. (See Figure 6.2.) Although Facebook quickly became the largest SNS in the world, there have been many others. (See Figure 6.3.) The growth of these SNSs has been enormous and also very fast.

WHILE YOU READ 1

Look for a word that ends in a noun suffix in this sentence. Highlight it.

2 With thousands of people connecting online, what is the impact on our personal relationships and on our daily lives? Many people are concerned about the answers to these questions. Some say that we care more about our online relationships, and we don't pay enough attention to the people we live and work with. They believe that online relationships are not as deep and permanent as our face-to-face relationships. Others believe that social networking is just changing how we develop and maintain relationships. So, do SNSs create a new kind of community? Or are they a poor substitute for real relationships?

II. Positive Impact of SNSs

3 In 2009, researchers did a study to find answers to these questions. They got some surprising results. They found several **benefits** to SNS use. They found that compared to people who did *not* use SNSs:

WHILE YOU READ 2

Does *benefits* signal (a) an advantage or (b) a disadvantage?

- Members of SNSs had more close relationships.
- They got more support from others (for example, help when they were sick or were in trouble).

Figure 6.2 Global Facebook Users at the End of 2013

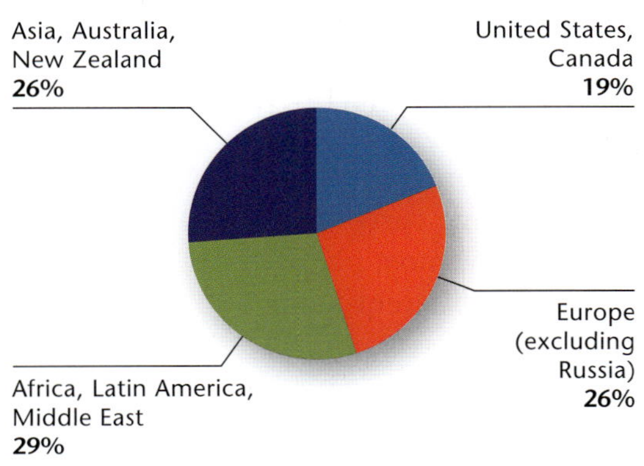

Source: Pew

Figure 6.3 Social Networking Sites – Users Worldwide (in millions) January 2014

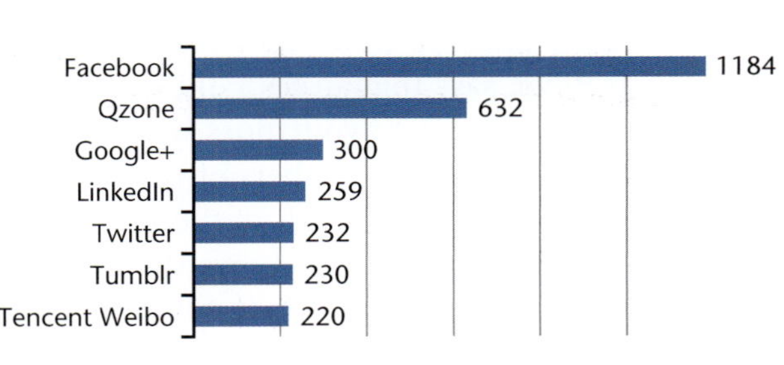

Source: Statistica.com

- They were more politically active.
- They renewed and then kept old relationships (for example, with people they went to school with).

According to the authors, SNSs are not a substitute for more traditional relationships. Instead, online relationships expand and add to them. Other studies have found similar results. They also suggest that SNSs reflect, and even magnify, how we interact with others offline. In other words, people who have a lot of friends and are very social also have a lot of friends online. Their SNS use significantly increases the number of relationships they have. People who don't have many friends offline will probably not change their behavior when they are online.

III. Negative Impact of SNSs

4 Other studies have shown some negative effects of SNS **use**. A study in 2013 found that people often felt worse after they spent time on an SNS. The authors offer a possible explanation for this result. They say SNSs allow us to know a lot about other people. They also allow us to tell others a lot about ourselves. As a result, people can easily compare their lives to the lives of other people. The authors believe that when people look at other people's SNS pages, they may start to feel depressed. They see pictures of other people's parties and vacations. They begin to think that other people have more friends and more fun than they do. They believe that others are more successful.

WHILE YOU READ 3

Look for a word that signals a disadvantage in this sentence. Highlight it.

5 When we interact on SNSs, we can't see how people respond to our messages. We can't see their faces, their smiles, or their tears. This creates a social distance that may also have a negative impact. It may encourage people to say things they would not say face to face. This occurs more often on sites that allow users to post pictures and messages anonymously, that is, without giving their identity. This has become a problem, especially with school-age users, who sometimes use these sites to make fun of other users. So, do SNSs increase our happiness? Or, on the other hand, do they make us feel small and **lonely**? There is probably not one clear answer for everyone.

WHILE YOU READ 4

Look for a phrase that introduces a disadvantage in this sentence. Highlight it.

IV. The Future of SNSs

6 One thing is clear, however. SNSs will continue to have an important role in our lives. More than 3 billion people use them. As more and more people gain access to the Internet, that number will certainly increase. However, SNSs may become more specific in the future. One Internet researcher, Danah Boyd, says that an SNS like Facebook may have too many functions. You would not invite your boss, your grandmother, your friend from elementary school, and members of your football team to the same party. Why should you interact with all of them on the same SNS? Today, most people use only one SNS, but Boyd says she uses different SNSs for different functions. More people are likely to follow her example in the future.

Reading Skill Development

Main Idea Check

Match the main ideas below to paragraphs 2–6 in Reading 3. Write the number of the paragraph on the blank line.

_____ A Other studies show the disadvantages of SNSs.

_____ B Some studies show the advantages of SNSs.

_____ C Communication on SNSs is not face-to-face, and this can cause problems.

_____ D As SNSs become more popular, people may use them in different ways.

_____ E People wonder how SNSs affect their daily lives.

A Closer Look

Look back at Reading 3 to answer the following questions.

1 Facebook has 750 million users. **True or False?** (Par. 1)

2 Most Facebook users live in the United States. **True or False?** (Par. 1)

3 According to paragraph 2, what is one concern about online relationships?
 a People share too much personal information online.
 b Online relationships are creating a new kind of community.
 c Online relationships do not last as long as face-to-face friendships.
 d People spend too much time communicating about work online.

4 What is true about people who use SNSs according to the 2009 study? Choose two answers. (Par. 3)
 a They have fewer close friends.
 b They often talk to former classmates.
 c They have little interest in politics.
 d They share their problems with their friends online.

5 What is true about people who use SNSs according to the 2013 study? Choose two answers. (Par. 4)
 a Their use of SNSs makes them feel happy.
 b They post pictures of themselves having fun on SNSs.
 c They go to more parties and social events because of their SNS use.
 d They sometimes feel jealous of their friends.

6 According to paragraph 5, SNSs that allow users to post pictures and messages anonymously can be a problem for young people. **True or False?**

7 According to Danah Boyd, how will SNS use probably change in the future? (Par. 6)
 a Many people will realize the disadvantages of SNSs and stop using them.
 b Most people around the world will use the same SNS.
 c People will use different SNSs for different purposes.
 d People will use SNSs mostly for educational and professional reasons.

Skill Review

In Skills and Strategies 12, you learned that writers sometimes explain advantages and disadvantages. In one reading or paragraph, a writer may give only advantages, only disadvantages, or both advantages and disadvantages.

A **Read paragraphs 2–5 again. Write the paragraph numbers on the blank lines.**

_____ 1 Which paragraph(s) give(s) only advantages?

_____ 2 Which paragraph(s) give(s) only disadvantages?

_____ 3 Which paragraph(s) give(s) both advantages and disadvantages?

B **Complete the chart with five advantages and five disadvantages of SNSs from paragraphs 2–5. Write the number of the paragraph where you find each advantage or disadvantage. The first one is an example.**

ADVANTAGES OF SNSs	DISADVANTAGES OF SNSs
	We don't pay attention to the people we live and work with (Par. 2)

C **Compare your answers with a partner's.**

Definitions

Find the words in Reading 3 that complete the following definitions.

1 ________________ are groups of people or computers that are connected and can share information. (*n pl*) Section I heading

2 Something that is ________________ is very large. (*adj*) Par. 1, last sentence

3 If you are ________________ about something, you are worried about it. (*adj*) Par. 2, sentence 2

4 To ________________ is to increase in size or amount. (*v*) Par. 3, sentence 10

5 To ________________ something is to show or to be a sign of it. (*v*) Par. 3, sentence 12

6 If someone feels unhappy for a long time, he or she is ________________. (*adj*) Par. 4, sentence 7

7 If you do something without giving your name, you do it ________________. (*adv*) Par. 5, sentence 5

8 A / An ________________ is a group of people who do a sport or activity together or who work together to do something. (*n*) Par. 6, sentence 7

Words in Context

Complete the sentences with words and phrases from Reading 3 in the box below.

billion	magnify	offline	substitute
interact	make fun of	site	vacation

1 A very famous writer was born in this building; it is a historic ________________.

2 The population of China is more than a ________________ people.

3 Even though the students have a two-month ________________ during the summer, the building is still open for meetings and special activities.

4 The teacher was sick on Wednesday, so a ________________ taught the class.

5 If people become sick, it can ________________ their problems, that is, make their problems seem bigger.

6 The computer could not connect to the Internet, so we had to work ________________.

7 Actors at the theater do not usually ________________ with the audience members.

8 The other students ________________ my friend because he has big ears.

Academic Word List

The following are Academic Word List words from all the readings in Unit 6. Use these words to complete the sentences. (If necessary, review the AWL words in Key Vocabulary on pages 257–267.)

aid (*n*)	document (*n*)	immigrant (*n*)	site (*n*)	tradition (*n*)
depressed (*adj*)	enormous (*adj*)	network (*n*)	substitute (*n*)	volunteer (*n*)

1 Some students do not have much money to pay for school, but fortunately they receive financial ________________ from their university.

2 The student is a ________________ at a home for elderly people on the weekends.

3 Our grandfather was a / an ________________; he was born in Brazil but came to the United States at age eighteen.

4 After many months of looking for work with no success, Mr. Fitzgerald became ________________.

5 Some people use honey as a ________________ for sugar in their tea because of honey's health benefits.

6 The home is ________________; it has seven bedrooms and five bathrooms.

7 All the computers in the office are connected by a / an ________________.

8 All students must sign this ________________ and then deliver it to the main office.

9 The trucks delivered the supplies to the construction ________________.

10 In North America, women usually wear a white dress on their wedding day; it is a / an ________________.

Beyond the Reading

Critical Thinking

> **AGREEING AND DISAGREEING**
>
> When the writer or someone in a text expresses an opinion, ask yourself if you agree or disagree with the opinion.

In Reading 3, you learned about the growth of social networks and about their advantages and disadvantages.

Work in a small group. Say if you agree or disagree with the following statements. Explain your opinion.

1 Online relationships are not as deep and permanent as face-to-face relationships.

2 If you have a personal problem, you should share it with friends online.

3 If people do not have many friends online, they probably do not have many friends in real life.

4 When people share information about their lives on social networks, they make their lives seem more interesting than they really are.

5 Schoolchildren should not be allowed to use anonymous websites.

6 It is better to use different social networks to communicate with different people than to use one social network to communicate with everyone you know.

Research

A Study your own communication for one week. Write down how much time you spend each day communicating with people face-to-face and how much time you spend communicating on social networks.

	SUN	MON	TUES	WED	THUR	FRI	SAT
Time spent communicating face-to-face							
Time spent on social networks							

B Share the results with other students in a small group. Answer the questions.

1 Overall, do you and the others in your group spend more time communicating face-to-face or on social networks?

2 Does your research support the idea that people who are social in real life use social networks the most?

Writing

Write a short report about your research. Compare your use of social networks with that of other members of your group.

Improving Your Reading Speed

Good readers read quickly and still understand most of what they read.

A Read the instructions and strategies for Improving Your Reading Speed in Appendix 3 on page 270.

B Choose one of the readings in this unit. Read it without stopping. Time how long it takes you to finish the text in minutes and seconds. Enter the time in the chart on page 272. Then calculate your reading speed in number of words per minute.

CONTRAST CONNECTORS

Writers often connect ideas by showing a contrast between them. A contrast shows how two ideas are different. To make the differences clear, writers often use signals such as *unlike, but, however,* and *in contrast* to make these connections. You learned these words and phrases in Skills and Strategies 5 on page 66. As you learned in Skills and Strategies 12 on page 181, writers also use *on the one hand* and *on the other hand* to introduce contrasting ideas.

Exercise 1

Read the following paragraphs. Highlight any words or phrases that signal contrasts.

1 Researchers have been studying the use of social networks in schools. On the one hand, they have found that social networks have many benefits in this context. One benefit is that students can communicate with many classmates at the same time. However, there are also negative aspects. For instance, some students use SNSs to send hateful messages or to reveal their classmates' personal information.

2 Women tend to use social networks more than men. For example, one study of Internet users in the United States found that 76 percent of women use Facebook, but just 66 percent of men do so. Why is that? One researcher gave the following explanation. Women, unlike men, tend to build relationships by sharing personal information. As a result, SNSs offer a real advantage to women.

3 Researchers say there are two types of social network users: regular users and a special group they call power users. Regular users visit social networks about once a week. In contrast, power users use social networks almost every day. They share more photos, send more messages, and request more friends to join their networks. This creates benefits for regular users. Because of power users, most social network users receive more messages than they send.

Exercise 2

Make a clear paragraph by putting sentences A, B, and C into the best order after the numbered sentence. Look for pronouns and words and phrases that signal contrast, time, or addition to help you. Write the letters in the correct order on the blank lines.

1 Emmanuel Nnaemeka Nnadi is a scientist from Nigeria. ___ ___ ___

A He wanted to talk to other *Candida* experts about his research.	**B** However, most *Candida* experts lived in other parts of the world.	**C** In 2011, he was studying a disease-causing organism named *Candida*.

2 How could Nnadi communicate with scientists in many different countries, all at the same time? ___ ___ ___

A The answer was social networking.	**B** He then entered his personal information and became a member.	**C** First, Nnadi went online and found a site called ResearchGate.

3 ResearchGate is a special type of social network. ___ ___ ___

A However, it is gaining 10,000 new members every day.	**B** It has 5 million members, much fewer than Facebook or Twitter.	**C** Unlike other social networks, ResearchGate is open only to scientists.

4 ResearchGate helps scientists in many ways. ___ ___ ___

A Another benefit is that they can ask each other for help and suggestions.	**B** One advantage is that they can share research findings.	**C** For example, Nnadi asked for help with his research into *Candida*.

5 Nnadi posted messages about his research and waited for a reply. ___ ___ ___

A His first response was from an Italian scientist named Orazio Romeo.	**B** Romeo was also interested in studying *Candida*.	**C** Nnadi and Romeo have been research partners ever since.

7 MONEY

SKILLS AND STRATEGIES

- Noticing Parts of Words: Verb Suffixes
- Finding Causes and Effects

Skill Practice 2

Look again at the words you highlighted in Skill Practice 1. Write the correct words in the blanks to complete the definitions. The first one is an example.

1 When you *computerize* something, you use a computer to do something that was done by people or other machines before.

2 When you ______________ something, you make it longer than before.

3 If an object ______________ something, it represents it or acts as a symbol of it.

4 If you ______________ something, you add color to it.

5 When you ______________ something, you make it shorter than before.

6 When you ______________ something, you make it simple or easy to do.

7 If you ______________ something, you make it beautiful.

8 If you ______________ something, you make it stronger.

9 When you ______________ a system or building, you make it more modern.

Before You Read

Connecting to the Topic

Discuss the following questions with a partner.

1 How do you pay for most of the things that you buy? For example, do you usually pay with cash (paper money and coins), a credit card, a check, or some other form of payment?

2 Is this different from how your parents or grandparents paid for things?

3 Imagine a world without money. How could people get the things that they need? Could the world work without money?

Previewing and Predicting

> Remember to preview the title and quickly look at any art, such as photos or drawings. If the art has any words below it, you should read them, too. They can help you predict what the reading will be about.

A Read the title of Reading 1 and look at the illustrations. Then answer the following question.

What are these illustrations of?

____

B What do you think this reading will be about? Put a check (✓) next to the topic or topics that you think will be included in the reading.

_____ a How money has changed

_____ b The dangers of credit cards

_____ c Different forms of money

_____ d Money today and in the future

_____ e Money and farming

C Compare your answers with a partner's.

While You Read

As you read, stop at the end of each sentence that contains words in bold. Then follow the instructions in the box in the margin.

READING 1

The History of Currency

1 Look in your wallet. You probably have paper money and coins. They are the currency of today's world. It is hard to visualize life without **money**. Yet, humans existed for a long time without money. Imagine a farmer thousands of years ago. He specializes in **tomatoes**. He likes his tomatoes, but sometimes he wants to eat chicken or fish. Without money, how can he do this? He could go to a fisherman and offer him some tomatoes in exchange for fish. This is called barter. It is the direct exchange of one thing for another. It is likely that most economic systems began this way.

2 But what if the fisherman doesn't want any tomatoes? Or what if it is the middle of winter and the farmer has no tomatoes to offer him? In order to resolve this problem, long ago, communities often chose one special thing as a medium of exchange – a thing that can be used as payment. They chose sugar, or oil, or skins of animals. These are all goods that have their own value. In this kind of system, the value of other things – like tomatoes, fish, shoes, or tools – is measured in terms of how much sugar, oil, or animal skins they are worth. Around 9000 BCE, people started using cows as a medium of exchange. In many parts of the ancient world, they were the basic unit of value.

3 Cows, however, are not quite the same thing as money. Cows are not a convenient medium of exchange. They are big, heavy, and alive. It is difficult to buy a tomato with a cow. Kinds of currency – coins and paper money, like the euro or dollar – are much more convenient. Yet, paper money does not have any real value. You can't eat a dollar or wear a yen. The key characteristic of money is that the users specify the **value**. Gold is valuable because the users agree that it is valuable. It is true that gold can be used as a metal, but many other metals are more useful. Cultures all over the world chose gold to measure the value of goods.

4 Gold was not the only material used as currency long ago. People in many parts of the world used shells. Shells were used as a medium of exchange in China and Africa as early as 1200 BCE. These were special shells, called cowries, that came from islands in the Pacific and Indian oceans. They were somewhat rare, so they became valuable. People measured the value of goods in the number of cowrie shells. Like the money we use today, they were small and easy to carry. Another benefit was that people could store shells as a supply of valuable things to use for trade in the **future**. This was a big step forward for our tomato farmer. He could wait for his tomatoes to ripen and then exchange them all for shells. He could then use the shells to buy food and other things all year. He could also save his shells for the future.

5 Shells continued to be used as money in some areas until the nineteenth century. However, coins and other metal pieces became the dominant form of money in most parts of the world. The first paper money appeared in

WHILE YOU READ 1

Look for a word with a verb suffix in this sentence. Highlight it.

WHILE YOU READ 2

Look for a word with a verb suffix in this sentence. Highlight it.

WHILE YOU READ 3

Look for a word with a verb suffix in this sentence. Highlight it.

WHILE YOU READ 4

Look for an advantage signal in this sentence. Highlight it.

China around 800 CE, but paper currency was not widely used in Europe until the seventeenth century. At that time, paper money was still a substitute for gold. A person with a paper banknote could go to a bank and ask for its value in gold. Today, the value of money has been separated from gold. Financial experts say soon we will have no more paper money or coins. Already many people use credit cards more than paper money. Some experts theorize that, in the future, people will buy and sell everything electronically using computers and smartphones. This will make banking more convenient. Perhaps we will see paper money only in museums, like the shell money of the past.

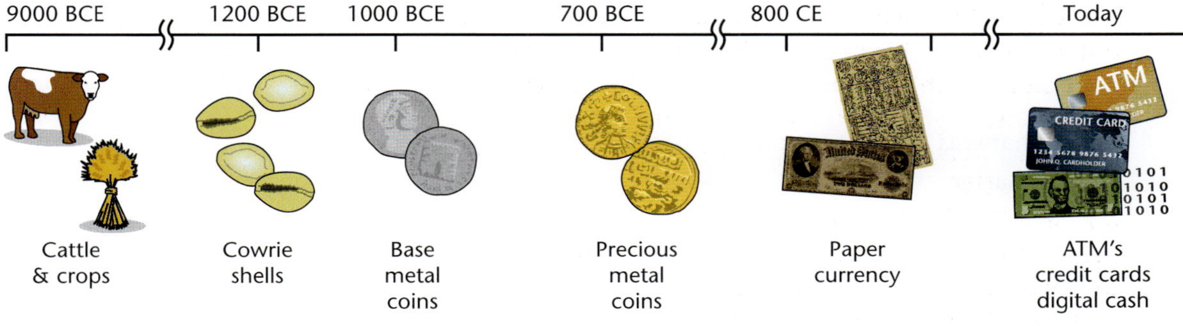

Main Idea Check

Match the main ideas below to paragraphs 2–5 in Reading 1. Write the number of the paragraph on the blank line.

_____ A One form of money was the shell.

_____ B Over time, people started to pay for goods with coins and certain metals.

_____ C Today, most people use paper money, and in the future, they may use electronic forms of money.

_____ D To solve problems with the barter system, people chose one special thing as a medium of exchange.

A Closer Look

Look back at Reading 1 to answer the following questions.

1 What was the first form of exchange? (Par. 1)

a Barter
b Shells
c Cows
d Notes

2 What problems with barter does the writer mention? Choose two answers. (Par. 2)

a If you only have one thing to trade, people may not want to trade with you.
b You may not always have something to trade.
c Some goods are not easy to transport and care for.
d It is hard to trade something big and valuable for smaller, less valuable things.

3 Which of the following is likely to happen in the future? (Par. 5)

a People in every country will use the same paper money.
b People will return to the barter system.
c People will pay for things using small computers or phones.
d People will use plastic coins instead of paper money.

4 According to the whole reading, which of the following have been used as a medium of exchange? Choose four answers.

a Animal skins
b Sugar
c Oil
d Books
e Gold
f Stones

5 Put the mediums of exchange (A–E) in the order that humans began to use them. Write the correct letter in each box.

☐ → ☐ → ☐ → ☐ → ☐

A Barter
B Cows
C Electronic payments
D Paper money
E Shells

Skill Review

In Skills and Strategies 13, you learned about the suffixes *-en*, *-ify*, and *-ize*. These suffixes can help you identify verbs and understand the meaning of those verbs.

A Look at Reading 1 again. Write a word with a verb suffix next to each definition. The first one is an example.

1 To create a picture or visual image in your mind = *visualize* (Par. 1)
2 To spend most of your time doing one thing = ________________ (Par. 1)
3 To say or describe something in a detailed way = ________________ (Par. 3)
4 To become ripe = ________________ (Par. 4)
5 To develop a theory about something = ________________ (Par. 5)

B Complete the sentences below with the words from A.

1 Some people ________________ that the first coin was created around 5000 BCE, but no one is sure.
2 We do not know when the meeting will start because the manager did not ________________ an exact time.
3 When the tomatoes ________________, their color will change from green to red.
4 This restaurant serves a variety of dishes, but they ________________ in seafood.
5 I listened to the builder describe his house, and I tried to ________________ it.

Definitions

Find the words in Reading 1 that complete the following definitions.

1 A / An ________________ is a kind of money used by a particular country or group of people. (*n*) Par. 1, sentence 3

2 A / An ________________ problem is a problem that relates to money, trade, or business. (*adj*) Par. 1, last sentence

3 If you ________________ a problem or difficulty, you find a way to end it. (*v*) Par. 2, sentence 3

4 If something is ________________, it is easy to use or makes life less complicated. (*adj*) Par. 3, sentence 2

5 A / An ________________ object is not common or is hard to find. (*adj*) Par. 4, sentence 5

6 The ________________ currency is the main or most important currency. (*adj*) Par. 5, sentence 2

7 A / An ________________ is a piece of paper money. (*n*) Par. 5, sentence 5

8 If something is done ________________, it is done through the Internet or some other system using computer equipment. (*adv*) Par. 5, sentence 9

Words in Context

Complete the sentences with words from Reading 1 in the box below.

barter	financial	key	somewhat
credit card	forward	medium of exchange	wallet

1 Hard work is the ________________ factor for success.

2 Gold has long been of great value, and many cultures have used it as a ________________.

3 A person may keep money, bank cards, and identification in his or her ________________.

4 Many students would like to work for a bank or another ________________ institution.

5 A young person should not receive a ________________ until he or she learns to carefully manage money.

6 In societies with no money, people often exchanged goods using the ________________ system.

7 The price was ________________ higher than we expected, but not much.

8 We cannot go back, so we must move ________________.

Critical Thinking

> **APPLYING INFORMATION**
>
> You use critical thinking skills when you apply information you have just learned to new situations.

In Reading 1, you learned about the history of money and different forms of currency and exchange.

A Work in a small group. Make a list of ten objects that you can find in your homes. Then work together to answer the questions.

1 Which object on the list would be the most effective medium of exchange? Why?

2 Which object on the list would be the least effective medium of exchange? Why?

B Share one thing from your discussion with the rest of the class.

Research

Do an Internet search for strange or unusual currencies. Find some unusual currencies humans used in the past. Choose one of the currencies. Where and when did people use it?

Writing

Write a short report about your research. Be sure to include the history of the currency you chose.

Before You Read

Connecting to the Topic

Read the definition of *counterfeit*, and then discuss the following questions with a partner.

> **counterfeit** (*adj*) copied to look exactly like something valuable, especially money

1 Have you ever seen counterfeit money? Did it fool you?

2 Do you think it would be difficult to copy money? Explain your answer.

3 How do you think the police find out that money is counterfeit?

4 Do you know about any steps that your country has taken to make sure that no one makes counterfeit money?

Previewing and Predicting

Read the title of a reading. Then look at any photos or drawings, and read their descriptions. They can help you predict what the reading will be about.

A Read the title of Reading 2, and look at the photographs. Then answer the following question.

What are these photographs of?

____

B What do you think this reading will be about? Put a check (✓) next to the topic or topics that you think will be included in the reading.

_____ a Shopping
_____ b Copying money
_____ c Modern banknotes
_____ d Credit cards
_____ e Marketing

C Compare your answers with a partner's.

While You Read

As you read, stop at the end of each sentence that contains words in bold. Then follow the instructions in the box in the margin.

READING 2

Counterfeit Money

1 In 2004, Alice Pike went shopping at a Walmart in Georgia. The total for her purchases was about $1,600. She handed the cashier a $1 million **bill**. There was just one problem. The United States does not print $1 million bills. Pike's money was counterfeit. Experts estimate that about 0.1 percent of all paper money is fake. In the United States, that comes to about $70 million. Alice Pike's fake bill was easy to identify, but what about a $100 or $50 **banknote**? With a good scanner and printer, wouldn't it be easy to just copy paper money?

WHILE YOU READ 1

Which definition of *bill* is the writer using?
a) A banknote
b) A piece of paper that tells you how much you must pay

2 Not really. Although it might be possible to produce a copy that you could spend in a very dark place, in general, it is difficult to produce a realistic copy of a bill. The government offices that print money use advanced technology. This makes paper money hard to copy. National and regional issuers of money, like the European Bank and the United States Treasury, have taken a number of steps to make it difficult for counterfeiters to make copies that are good enough to spend.

WHILE YOU READ 2

Look for a word with a verb suffix in this sentence. Highlight it.

3 The designs on bills are extremely detailed and complex. They are filled with tiny lines that you can see only with a microscope. For example, inside the numbers on the U.S. $100 bill are tiny numbers – *100* – repeated over and over. The images on bills are printed with special ink. It is absorbed by the paper but also sits on top of the paper. As a result, the images are slightly raised. You can feel the images with your fingers. The ink has other special characteristics. It makes the colors on bills change as you move them in the light.

4 The paper is also very unusual. It is not like regular paper, which is made from wood. The paper in money comes from cloth – cotton and linen. It is extremely thin but very strong. This strength is necessary because the bills must pass through thousands of hands and, sometimes, even through a washing machine. The paper feels special. People who handle money all the time, like bankers, say they can feel the difference between real and counterfeit money. Some countries are now using polymer, which is a kind of plastic, instead of paper in their bills. Plastic bills have many positive aspects; they last longer than paper, and they are harder to **copy**. Australia was the first country to use polymer bills. Today, Canada, Vietnam, and Israel also do so.

WHILE YOU READ 3

Look for an advantage signal in this sentence. Highlight it.

5 The newest bills have several other special features that counterfeiters find very difficult to copy. Most bills have a special sign called a watermark. This is an image that is inside the paper. You can see it when you hold the note up to a bright light. You can see other details, too, if you look carefully. For example, the numbers on the front of euros look broken. The other pieces of the numbers are on the back. So, if you hold them up to the light and look through them, the numbers look complete. Many countries have also added security strips or holograms to their bills.

Holograms are images that reflect light in a special way. The images look three-dimensional instead of flat. (See photos.)

Bill with a blue security strip

Bill with a hologram

6 Other features become apparent only with special tools. An ultraviolet light reveals aspects of bills that you cannot see in ordinary light. Special pens can distinguish between the paper in real money and the paper in counterfeit money. This kind of tool is important because it is simple, inexpensive, and easy to use. Cashiers in supermarkets can use such pens to check the money that customers give them – like the $1 million bill from Alice Pike.

Main Idea Check

Match the main ideas below to paragraphs 2–6 in Reading 2. Write the number of the paragraph on the blank line.

_____ A Bills are made from special materials.

_____ B New bills have special details that make them especially hard to copy.

_____ C Governments use technology to make it difficult to copy bills.

_____ D Bills are printed with special designs and ink on them.

_____ E People can use special equipment to tell if money is real or not.

A Closer Look

Look back at Reading 2 to answer the following questions.

1 A high percentage of money in the U.S. is counterfeit. **True or False?** (Par. 1)

2 It is easy to copy bills with a printer and scanner. **True or False?** (Par. 2)

3 What are some ways to tell if a U.S. bill is real or not? Choose three answers. (Par. 3)

a Look at it very closely
b Weigh it
c Touch the images
d Rub it with a warm towel
e Look at it under a bright light
f Ask someone who works at a bank

4 Some bills are made of plastic. **True or False?** (Par. 4)

5 Why are bills becoming more difficult to counterfeit? (Par. 5)

a They have specific weights and sizes.
b They are visually more complex.
c They are made in secret locations.
d They are produced in limited quantities.

6 Which word best describes cashiers' tools for checking money? (Par. 6)

a Convenient
b Costly
c Confusing
d Complex

Skill Review

In Skills and Strategies 13, you learned about the verb suffixes *-en*, *-ify*, and *-ize*. These suffixes can help you understand words. They can also increase your vocabulary.

A **The words below are from Reading 2. Add the suffix *-en*, *-ify*, or *-ize* to each word to form a new verb. The first one is an example.**

1 strength *strengthen*
2 dark ______
3 general ______
4 sign ______
5 bright ______
6 real ______
7 flat ______

B **Use the verbs you formed in A to complete the sentences below.**

1 The use of plastics such as polymer will ______ bills.
2 The student wants to ______ her dream of working for the treasury.
3 My grandparents ______ about young people; for example, they say all young people are impatient.
4 When gray clouds ______ the sky, rain might be coming.
5 Be sure to ______ the pizza dough before you put on the sauce.
6 We opened the curtains to ______ the classroom.
7 In the U.S., red lights mean "stop" or "danger." Does the color ______ danger in your country, too?

Vocabulary Development

Definitions

Find the words in Reading 2 that complete the following definitions.

1 ________________ are things that you buy. (*n pl*) Par. 1, sentence 2

2 ________________ money is not real, but is made to look real to trick people. (*adj*) Par. 1, sentence 6

3 A ________________ is a piece of equipment that copies words and pictures from paper into a computer. (*n*) Par. 1, last sentence

4 If something is ________________ difficult, it is very difficult, or much more difficult than usual. (*adv*) Par. 3, sentence 1

5 A ________________ is a piece of scientific equipment that uses glass lenses to make small objects look bigger. (*n*) Par. 3, sentence 2

6 A ________________ picture has length, depth, and height. (*adj*) Par. 5, last sentence

7 If something is ________________, it is clear, obvious, or easy to notice. (*adj*) Par. 6, sentence 1

8 If people with light-colored skin spend a lot of time in the sun, ________________ light can burn their skin. (*adj*) Par. 6, sentence 2

Words in Context

Complete the sentences with words from Reading 2 in the box below.

cashier	fake	handle	slightly
cloth	features	regional	treasury

1 The new computer has special ________________ like a camera and music player.

2 His ________________ accent shows that he grew up in the South.

3 It looks like a real gold watch, but actually it is ________________.

4 You must wash your hands before you ________________ food.

5 They work for the government in the ________________ department.

6 My brother and I weigh the same amount, but he is ________________ taller.

7 I had no cash to pay for my purchases, so I gave the ________________ my credit card.

8 The professor cleaned the blackboard with an old piece of ________________.

Critical Thinking

In Reading 2, you learned about the ways that governments make paper money difficult to copy.

PERSONALIZING

Thinking about how new information applies to your own life can help you understand the text better.

A Work in a small group. Ask and answer questions.

1 Have you ever seen a cashier looking at money to see if it was counterfeit? What technique did the cashier use to check the money?

2 How would you feel if someone told you that your money was counterfeit?

3 Imagine you own a store. What things will you do to check for counterfeit money?

4 What other products do people copy illegally? Make a list.

5 Look at the items on your list from number 4. How can a buyer check those things to know if they are real or fake?

B Share some ideas from your discussion with the rest of the class.

Research

Do some research on the paper money in your home country. Compare a bill that was made very recently with a bill of the same value from many years ago. Make a list of all the differences you see. Then answer the questions.

1 What kind of security features do you see in the new bill?

2 Which of those security features did the old bill have?

3 How much more difficult is the new bill to copy than the old one, in your opinion?

Writing

Write a short report on the results of your research. Include pictures of the bills if you can.

Finding Causes and Effects

When writers want to explain why something happened and why that thing was important, they often give causes and effects. Causes are explanations of why something happened. Effects (the changes, reactions, or results) show why the things were important. Writers often introduce causes and effects with signal words such as *because*, *due to*, *so*, and *that's why*.

Examples & Explanations

One school in New York City prints its own money and gives it to students. The school does this because it wants to influence students' behavior and attendance.

In this paragraph, the writer gives a cause: *The school wants to influence students' behavior and attendance.* The writer introduces the cause with a signal, *because*. Other cause signals are *due to* and *reason*.

The school now pays students to come to class and behave well. The students can use the money for special lunches and school supplies. As a result, attendance has increased significantly, and students are paying more attention in class.

In this paragraph, the writer gives a cause, *the school pays students to come to class and behave well*, and some effects: (1) *attendance has increased significantly*, and (2) *students are paying more attention in class*. The writer uses the signal phrase *as a result* to introduce the effects. Other common signals of effects are *so*, *this makes*, and *that is why*.

The students who arrive earliest receive the most money, so there is usually a line by the door when the school opens in the morning. The plan makes the students feel excited about school.

Writers may introduce the effects before the cause, or the cause before the effects. In this paragraph, the writer introduces the cause first: *Students who arrive earliest receive the most money.*

The Language of Cause and Effect

Here are some common words and phrases that signal cause and effect.

WORDS AND PHRASES THAT SIGNAL CAUSES	WORDS AND PHRASES THAT SIGNAL EFFECTS
because *cause* *due to* *reason*	*as a result* *effect* *so* *that is why* *this makes*

Strategies

These strategies will help you find causes and effects while you read.

- Look for signals that writers use to introduce causes and effects. Study and learn the signal words and phrases in the chart.
- If the writer does not use signal words, there may be still be a cause and effect relationship. Think carefully about the relationship between ideas in a text as you read. Ask yourself: *Which idea is the cause? Which idea is the effect?*
- If a reading has many causes and effects, make a list of them while you read.

Skill Practice 1

Read the following paragraphs. Find two cause or effect signals in each paragraph. Highlight the cause signals. Underline the effect signals.

1 Espinal, in the south of Mexico, was a small town with a big problem. The economy was not growing. The reason was that people did not have enough money to pay for products and services. A local professor wanted to solve the problem, so he asked his students to create a new type of money for the town.

2 The students made a new form of money called túmin. They chose this name because it means "money" in Totonac, the local language. The creators of the túmin valued creativity. That is why each bill has a picture of Diego Rivera, a famous artist.

3 Many businesses in Espinal agreed to accept túmin. As a result, it is very popular. People can use it to buy groceries, visit the doctor, or pay for a haircut. People in Espinal like the new currency. As one café owner says, "The túmin has changed my life because it has helped me. Now, the price of things is more affordable."

Skill Practice 2

Read the paragraphs in Skill Practice 1 again. Then answer the questions.

1 Why was the economy of Espinal not growing?

____

2 Why did the students choose the name *túmin*?

____

3 Why are túmin printed with pictures of an artist?

____

4 When local business agreed to accept túmin, what was the result?

____

5 What effect has the túmin had on the café owner?

____

Before You Read

Connecting to the Topic

Discuss the following questions with a partner.

1 What does the money from your country look like? What images appear on it?

2 How do you think choices are made about the images on the coins and bills in your country?

3 What do you think the design of the money expresses about your country?

Previewing and Predicting

When you preview a longer reading, remember to look at section headings. These headings can help you predict what the reading will be about. Remember that looking at the art can also help you make predictions about the reading.

A Read the title and the section headings of Reading 3. Also look at the art and the words below it. Decide what topics you think will be in each section. Then write the number of the section (*I–III*) next to the topic(s) that will be included in it.

SECTION	TOPIC
	Famous buildings on paper money
	Famous people on paper money
	The design of the euro
	Scenes of daily life on paper money
	Money as an expression of national identity
	Scenes of nature on paper money

B Compare your answers with a partner's.

While You Read

As you read, stop at the end of each sentence that contains words in bold. Then follow the instructions in the box in the margin.

READING 3

Money, Art, and Identity

1 One of the things that you notice when you visit a different country is the money. You notice the face of Mao Zedong on the Chinese yuan. You notice the bright, tropical colors of the Samoan tala, or the single green color of much American paper money. Bills are like small works of art. They are detailed and beautiful. They tell stories of their country. What is the reason for the images that appear on **them**? These images are statements about a country's identity.

WHILE YOU READ 1

Look for a cause or effect signal in this sentence. Highlight it.

I. National Faces

2 Probably the most common image on bills is the face of a famous person. This person is often a past or current leader. Because Great Britain once had colonies all over the world, Queen Elizabeth is the most common face on paper money **today**. Thailand and Morocco also display their kings on the front of their bills. Kings and queens are popular choices, but other famous people appear as well. Often, countries choose heroes from the past. For example, Simón Bolivar appears on Venezuelan money because of his importance in the country's fight for independence. For similar reasons, the Indian rupee shows the face of the Mahatma Gandhi; and the Iranian rial shows the Ayatollah Khomeini. Sometimes, governments choose a famous scientist, writer, or artist. The scientist Lord Kelvin appears on the Scottish pound; the writer Jane Austen has been chosen to appear on the British ten-pound note. The front of the Mexican 500-peso note shows the head of the artist Diego Rivera, and his wife, the artist Frida Kahlo, appears on the back.

WHILE YOU READ 2

Look for a cause or effect signal in this sentence. Highlight it.

3 Not only famous people appear on paper money. Often there are images of ordinary people doing ordinary things. These images of ordinary people may be part of a political or cultural message that the government wants to send. In the 1960s, Chinese bills often showed pictures of workers and farmers. These images were very important due to the Chinese political situation at that **time**. Such images of everyday life on paper money continue today. The picture on the Canadian five-dollar bill of children with hockey equipment is due to the sport's popularity in Canada. The money of the island

WHILE YOU READ 3

Look for a cause or effect signal in this sentence. Highlight it.

nation of Comoros shows beautiful scenes of island life. As a result of these images, ordinary people seem important. The idea behind these images is that not only famous people matter.

II. National Identity

4 Sometimes, instead of a famous face, bills show other things that are important in a country. What does the country produce? What are some important accomplishments? Some notes show famous landmarks, such as the Petronas Towers in Malaysia, the Great Hall of the People in China, and the Bolshoi Theater in Russia. That is also why there may be images of agriculture, industry, or structures, such as bridges and **airports**. A Kuwaiti banknote shows oil refineries. A power plant appears on one bill from Kyrgyzstan. Governments choose these images so that they can highlight important aspects of their economies.

WHILE YOU READ 4

Look for a cause or effect signal in this sentence. Highlight it.

5 Some countries, such as South Africa, Tanzania, and Costa Rica, have included images of buildings or industry on their money in the past. Recently, however, they have begun to replace these images. Today, new bills show pictures from nature, in particular, plants and animals that live in their country. On the South African rand, Nelson Mandela appears on the front, but on the back are lions, tigers, elephants, leopards, and rhinoceroses. Tanzania has a similar collection of animals on its banknotes. Birds, fish, and monkeys are also common choices. Animals are an important part of these African countries' identities.

III. One Case – The Euro

6 Usually, a single government is responsible for printing money. That government decides what kind of message it wants its bills to carry. It then chooses appropriate images, in other words, images that support the message. However, the establishment of the European Union in the 1990s presented a problem: the euro. Many different countries had to decide on a single set of bills. They had to show the identity of all of these countries. There was a competition to design them. The final decision was to show structures such as bridges and gates from different historical periods. These are not structures that exist in any of the countries. Instead, they are representative of architecture in general across Europe. As a result, the euro is able to express a shared identity for the whole region.

Reading Skill Development

Main Idea Check

Match the main ideas below to paragraphs 2–6 in Reading 3. Write the number of the paragraph on the blank line.

_____ **A** Some bills show sources of national pride such as famous landmarks.
_____ **B** The euro had to reflect the identities of many countries.
_____ **C** Other bills show images of average citizens.
_____ **D** Bills may show the natural beauty of a country and its animals.
_____ **E** Bills often show images of important or well-known individuals.

A Closer Look

Look back at Reading 3 to answer the following questions.

1 According to paragraph 1, which word best describes banknotes?
   a Famous
   b Tropical
   c Artistic
   d Common

2 Who appears on more bills than anyone else? (Par. 2)
   a Mao Zedong
   b Queen Elizabeth
   c Mahatma Gandhi
   d Ayatollah Khomeini

3 What reason does the reading give for featuring ordinary people on some countries' bills? (Par. 3)
   a Those countries have unpopular leaders.
   b The countries want to show that everyone there is important.
   c Those ordinary people did amazing things to become heroes.
   d The countries want to show visitors their typical lifestyle.

4 The bridges and gates on the euro are all real landmarks. True or False? (Par. 6)

5 What image does each country have on its currency? Match the country in the left column with the image in the right column. (Pars. 2–5)

	Country	Image
_____	1 Great Britain	a A well-known writer
_____	2 Canada	b Married artists
_____	3 Mexico	c Wild animals
_____	4 Russia	d A winter sport
_____	5 Kyrgyzstan	e A power plant
_____	6 Tanzania	f A famous theater

Skill Review

In Skills and Strategies 14, you learned that writers use words and phrases that signal cause-and-effect relationships between ideas.

A Read the following sentences. Highlight any cause or effect signals. Then write *C* over the part of the sentence that tells the cause. Write *E* over the part of the sentence that tells the effect.

1 The picture on the Canadian five-dollar bill of children with hockey equipment is due to the sport's popularity in Canada.

2 Sometimes, bills show what is important in that country; that is why some notes show famous landmarks, such as the Petronas Towers in Malaysia, the Great Hall of the People in China, and the Bolshoi Theater in Russia.

3 Governments choose images of power plants and oil refineries so that they can highlight important aspects of their economies.

B Complete the chart with ideas from Reading 3. Write the cause of each effect, or the effect of each cause. The first one is an example.

CAUSES	EFFECTS
Great Britain once had colonies all over the world.	Queen Elizabeth is the most common face on paper money today. (Par. 2)
Simón Bolivar was important in Venezuela's fight for independence. (Par. 2)	
	In the 1960s, images of farmers and workers were very important in China. (Par. 3)
Some bills show images of ordinary people. (Par. 3)	
	The euro is able to express a shared identify for the whole region. (Par. 6)

Definitions

Find the words in Reading 3 that complete the following definitions.

1 If something is ________________, it comes from the hottest part of the world. (*adj*) Par. 1, sentence 3

2 ________________ are people who are brave, respectable, and admirable. (*n pl*) Par. 2, sentence 6

3 ________________ are places that people easily recognize. (*n pl*) Par. 4, sentence 4

4 ________________ are very tall, narrow buildings. (*n pl*) Par. 4, sentence 4

5 If an organization is ________________ for something, it is their job or duty to do that thing. (*adj*) Par. 6, sentence 1

6 If something is ________________, it is suitable for a particular situation. (*adj*) Par. 6, sentence 3

7 ________________ are the parts of an outside wall that open like a door. (*n pl*) Par. 6, sentence 8

8 ________________ is the design and style of buildings. (*n*) Par. 6, sentence 10

Word Families

A **The words in bold in the chart are from Reading 3. The words next to them are from the same word family. Study and learn these words.**

NOUN	VERB
colony (Par. 2)	*colonize*
highlight	***highlight*** (Par. 4)
refinery (Par. 4)	*refine*
replacement	***replace*** (Par. 5)
structure (Par. 4)	*structure*

B **Choose the correct form of the words from the chart to complete the following sentences.**

1 The cash machine at the bank broke down, and they had to ________________ it with a new one.

2 The students should ________________ all the important information in the economics textbook.

3 The island of Mauritius used to be a French ________________, so the people there speak French.

4 The sugar ________________ employs more than 1,000 workers.

5 The Director of the Treasury retired, and today we met his ________________, who used to be the assistant director.

6 The new library building is not finished yet; you can only see the basic ________________.

7 The computer program has many small problems that keep it from working perfectly; the engineers need to ________________ it.

8 During the Age of Exploration, Europeans started to ________________ the world by taking over countries on other continents.

9 We enjoyed the ending of the movie the most; it was the ________________ of the film.

10 One way to ________________ a paragraph is to start with a topic sentence, follow with body sentences, and end with a concluding sentence.

Academic Word List

The following are Academic Word List words from all the readings in Unit 7. Use these words to complete the sentences below. (If necessary, review the AWL words in Key Vocabulary on pages 257–267.)

apparent (*adj*)	currency (*n*)	financial (*adj*)	purchase (*n*)	resolve (*v*)
appropriate (*adj*)	feature (*n*)	highlight (*v*)	regional (*adj*)	structure (*n*)

1 Customers receive a free drink with the ________________ of a sandwich.

2 The ________________ in England is called the pound sterling.

3 The banker gave us ________________ advice: save money and invest carefully.

4 Visiting the Great Wall was the ________________ of our trip to China.

5 The child used the blocks to build a simple ________________.

6 It is usually not ________________ to wear shorts to a wedding.

7 She is coughing and sneezing a lot; it is ________________ that she does not feel well.

8 The computer lab is the best ________________ of our new school building.

9 The students had an argument, but the teacher helped them ________________ it.

10 We were surprised by the ________________ differences in the English language as we traveled around the United States.

Critical Thinking

In Reading 3, you learned about the images that countries feature on their currencies.

A Imagine the following places created their own currency. What images do you think each place's currency should have? Explain your ideas to a partner.

1 Your region of your home country
2 Your hometown
3 Your neighborhood
4 Your school
5 Your class

B Share one of your ideas with the rest of the class.

APPLYING INFORMATION

You use critical thinking skills when you apply information you have just learned to new situations.

Research

Do some research on currencies in other countries. Choose five countries that were not mentioned in Reading 3. What does the currency look like in each country? What types of images are shown on each country's currency?

Writing

Write a short report on your research. What types of images are most often shown on currency?

Improving Your Reading Speed

Good readers read quickly and still understand most of what they read.

A Read the instructions and strategies for Improving Your Reading Speed in Appendix 3 on page 270.

B Choose one of the readings in this unit. Read it without stopping. Time how long it takes you to finish the text in minutes and seconds. Enter the time in the chart on page 272. Then calculate your reading speed in number of words per minute.

CAUSE-AND-EFFECT CONNECTORS

Writers connect ideas by showing causes and effects. They show how one event (the cause) leads to another event (the effect). Writers often use signal words like *because*, *due to*, *so*, *as a result*, and *that is why* to help readers understand which ideas are causes and which ideas are effects. You learned these signal words in Skills and Strategies 14 on page 213.

Exercise 1

Read the following paragraphs. Highlight the signals of causes and effects. Then write *C* above the causes and *E* above the effects. The first one is an example.

1 Like that of the United States, the Canadian currency is called the dollar. However, Canada's dollars are very different from those of its neighbor to the south. Because Canada used to be a British colony, there is an image of Queen Elizabeth on the front of the Canadian 20-dollar bill.

2 In 1987, Canada decided to replace its one-dollar bill with a metal coin of the same value. The government wanted a new image for the back of this coin. So it chose something familiar to most Canadians: the common loon, a type of bird that lives near water. Canadians started calling their dollars *loonies* due to the image of the loon. The name became very popular.

3 At the 2002 Winter Olympics in Salt Lake City, a worker for the Canadian national hockey team wanted to give the players good luck. So, he hid a loonie under the ice before a game. The team won that day, and both the Canadian men's and women's hockey teams went on to win gold medals. When the worker later revealed the story of the hidden coin, many Canadians were convinced that the team had won because of the "lucky loonie." As a result of that experience, the Canadian government now produces a special coin for every Olympics. The coin shows an image of the Olympics on the back.

Exercise 2

Make a clear paragraph by putting sentences A, B, and C into the best order after the numbered sentence. Look for cause-and-effect signals, pronouns, category words, and additional information signals to help you. Write the letters in the correct order on the blank lines.

1 Currency has many uses. ___ ___ ___

A	B	C
It also helps a country's economy grow.	It allows people to make purchases.	To some people, currency even has artistic and historical value.

2 Some forms of currency are special because they are rare. ___ ___ ___

A	B	C
For example, the U.S produces a very small number of two-dollar bills.	In fact, they often pay more than two dollars for these unique bills.	Because two-dollar bills are so rare, collectors often seek them out.

3 Other forms of currency are special because they reflect important moments in history. ___ ___ ___

A	B	C
Companies and local governments started printing this money because Germans did not trust the national money at the time.	Due to the large variety of producers, the emergency money featured everything from pictures of German farm workers to humorous images.	An example is German emergency money from the first World War.

4 Collectors may also enjoy a form of currency simply because it is unusual. ___ ___ ___

A	B	C
Another unusual bill was printed in Northern Ireland with a picture of soccer star George Best – maybe the only bill in history to show an athlete.	One unusual form of currency was a bill printed by the Thai government in 1987.	At 16 centimeters by 16 centimeters (6.3 inches), this Thai note was perhaps the largest bill ever produced.

5 Finally, a form of currency may have special artistic value. ___ ___ ___

A	B	C
One example is the ten-dollar bill in the Cook Islands.	Another example is the Polish bank note that shows composer Frederic Chopin with images of musical notes.	The bill celebrates island culture by showing a woman riding a shark.

8

SPACE

SKILLS AND STRATEGIES

- Noticing Parts of Words: Adjective Suffixes
- Finding Problems and Solutions

Noticing Parts of Words: Adjective Suffixes

In previous Skills and Strategies, you learned about some suffixes that show a word is a noun (page 164) or a verb (page 196). Certain suffixes can also help you identify adjectives. Examples of adjective suffixes are *-able*, *-ful,* and *-less*. Good readers use these suffixes to help them understand a word's meaning.

Examples & Explanations

Today, life in space is more enjoy**able** than in the past. Companies may soon turn space vacations into a profit**able** business as customers seek fun and adventure in space.

One common adjective suffix is *-able.* It means "able to be done." It connects to root words such as *enjoy* or *profit*.

enjoyable = giving pleasure; able to be enjoyed
profitable = able to be used in making a profit

Is space exploration really use**ful**? Some people believe so. They think it leads to important scientific discoveries. Other people say space travel is waste**ful**. They think it is better to solve problems here on Earth than spend money on space exploration.

Another common adjective suffix is *-ful*. It means "having a lot of something" or "full of something." It can connect to root words such as *use* and *waste.* If you know these root words, and the meaning of the suffix *-ful*, you can figure out the meaning of *useful* and *wasteful*.

useful = having a lot of use; helping you do something
wasteful = having a lot of waste; unnecessarily using money or resources

On a cloud**less** night, we can see the stars and other planets. Humans may one day visit these stars and planets. The opportunities for space exploration are end**less**.

Another common adjective suffix is *-less*. It means "without something" or "not having." In this example, it connects to the root words *cloud* and *end*.

cloudless = without clouds
endless = without an end; never finishing

Common Adjective Suffixes

Here are some common adjective suffixes and examples.

ADJECTIVE SUFFIX	MEANING	EXAMPLE WORD
-able	*able to be done*	*enjoyable, drinkable, comfortable, profitable*
-ful	*having a lot of something; full of something*	*useful, wasteful, thoughtful, careful*
-less	*without something; not having*	*cloudless, endless, useless, tasteless*

Strategies

These strategies will help you notice adjective suffixes. They may help you understand the meanings of words while you read.

- Study and learn the suffixes in the chart. You may also want to copy this chart in your vocabulary notebook. When you find new adjectives with these suffixes, add them to the chart.
- To learn more adjective suffixes, check a learner dictionary or website that lists common English suffixes.
- Use your knowledge of root words and suffixes to help you understand unknown words.

Skill Practice 1

Read the following text. Highlight seven words that have the adjective suffixes –*able*, -*ful*, and -*less*. The first one is an example.

1 Some people say space exploration is a useless waste of money. However, the technology of space exploration benefits many people.

2 One advantage of space programs has been the development of satellites. Scientists use them to get information about the weather. As a result, the weather is much more predictable than it was in the past. When powerful storms happen, people know days in advance.

3 Space programs have also created important camera technology. This technology is usable in hospitals. The special cameras can look inside patients' bodies. Many medical examinations that used to be stressful for patients are now painless.

4 Because space technology is so useful here on Earth, many people believe that space programs are worth the high cost.

Skill Practice 2

Write definitions for the words you highlighted in Skill Practice 1. Use your knowledge of adjective suffixes to help you. The first one is an example.

1 *useless* = not having any use

2 *predictable* = ______

3 *powerful* = ______

4 *usable* = ______

5 *stressful* = ______

6 *painless* = ______

7 *useful* = ______

Before You Read

Connecting to the Topic

Discuss the following questions with a partner.

1 Did you learn about space travel in school? Were you excited by the idea? Explain your answer.

2 Do you think it is a good idea to spend money on space exploration?

3 What kinds of things do you think we might learn from space exploration?

4 Do you think ordinary human beings will ever be able to live in space, on the moon, or on another planet? Why or why not?

Previewing and Predicting

Remember that one way to preview is to read the title and the first paragraph of a reading. The first paragraph can often tell you what the whole reading will be about.

A Read the title and first paragraph of Reading 1 on page 230. Then put a check (✓) next to the topic that best describes what you think the reading will be about.

_____ a Arguments against spending money on a space program

_____ b Benefits of space programs

_____ c The history of space programs

_____ d The story of one astronaut's journey

B Compare your answers with a partner's.

While You Read

As you read, stop at the end of each sentence that contains words in bold. Then follow the instructions in the box in the margin.

Who Benefits from Space Exploration?

1 For more than a century, space and space travel have fascinated people around the world. There have been countless books and movies about exploration beyond **Earth**. Recently, however, the public's interest in space exploration has declined. Many people are asking if space exploration is worth the money. A space program is very expensive. Fifty percent of the people in a 2014 survey in the United States said the government should not spend billions of dollars to send people to the moon, Mars, and other places in space. Yet, a review of past achievements and current projects shows many benefits of space exploration.

An American astronaut on the moon

WHILE YOU READ 1

Look for a word with an adjective suffix in this sentence. Highlight it.

2 It has taken time for some of the benefits of space exploration to reach the public. However, much of the technology that is part of our lives today began in programs at NASA (the United States space agency) and the ESA (European Space Agency). These agencies have developed new tools and materials. Many of them were later adapted for everyday uses on Earth. For example, NASA needed to create vehicles that would be drivable on **Mars**. During this process, NASA developed a special material that you can still find today in most car tires. The material makes tires last longer and makes driving safer. Astronauts need a small camera to take clear pictures in space. The camera in your cell phone uses this technology today. Astronauts also need clean water on their trips into space, so scientists developed ways to make reusable **water**. That technology is now used here on Earth. NASA also developed new techniques to analyze pictures of the moon and planets. These techniques are now used in hospitals to look inside the body and the brain. These and many other ideas were originally developed for astronauts and space exploration, but they have made life better for all of us.

WHILE YOU READ 2

Look for a word with an adjective suffix in this sentence. Highlight it.

WHILE YOU READ 3

Look for a cause-and-effect signal in this sentence. Highlight it.

3 Today, researchers are using the space environment to develop materials specifically for use on Earth. There is very little gravity in space. Scientists are investigating whether some things work better in this environment. They have discovered that low gravity can be an advantage. For example,

crystals of materials like silicon grow better in a weightless environment. Crystals are very important in complex computers, but they need to be perfect. If the crystals are not perfect, the computers won't work. In space, crystals grow perfectly, whereas when they grow on Earth, they often develop small cracks. Researchers are also growing crystals of proteins. They are hopeful they can use these crystals to develop more effective drugs in the future.

4 Although most successful space programs began as government projects, today the responsibility for space exploration is moving to private **companies**. These companies hope that they can make a profit from exploration, research, and technology in space. One mining company hopes to find and use natural resources, such as valuable metals, in space. Some of the rocks in space contain other minerals that can be used on Earth. Other companies hope to make money in a more surprising way – in tourism. Several companies are trying to build a spaceship that can be used over and over again, like an airplane. One of them, Virgin Galactic, is already selling tickets for tourists who want to take a trip into space. The price of the ticket? About $250,000.

WHILE YOU READ 4

Look for a word with an adjective suffix in this sentence. Highlight it.

The future of tourism?

Main Idea Check

Match the main ideas below to paragraphs 2–4 in Reading 1. Write the number of the paragraph on the blank line.

_____ A Private companies are increasingly involved in space exploration.

_____ B Some useful materials can only be developed in space.

_____ C Technology from space programs is also used here on Earth.

A Closer Look

Look back at Reading 1 to answer the following questions.

1 Interest in space exploration is increasing. **True or False?** (Par. 1)

2 Most people think space exploration is worth the money. **True or False?** (Par. 1)

3 When does technology from space programs help people on Earth? (Par. 2)
   a Immediately
   b Eventually
   c Rarely
   d Never

4 Which of the following have resulted from space technology? Choose four answers. (Par. 2)
   a Fewer car accidents
   b Fresher food in supermarkets
   c Less waste of water
   d Smaller cameras
   e Warmer clothing
   f Less painful visits to hospitals

5 Which of the following are possible uses of crystals? Choose two answers. (Par. 3)
   a Use in advanced technology
   b Use in medicine
   c Use in food
   d Use in entertainment

6 According to paragraph 4, what will private companies look for in space?
   a Tools and equipment
   b Gold and silver
   c Plants and animals
   d Food and water

Skill Review

In Skills and Strategies 15, you learned about the suffixes *-able*, *-ful*, and *-less*. These suffixes can help you identify and understand adjectives.

A **Look at Reading 1 again. Write a word with an adjective suffix next to each definition.**

1 very many = ________________ (Par. 1, sentence 2)

2 able to be driven = ________________ (Par. 2, sentence 5)

3 capable of being used again = ________________ (Par. 2, sentence 11)

4 having no weight = ________________ (Par. 3, sentence 5)

5 having hope or a positive feeling = ________________ (Par. 3, last sentence)

6 achieving a lot = ________________ (Par. 4, sentence 1)

B **Complete each sentence with a word from A.**

1 Some spaceships can only be used one time, but others are ________________.

2 The first test of the spaceship was a failure, but the second test was ________________.

3 People feel ________________ in outer space because of the weak gravity.

4 The number of stars in the sky is ________________.

5 Without tires, a car is not ________________.

6 Some people worry about the future; others are more ________________.

Definitions

Find the words in Reading 1 that complete the following definitions.

1 A / An ________________ is a list of questions that you ask a large number of people so you can learn about their opinions. (*n*) Par. 1, sentence 6

2 ________________ are carefully planned pieces of work that people complete over time in order to achieve a particular purpose. (*n pl*) Par. 1, last sentence

3 ________________ are thick, round pieces of rubber that you put on wheels and then fill with air. (*n pl*) Par. 2, sentence 6

4 When you ________________ something, you study its details very carefully so you can learn more about it. (*v*) Par. 2, sentence 12

5 ________________ are large, round objects in space that move around the sun or another star. (*n pl*) Par. 2, sentence 12

6 ________________ is the force that pulls objects toward a planet or makes objects fall to the ground. (*n*) Par. 3, sentence 2

7 ________________ are clear rocks that form in nature. (*n pl*) Par. 3, sentence 5

8 ________________ are valuable or useful substances that are dug out of the ground. (*n pl*) Par. 4, sentence 4

Words in Context

Complete the sentences with words from Reading 1 in the box below.

adapt	fascinate	program	vehicle
crack	investigate	technique	whereas

1 An airplane is a much faster ________________ than a car or ship.

2 Stories about space exploration do not interest everyone, but they ________________ some people.

3 A small rock hit the window, and now the glass has a ________________.

4 The government wants to know why the spaceship failed to work, so they are going to ________________ the problem.

5 Life in space is very different from life on Earth, so astronauts have to ________________ to the different conditions.

6 There is a government ________________ that gives free books to schoolchildren.

7 The doctor's new ________________ for looking at patients' brains is much less painful than the old method.

8 ________________ only governments did space exploration in the past, private companies are becoming more involved today.

Beyond the Reading

Critical Thinking

In Reading 1, you learned about technology that was created by space programs and how it benefits people on Earth.

> **PERSONALIZING**
>
> Thinking about how new information applies to your own life can help you understand the text better.

A Work with a partner to answer the following questions.

1 Which of the technologies that were mentioned in Reading 1 do you use in your own life?
2 Do you think your home country needs a space program? Why or why not?
3 Would you like to visit space as a tourist? Explain.
4 Would you like to work for a company that looks for valuable metals and other minerals in space? Explain.
5 What other valuable things could private companies look for in space?

B Share an idea from your discussion with the rest of the class.

Research

Reading 1 explained that people on Earth benefit from the technology of space programs. Find out about some other examples of technology from space programs that are also used here on Earth. Choose one type of technology. Answer the questions.

1 When was this technology originally created?
2 What was its original purpose in space?
3 How is it used here on Earth?

Writing

Write a short report about the technology that you researched.

Before You Read

Connecting to the Topic

Discuss the following questions with a partner.

1 Would you like to spend time at the International Space Station? Explain your answer.

2 What do you think would be the most difficult part about living there?

3 What do you think would be the most enjoyable?

Previewing and Predicting

Remember that one way to preview is to look at the first paragraph of a reading and the first few sentences of each remaining paragraph. Writers often tell main ideas in these parts of the reading.

A Look at the first paragraph and the first few sentences of paragraphs 2–5 in Reading 2. Then put a check (✓) next to the topic or topics that you think the reading will discuss.

_____ **a** Scientific discoveries in space
_____ **b** Living conditions on the space station
_____ **c** Eating in space
_____ **d** Sleeping in space
_____ **e** The future of the space station
_____ **f** Washing and cleaning in space

B Compare your answers with a partner's.

While You Read

As you read, stop at the end of each sentence that contains words in bold. Then follow the instructions in the box in the margin.

Living in Space

1 In 1961 Yuri Gagarin, a Russian pilot, became the first person to visit space. He took one trip around the earth. It lasted less than two hours. He didn't need to eat, drink, sleep, take a shower, or use a toilet. Today, astronauts live for up to six months on the International Space Station (ISS). The ISS is a project that is shared by Canada, Europe, Japan, Russia, and the United States. In some ways, the daily lives of these astronauts are not very different from our lives here on Earth. They eat, sleep, and work. However, they face special challenges in their daily routines.

2 One of the biggest problems in space is meals. With zero gravity, astronauts can't just set dinner down on the table. It would float away. Very small pieces of food are especially dangerous. They may float into computers or other equipment and cause problems. Similarly, liquids are a threat. They can get inside computers or other electronic equipment and cause serious damage.

3 Because of these challenges, in the early days of space travel, the food was pretty **terrible**. Astronauts squeezed food out of little tubes. Meat, vegetables, and fruit all looked very similar, and they resembled toothpaste. Today, things are much better. Researchers have found ways to package food that is very much like the food we have on Earth. The space agencies have even invited famous chefs to prepare meals for the astronauts on the ISS. Astronauts' senses of smell and taste become weaker in space, so they

WHILE YOU READ 1

Which part of this sentence gives a cause?
a) The first part
b) The second part

Space food

often prefer stronger **flavors**. Many astronauts report that they like salty, sour, and spicy foods in space even if they don't like them very much on Earth. Eating well is essential for the astronauts' health, so it is important to give them tasty meals.

4 Staying clean is another challenge. No one wants to live for six months without a shower. Smells have nowhere to go on the ISS. There are also practical reasons to keep everyone and everything **clean**. Studies have shown that bacteria grow very quickly in an environment like the ISS. If the astronauts do not keep their environment clean, they could get sick. Scientists have developed a special system for washing and cleaning without water. When they must use water, such as to brush their teeth, they are careful about where it **goes**. They cannot rinse and then spit the water into the sink. Instead, they have to spit it onto a cloth that absorbs all of the liquid.

5 Even sleeping requires special equipment. Astronauts cannot just lie down on a bed. They would float away. They might bump into some important equipment or hurt themselves. When they go to sleep, they have to tie themselves down. However, they don't actually have to lie down. Without gravity, they can also sleep standing up. Many astronauts report that it is hard to sleep in space. There is a lot of noise, not very much fresh air, and a sunrise every 90 minutes. Living in space has many challenges, but today's astronauts have a much more comfortable life than astronauts in the early days of space **exploration**.

WHILE YOU READ 2

Which part of this sentence gives a cause?
a) The first part
b) The second part

WHILE YOU READ 3

Look for a cause-and-effect signal in this sentence. Highlight it.

WHILE YOU READ 4

Look for a word with an adjective suffix in this sentence. Highlight it.

WHILE YOU READ 5

Look for a word with an adjective suffix in this sentence. Highlight it.

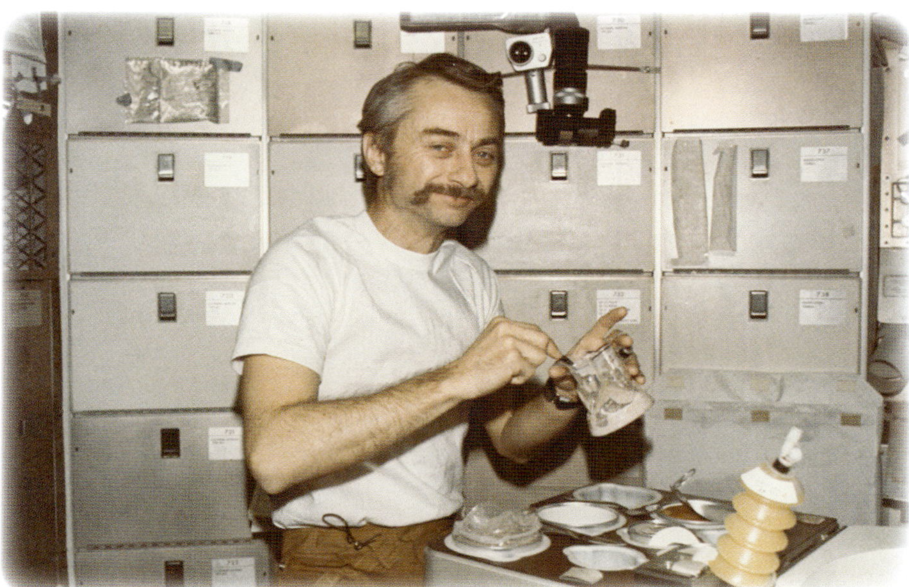

An astronaut preparing a meal in space

Reading Skill Development

Main Idea Check

Match the main ideas below to paragraphs 2–5 in Reading 2. Write the number of the paragraph on the blank line.

_____ A Sleeping in space can also be difficult.
_____ B In zero gravity, astronauts have to eat very carefully.
_____ C Keeping clean in space is a challenge.
_____ D Astronauts eat much better today than they did in the past.

A Closer Look

Look back at Reading 2 to answer the following questions.

1 Why is space travel more complicated for astronauts today than it was for Yuri Gagarin in 1961? (Par. 1)
   a They take a trip around the earth.
   b They expect tastier meals.
   c They communicate with more people.
   d They stay in space a longer time.

2 Why are small pieces of food dangerous in zero gravity? (Par. 2)
   a They can get in astronauts' eyes and ears.
   b They can damage computers.
   c They are covered in bacteria.
   d They are difficult to clean up.

3 Why is astronauts' food better today than it was in the past? Choose three reasons. (Par. 3)
   a Expert cooks prepare the meals.
   b The food has especially strong flavors.
   c Scientists have found new ways to keep food fresh.
   d The food comes in tubes and is easy to eat.
   e The meat, fruit, and vegetables all look the same.

4 Match the beginning of a sentence in Column A with its correct ending in Column B. (whole reading)

	Column A	Column B
_____	1 In space, the sun rises	a without using much water.
_____	2 The International Space Station is	b used to look like toothpaste.
_____	3 The first person to travel to space	c every 90 minutes.
_____	4 When astronauts go to sleep,	d unless astronauts clean carefully.
_____	5 Astronauts have to clean things	e was a Russian pilot.
_____	6 Astronauts' meals	f they sometimes stay standing up.
_____	7 Bacteria grow quickly	g can be damaged by small pieces of food.
_____	8 Computer equipment in space	h home to astronauts from many different countries.

Skill Review

In Skills and Strategies 15, you learned about the adjective suffixes *–able, -ful,* and *-less*. These suffixes can help you understand words. They can also increase your vocabulary.

A **Add the suffixes –*able*, -*ful*, and –*less* to the words below to create adjectives. Each word can combine with more than one suffix. The first one is an example.**

1 care *careful* *careless*

2 color ______ ______

3 fear ______ ______

4 flavor ______ ______

5 forget ______ ______

6 help ______ ______

7 power ______ ______

8 use ______ ______ ______

B **Complete each sentence with the most appropriate adjective form of the word in parentheses.**

1 Outer space is a dangerous place, so astronauts have to be ______. (care)

2 Clean, pure water is ______. (color)

3 Yuri Gagarin's family was ______ that he would not survive his space mission. (fear)

4 Astronaut food used to be terrible, but today it is quite ______. (flavor)

5 The professor is very ______ and often can't remember students' names. (forget)

6 Newborn babies are completely ______ without their parents. (help)

7 The people near the river were ______ against the rising flood. (power)

8 Camera technology from space programs is also ______ here on Earth. (use)

Vocabulary Development

Definitions

Find the words in Reading 2 that complete the following definitions.

1 A / An ________________ is something that is likely to cause harm or damage. (*n*) Par. 2, sentence 6

2 ________________ are difficult problems that you have to work hard to solve. (*n pl*) Par. 3, sentence 1

3 ________________ are pipes made of metal, glass, or plastic that can hold liquids and other soft substances. (*n pl*) Par. 3, sentence 2

4 ________________ is a substance that you use to clean your teeth. (*n*) Par. 3, sentence 3

5 ________________ are skilled and trained cooks who usually work in restaurants or hotels. (*n pl*) Par. 3, sentence 6

6 ________________ are very small living things that can cause disease. (*n pl*) Par. 4, sentence 5

7 When you ________________, you force liquid suddenly out of your mouth. (*v*) Par. 4, sentence 9

8 A ________________ is the time in the morning when the sun appears and the sky becomes light. (*n*) Par. 5, sentence 9

Words in Context

Complete the sentences with words or phrases from Reading 2 in the box below.

float	practical	rinse	terrible
lie down	resemble	squeeze	tie

1 We want to invite everyone for dinner, but it is not very ________________ with our small apartment.

2 Children have to learn to ________________ their shoes.

3 To make orange juice, take fresh oranges and ________________ them so the liquid comes out.

4 If you put wood in water, it will ________________.

5 The weather was ________________; it was cold and windy, and it rained all day.

6 Before we eat an apple or a pear, we usually ________________ it with water.

7 The children ________________ their mother; they have the same hair, eyes, and nose.

8 The boy was tired, so he decided to ________________ and take a short nap.

Critical Thinking

In Reading 2, you learned about the challenges of living in space.

PERSONALIZING

Thinking about how new information applies to your own life can help you understand the text better.

A Work with a partner to answer the following questions.

1 Would you like to be an astronaut? Explain.

2 Imagine you can visit the ISS. How long would you like to stay there?

3 Imagine you are living on the ISS. How will you sleep? Will you tie yourself to a bed?

4 What foods do you think you would enjoy eating in space?

5 Which of the challenges of living in space do you think is most difficult? Explain.

6 What qualities does a person need to be an astronaut? Make a list.

B Share your answers with the rest of the class.

Research

Visit the website for the International Space Station (www.nasa.gov). Find some current information about the ISS. Which astronauts are staying there? What countries do they come from? What projects are they working on?

Writing

Write a short report about your research.

Finding Problems and Solutions

Writers sometimes explain problems and solutions. Several problems (usually related) may appear in one reading. Similarly, a single reading may explain several solutions. Good readers can find signal words to help them understand problems and solutions in a reading.

Examples & Explanations

As anyone who has taken a long drive or flight knows, travel is often uncomfortable. When people travel to space, staying comfortable becomes a serious problem.

In this paragraph, the writer gives a problem: *staying comfortable in space*. Writers usually give problems first and then solutions.

One challenge is the extreme temperatures in space. Astronauts orbiting Earth see a sunrise or a sunset every 45 minutes, and the change in temperature between day and night can be 275°F (135°C). To keep astronauts safe and comfortable, the International Space Station (ISS) is covered in special materials that keep out extreme heat and cold. The temperature inside is a constant 70°F (21°C).

In this paragraph, the writer introduces the problem of temperature. The writer uses the signal word *challenge* to introduce it. Writers also use words like *problem* and *difficulty* to signal problems.

Another problem related to comfort is clothing. Astronauts cannot wash clothes in space. To resolve this problem, they have to bring extra clothing with them. They also wear each article of clothing several times. For example, ISS astronauts only change their shirts every ten days and their socks and underwear every other day.

In this paragraph, the writer introduces the problem of clothing and then gives a solution. The writer uses the signal word *resolve* to introduce the solution. Writers also use words like *solution* and *solve* to signal solutions.

In the second and third paragraphs, the writer introduces two problems, temperature and clothing, and some solutions. All of the problems and solutions are related to the topic of the reading – staying comfortable in space.

The Language of Problems and Solutions

SIGNAL WORDS FOR PROBLEMS		SIGNAL WORDS FOR SOLUTIONS	
challenge	*difficulty*	*improve*	*solution*
danger	*problem*	*resolve*	*solve*

Strategies

These strategies will help you identify problems and solutions while you read.

- Remember that writers usually give problems first and then solutions. Writers may give all the problems first and then the solutions at the end, or they may give a solution after each problem.
- Study and learn the signals in the chart above. Use them to help you identify problems and solutions while you read.
- If a reading has several problems or solutions, make a list of them while you read. Ask yourself: *How are they related?*

Skill Practice 1

Read the following paragraphs. In each paragraph, highlight one problem signal and one solution signal.

1 It is not easy to build a perfect tool, especially if that tool has to work in space. One challenge is that the tool has to be very strong but also light enough to carry into space. Space scientists try to find the strongest and lightest materials possible so they can improve astronauts' tools. If the tool is used outside of the space station, it also has to survive the extreme temperatures of space. In direct sunlight, a piece of metal can become as hot as 500°F (260°C). One solution is for astronauts to protect themselves by covering tools with special blankets when they are working outside the space station.

2 Astronauts' bodies change in space and so can their moods. Astronauts are far away from their family and friends, and as a result, they often experience loneliness. There is also the problem of boredom. After many weeks in a small space station, astronauts can become very tired of their surroundings – and each other. However, modern technology is helping to improve astronauts' moods. Astronauts can now bring laptop computers to space and watch their favorite shows and movies. They can also use email to communicate with their friends and family back home. On some trips to space, they can even make phone calls.

3 On Earth, bad smells are part of everyday life. In space, however, smells can be a matter of life and death. In space, smells do not go away. A bad smell can stay in a space station for weeks, or even months. An even greater danger is that smells can change in space. If a smell becomes unpleasant, astronauts may need to end their trip early. NASA has found an interesting solution to bad smells in space: smell tests. George Aldrich works at NASA's research center in New Mexico. He has a very strong sense of smell. He works with a team of other scientists to test how the objects that astronauts use will smell in space. If the objects do not pass Aldrich's smell test, they have to stay on Earth.

Skill Practice 2

Read the paragraphs in Skill Practice 1 again. How does the writer organize ideas in each paragraph? Choose the best answer. Use the problem or solution signals you highlighted to help you.

1 a The writer gives all the problems first, then all the solutions at the end.
  b The writer gives a solution after each problem.

2 a The writer gives all the problems first, then all the solutions at the end.
  b The writer gives a solution after each problem.

3 a The writer gives all the problems first, then all the solutions at the end.
  b The writer gives a solution after each problem.

Before You Read

Connecting to the Topic

Discuss the following questions with a partner.

1 Astronauts work in a low-gravity environment. How do you think that would feel? Do you think you would enjoy the experience?

2 How do you think it might change your body if you stayed in that environment for a long time? Explain your answer.

3 How do you think staying in space for several months might affect your mind and your emotions?

Previewing and Predicting

To preview a longer reading, start by reading the title and first paragraph. Then look at headings of sections.

A Read the title and first paragraph of Reading 3 on page 247. Then read the section headings. Decide what topics you think will be in each section. Then write the number(s) of the sections (*I*, *II*, *III*) next to the topics that you think will be in those sections. A topic may be in more than one section.

SECTION	TOPIC
	Serious health risks for astronauts
	How astronauts feel when they first arrive at the space station
	How astronauts feel after they return to Earth
	The effects of living on the space station on astronauts' health

B Based on the first paragraph, what factor do you think has the biggest effect on astronauts' health?

____

C Compare your answers with a partner's.

While You Read

As you read, stop at the end of each sentence that contains words in bold. Then follow the instructions in the box in the margin.

Health Effects of Living in Space

1 When Canadian astronaut Chris Hadfield returned to Earth after 146 days in space, he said holding his head up felt like a new experience. When humans spend a long time in space, their bodies change. They adjust to living in an environment with very little gravity, where their bodies are almost weightless. When they return to Earth, they have to adjust all over again. The experience of living in space has a variety of effects on the human body.

I. Immediate Effects

2 Some of the changes in the body happen right away. Usually, the first effect is space sickness. This is very much like seasickness. Seasickness is a feeling that some people get on a boat. The movement of the water upsets their stomachs. Living in a low-gravity environment can have the same effect. Many astronauts feel sick when they first go into space. For most of them, however, this feeling disappears after a few days. Another immediate impact is on sleep. Many astronauts find it difficult to sleep well in space. They must tie themselves to their beds so they don't float **away**. Also, it is never completely dark or completely quiet. However, most astronauts get accustomed to the environment after a while and begin to sleep better.

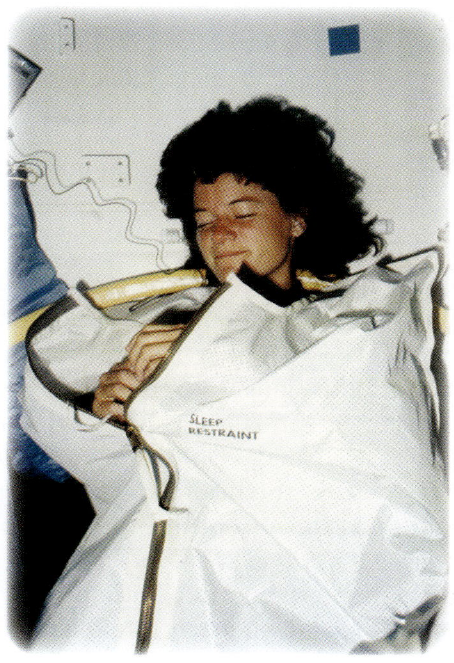

Sleeping astronauts

WHILE YOU READ 1
Which part of this sentence gives a solution to a problem?
a) The first part
b) The second part

II. Longer-Term Effects

3 In the early days of space travel, astronauts stayed in space for only a short time, so very little was known about the long-term effects of space travel. Now it is more common for them stay in space for several months. Researchers have investigated what happens to astronauts' bodies after these longer trips. The biggest impacts of spending a long time in space are on the circulatory system, that is, the movement of blood, as well as on muscles and bones.

4 The human circulatory system works very well in gravity. When blood goes into the lower body, our muscles help push it back up to the heart. But without gravity, the system is out of balance. Blood and other fluids rise, but there is no gravity to push them back down. So more fluids remain in the upper body. As a result, astronauts have big round faces, and their upper bodies become larger. But this effect is not permanent. When the astronauts return to Earth, their circulatory systems go back to normal.

5 Some more important impacts are on muscles and bones. On Earth, it takes effort to move the weight of our own bodies. This effort keeps our muscles and bones strong. In a low-gravity environment, in contrast, moving our bodies and lifting objects is almost effortless (very **easy**). As a result, astronauts' muscles become weak, and their legs become thin. Many of them joke about their "chicken legs." They also slowly lose bone. Scientists estimate that astronauts lose two percent of their bones every month they are in **space**. To try to slow this loss, astronauts do a lot of exercise while they are in space. Unfortunately, this does not really stop the changes in their muscles and bones. When the astronauts return to Earth, they get a big surprise. They have trouble walking and lifting their arms. Even holding their heads up is a challenge, just as Chris Hadfield **described**. After a few weeks back on Earth, their muscles recover. However, it may take up to two years to rebuild their bones.

WHILE YOU READ 

Look for a word with an adjective suffix in this sentence. Highlight it.

WHILE YOU READ 3

Which sentence gives a solution to a problem?
a) The sentence before
b) The same sentence
c) The next sentence

WHILE YOU READ 4

Look for a problem signal in this sentence. Highlight it.

III. Dangerous Effects

6 All of these effects are reversible, that is, the body returns to normal after some time back on Earth. One other effect may not be reversible, however. In space, there is a higher level of radiation than on Earth. Exposure to this radiation is dangerous, but medical experts are not sure of the long-term effects. So far, studies suggest that it may contribute to cancer and heart disease. It may also damage the eyes and perhaps the brain. With longer exposure, the health risks of radiation increase. That is why doctors monitor astronauts' health very carefully after they return to Earth.

7 As a result of all of these risks, most space programs limit the amount of time that astronauts spend in space. At some time in the future, we may have cities on the moon, on Mars, or in space. Scientists and medical experts will continue to study the effects of living in space on the human body. This knowledge can hopefully resolve any negative health effects of life in space and protect space travelers of the **future**.

WHILE YOU READ 5

Look for a solution signal in this sentence. Highlight it.

Reading Skill Development

Main Idea Check

Match the main ideas below to paragraphs 2–7 in Reading 3. Write the number of the paragraph on the blank line.

_____ A Astronauts may lose sleep and feel sick when they first arrive in space.
_____ B Astronauts' bones and muscles become weaker during long space trips.
_____ C A serious health problem for astronauts is radiation in space.
_____ D As astronauts take longer trips, we learn more about the effects of life in space.
_____ E Space programs look for solutions to the health problems that astronauts face.
_____ F The flow of blood in astronauts' bodies changes in space.

A Closer Look

Look back at Reading 3 to answer the following questions.

1 How long did Chris Hadfield stay in space? (Par. 1)
  a A few days
  b Several weeks
  c Several months
  d A few years

2 When do astronauts usually stop feeling sick and start sleeping better? (Par. 2)
  a After they eat a good meal
  b After they see a doctor
  c When they become accustomed to life in space
  d When they talk with their friends and family

3 What is the cause of each effect? Match the effect in the left column to a cause in the right column. (Pars. 2–6)

	Effect	Cause
_____	1 Astronauts have rounder faces.	a The circulatory system changes in space.
_____	2 Astronauts have difficulty sleeping.	b Astronauts experience muscle loss in space.
_____	3 Astronauts have "chicken legs."	c Astronauts must tie themselves to their beds.
_____	4 Astronauts have a higher risk of disease.	d There is dangerous radiation in space.

4 What caused Chris Hadfield's problem holding his head up? (Par. 5)
  a Space sickness
  b High levels of radiation
  c Lack of exercise
  d Muscle and bone weakness

5 Which of the following may cause permanent damage to astronauts' health? (Par. 6)

a Bone loss
b Space sickness
c Muscle loss
d Space radiation

Skill Review

In Skills and Strategies 16, you learned that writers sometimes explain problems and solutions. Writers usually give the problems first and then the solutions.

A **Complete the chart with ideas from Reading 3.**

PROBLEM	SOLUTION
	Astronauts give themselves a few days to get accustomed to their new environment so their stomachs feel better.
Astronauts will float away when they lie down in their beds because there is low gravity in space.	
	Astronauts do a lot of exercise while they are in space.
Space radiation can cause serious health problems.	
	Space programs limit the amount of time that astronauts spend in space.

B **Compare your answers with a partner's.**

Definitions

Find the words in Reading 3 that complete the following definitions.

1 If something ________________ your stomach, it makes your stomach hurt and feel sick. (*v*) Par. 2, sentence 5

2 If you are ________________ to something, you have experienced it enough for it to seem normal. (*adj*) Par. 2, last sentence

3 A / An ________________ problem is a problem that will continue into the future. (*adj*) Par. 3, sentence 1

4 A / An ________________ problem is a problem related to the movement of blood through the body. (*adj*) Par. 3, last sentence

5 ________________ are the parts of your body that help you move and connect your bones to each other. (*n pl*) Par. 3, last sentence

6 ________________ are liquids, such as water or blood. (*n pl*) Par. 4, sentence 4

7 If something is ________________, it requires very little strength or force to achieve. (*adj*) Par. 5, sentence 4

8 People with the disease ________________ have cells that grow uncontrollably. (*n*) Par. 6, sentence 5

Word Families

A **The words in bold in the chart are from Reading 3. The words next to them are from the same word family. Study and learn these words.**

NOUN	VERB
adjustment	***adjust*** (Par. 1)
balance (Par. 4)	*balance*
contribution	***contribute*** (Par. 6)
monitor	***monitor*** (Par. 6)
radiation (Par. 6)	*radiate*

B Choose the correct form of the words from the chart to complete the following sentences.

1 If the seatbelt in the car is too tight or too loose, you should ________________ it.

2 Solar ________________ can damage your skin and cause cancer.

3 The scientists created several technologies that the astronauts use; the government thanked them for their ________________ to the space program.

4 We made a / an ________________ to the schedule; the meeting will begin at 1 p.m. instead of noon.

5 The patient was connected to a heart ________________ so doctors could check on his recovery.

6 The heat from the wood fire will ________________ through the room.

7 Professional dancers rarely fall over because they have very good ________________.

8 The teacher will ________________ the students while they are taking the test.

9 Each student will ________________ a few dollars for the teacher's birthday present.

10 She can ________________ a book on top of her head.

Academic Word List

The following are Academic Word List words from all the readings in Unit 8. Use these words to complete the sentences. (If necessary, review the AWL words in Key Vocabulary on pages 257–267.)

adapt (*v*)	challenge (*n*)	monitor (*v*)	survey (*n*)	vehicle (*n*)
analyze (*v*)	contribute (*v*)	project (*n*)	technique (*n*)	whereas (*adv*)

1 Some people take public transportation because they do not have their own ________________.

2 The researchers wanted to know the public's opinion on space travel, so they created a ________________.

3 Space travel used to be very dangerous and difficult in the past, ________________ today it is much more comfortable.

4 The astronauts on the ISS just completed a six-month research ________________ about plant life in space.

5 We sent the cells to the laboratory so the researchers could ________________ them.

6 Scientists will continue to ________________ the movement of the storm; if it comes close to the city, they will release a warning.

7 Today photographers can print photographs using computers; in the past, they had to use a different ________________.

8 Understanding spoken English is not easy for language learners; in fact, it is a real ________________.

9 The survivors asked us to ________________ food, money, or clothing to the recovery effort.

10 When people move to a new country, they have to ________________ to a new way of life.

Critical Thinking

In Reading 3, you learned about the health effects of living in space.

EXPLORING OPINIONS

Critical readers form their own opinions about important topics in a text.

A Work with a partner to answer the following questions.

1 With so many health effects, why do you think astronauts continue to do their jobs?

2 Should people who experience seasickness become astronauts? Explain.

3 Is it a good idea to build cities on the moon? Why or why not?

4 In your opinion, what other jobs have health risks as serious as those that astronauts face?

B Share an idea from your discussion with the rest of the class.

Research

Do some research on space hotels.

- What types of space hotels are people planning?
- How will these hotels deal with the challenges of living in space?
- What will guests do at these space hotels?
- How much will they have to pay to stay at them?

Writing

Write a short report about your research. Include answers to the questions.

Improving Your Reading Speed

Good readers read quickly and still understand most of what they read.

A Read the instructions and strategies for Improving Your Reading Speed in Appendix 3 on page 270.

B Choose one of the readings in this unit. Read it without stopping. Time how long it takes you to finish the text in minutes and seconds. Enter the time in the chart on page 272. Then calculate your reading speed in number of words per minute.

MAKING CONNECTIONS

REVIEW OF CONNECTORS

In Units 1–7, you studied different types of connectors. You learned that writers connect sentences and ideas with words and phrases such as:

- Pronouns that refer to people, things, or ideas (See pages 31 and 62.)
- Category words (See page 95.)
- Additional information connectors (See page 129.)
- Time sequence connectors (See page 161.)
- Contrast connectors (See page 193.)
- Cause-and-effect connectors (See page 223.)

Exercise 1

Read the following paragraphs. Highlight any pronouns, and underline what they refer to. Circle any words or phrases that signal addition, time sequence, contrast, or cause and effect. The first three are examples.

1 In the near future, astronauts may visit the planet Mars. This is an exciting idea for many people. However, scientists must solve several problems. Their first challenge is to design a spaceship that can carry humans at least 34.8 million miles (54.7 million kilometers) from Earth to Mars. The spaceship will need to carry or produce a lot of fuel. It will also have to be made of very strong materials to survive the journey to Mars and back again.

2 Another problem is related to the physical and emotional condition of the astronauts during the journey. They will be in the spaceship for more than six months. How will they stay healthy – and happy – during the long trip? One solution could be for the astronauts to stay in a deep sleep. Some scientists are trying to develop new medical technology that lowers the temperature of the human body. This may allow the astronauts to stay asleep safely for weeks or even months at a time.

3 When they actually arrive at Mars, the astronauts will face another major challenge – the weather. Their view of Mars from space will be beautiful, but the weather on the planet's surface can change quickly. Powerful winds and sand storms are common. As a result, the astronauts will need a second, smaller spaceship to land on and explore Mars.

Exercise 2

Make a clear paragraph by putting sentences A, B, and C into the best order after the numbered sentence. Look for problem or solution signals, contrast signals, pronouns, and words that signal addition to help you. Write the letters in the correct order on the blank lines.

1 People who dream of living on Mars may soon have the chance to do so.

____ ____ ____

A	B	C
The company says it has received more than 200,000 applications.	The Mars One Project is looking for volunteers to create a colony on the red planet.	From those applications, just four people will be chosen for the first trip, scheduled to leave in 2023.

2 Building a colony on Mars will not be cheap. ____ ____ ____

A	B	C
Bas Lansdorp, the company founder, believes the show will be very popular and highly profitable.	He explains, "How many people do you think would want to watch the first humans arrive on Mars?"	However, Mars One has a creative solution to the problem: a TV show about the astronauts' lives.

3 Mars One will choose its astronauts very carefully. ____ ____ ____

A	B	C
The astronauts will have to live together in a small space.	That is why the company is looking for people who function well in a team.	They will also have to work together closely.

4 The astronauts will be living in a completely new environment on Mars. ____ ____ ____

A	B	C
For instance, Mars One plans to test its spaceship eight times before it makes the trip to Mars.	To prepare for the challenge, the astronauts will do eight years of training before they leave Earth.	Their equipment will also be carefully tested.

5 Because a trip to Mars is so complicated, many people doubt the Mars One Project will be a success. ____ ____ ____

A	B	C
But Lansdorp insists the project is his life-long goal.	"When I was 20 years old . . . I first started dreaming of this," he explains.	Some people say the company founder is not serious and just wants attention.

Key Vocabulary

The Academic Word List is a list of words that are particularly important to study. Research shows that these words frequently appear in many different types of academic texts. Words that are part of the Academic Word List are noted with an Ⓐ in this appendix.

UNIT 1 • READING 1

Procrastination

accomplish *v* to finish something successfully • *If we work together, we can* ***accomplish*** *more than if we each work alone.*

assignment Ⓐ *n* a piece of work or job that someone gives you to do • *Last night's homework* ***assignment*** *was very difficult.*

bill *n* a piece of paper that tells you how much you must pay for something • *I need to pay my electricity* ***bill*** *by the end of the week.*

deadline *n* a time by which something must be done • *We need to work more quickly because the* ***deadline*** *is in two days.*

due *adj* expected at a particular time • *I am going to work late tonight because the report is* ***due*** *in the morning.*

expert Ⓐ *n* someone who has a lot of skill in something or a lot of knowledge about something • *The professor is an* ***expert*** *in Chinese history.*

factor Ⓐ *n* one of the things that has an effect on a particular situation, decision, or event • *Price was the most important* ***factor*** *in my decision to buy this computer.*

guilty *n* feeling bad because you have done something wrong • *People often* ***guilty*** *after they lie or do something bad.*

lean *v* to move the top part of your body in a particular direction • *She* ***leaned*** *against the door for a moment to rest her back.*

perspective Ⓐ *n* the way you think about something • *It is a good idea to hear another person's* ***perspective*** *before you make a decision.*

positive Ⓐ *adj* feeling happy about your life and your future • *I have a very* ***positive*** *feeling about this idea; I think it is going to work.*

postpone *v* to arrange for something to happen at a later time • *Because of the bad weather, we are going to have to* ***postpone*** *the party until tomorrow.*

prefer *v* to like someone or something more than another person or thing • *Do you* ***prefer*** *coffee or tea with your breakfast?*

put off *v* to decide to do something at a later time • *You can't* ***put*** *it* ***off*** *any longer. You have to tell him the truth today.*

repair *v* to fix something that is broken or damaged • *My watch is broken but I have not had time to* ***repair*** *it.*

task Ⓐ *n* a piece of work, especially something unpleasant or difficult • *Her boss asked her to complete the* ***task*** *by Monday.*

UNIT 1 • READING 2

Memory and New Technology

access Ⓐ *n* the fact of being able to use or see something • *Students have* ***access*** *to the books in all of the university's libraries.* **access** Ⓐ *v* to get information, especially using a computer • *The police could not* ***access*** *the files on the computer.*

advice *n* suggestions about what you think someone should do or how they should do something • *I always listen to my friend because she usually gives me good* ***advice****.* **advise** *v* to make a suggestion about what you think someone should do or how they should do something • *My professor* ***advised*** *me to take a math course before I try physics.*

affect Ⓐ *v* to cause a change in someone or something • *Noise* ***affects*** *my ability to study, so I try to go somewhere quiet.*

consult Ⓐ *v* to go to a particular person, book, or object to get information or advice • *He is going to* ***consult*** *another doctor before he decides what to do.* **consultation** Ⓐ *n* a discussion with someone in order to get their advice or opinion • *After* ***consultation*** *with several experts, they decided to sell the company.*

impact Ⓐ *n* the effect that a person, event, or situation has on someone or something • *This decision is very important and its* ***impact*** *will last for a long time.*

instant *adj* happening immediately • *The new phone was an* ***instant*** *success. A million were sold in the first month.*

negative Ⓐ *adj* bad; causing damage to something • *The news about the war will have a* ***negative*** *effect on the economy.*

preserve *v* to keep something as it is • *The group is trying to* ***preserve*** *historic buildings in the center of the city.* **preservation** *n* keeping something the same or preventing it from being damaged or destroyed • *This new technology will help with the* ***preservation*** *of important government records.*

recent *adj* happening or starting from a short time ago • *This is the most* ***recent*** *picture of my granddaughter. It is from her birthday party last week.*

store *v* to put something somewhere and not use it until you need it • *You should not* ***store*** *tomatoes or bananas in the refrigerator.*

stress Ⓐ *v* to emphasize something in order to show that it is important • *Health experts **stress** the importance of healthy food and exercise.*

support *v* to help someone or something • *I am sure that my friends and family will **support** my decision.* **support** *n* agreement with an idea, group, or person • *The president's efforts have received **support** from other leaders all over the world.*

visual Ⓐ *adj* relating to seeing • *People who cannot hear depend on **visual** information in order to understand their environment.*

UNIT 1 • READING 3

Lying

avoid *v* to stay away from a person, place, or situation • *I try to **avoid** food that has a lot of sugar in it.*

benefit Ⓐ *v* to be helped by something • *Everyone in the country will **benefit** from cleaner air.*

detect Ⓐ *v* to discover or notice something, especially something that is difficult to see, hear, or smell • *Dogs can **detect** smells better than humans can.*

gap *n* an empty space between two things • *The new study will try to close the **gap** in our knowledge of this disease.*

image Ⓐ *n* the way that people think someone or something is • *We want to improve the city's **image** so that more people will want to visit.*

logical Ⓐ *adj* using reason • *When people listen to their feelings instead of their brains, they don't always behave in a **logical** way.*

maintain Ⓐ *v* to make a situation or activity continue in the same way • *She took very difficult courses but she was still able to **maintain** good grades.*

participant Ⓐ *n* someone who takes part in an activity • *The **participants** arrived about an hour before the race began.*

primary Ⓐ *adj* most important • *A police officer's **primary** job is to make sure that the city is safe.*

probability *n* how likely it is that something will happen • *There is a 50 percent **probability** of rain tomorrow.*

punishment *n* something that is done to someone to make them suffer because they have done something bad • *For teenagers, "no Internet" might be the best form of **punishment** when they behave badly.*

research Ⓐ *n* detailed study of a subject in order to discover information • *Medical **research** is helping stop dangerous diseases.*

reward *n* something good that you get or experience because you have worked hard or behaved well • *The person who finds the lost dog will get a **reward**.*

rude *adj* behaving in a way that is not polite and upsets people • *It some cultures, it is **rude** to look directly in another person's eyes.*

significantly Ⓐ *adv* by a large amount • *Average temperatures have increased **significantly** in the past hundred years.*

sum Ⓐ *n* the total amount that you get when you add two or more numbers together • *The **sum** of 17 and 18 is 35.*

UNIT 2 • READING 1

Fact or Fiction – Science

abandon Ⓐ *v* to leave behind or run away from someone or something • *A mother animal will not **abandon** her babies even if it is dangerous to stay with them.*

beneficial Ⓐ *adj* helpful or useful • *A few minutes of sun every day is **beneficial** for your health but too much sun is dangerous.*

drown *v* to die because you are under water and cannot breathe • *Babies can **drown** in just a small amount of water, so always watch children in the bath.*

evidence Ⓐ *n* something that makes you believe that something is true or exists • *The police are looking for **evidence** of the crime.*

familiar *adj* easy to recognize because you have seen or experienced it before • *I think we have met before because your face looks very **familiar**.*

fingernail *n* the hard, thin part on the top of the end of your finger • *Her **fingernail** broke when she tried to open the box.*

generation Ⓐ *n* a period of about 25 to 30 years; the time it takes for a child to become an adult • *He and I are from the same **generation**, so we remember a lot of the same events.*

immediately *adv* now or without waiting • *You need to go to the hospital **immediately**!*

lightning *n* a sudden flash of light in the sky during a storm • *During the storm last night, **lightning** hit a tree and started a fire.*

originate *v* to begin during a particular period or in a particular place • *Scientists have discovered a new fish, which they think **originates** in Alaska.*

persist Ⓐ *v* to continue to exist • *If your cold and fever **persist** for another day, you should go see a doctor.*

relevant Ⓐ *adj* related to or useful to what is happening or being talked about • *This new information could be **relevant** to my decision.*

repetition *n* the act of saying or doing something again • ***Repetition** of new words and facts can help you remember them.*

resist *v* to fight against or oppose something or someone • *This is a new kind of rice that **resists** many insects and diseases.*

twice *adj* two times • *I have already called him **twice**; perhaps I should call a third time.*

virus *n* a very small organism (creature) that causes disease • *This test will show if the infection is caused by a **virus**.*

UNIT 2 • READING 2

Fact or Fiction – History

ancient *adj* from a long time ago • *This wall is part of the **ancient** city that existed here two thousand years ago.*

astronaut *n* a person who travels into space • *The **astronauts** will return after one year at the space station.*

credit Ⓐ *n* praise for something that is accomplished • *Two scientists took **credit** for last week's important discovery.*

culture Ⓐ *n* the habits, traditions, and beliefs of a country, society, or group of people • *We travel a lot because we like learning about different **cultures**.*

establish Ⓐ *v* to bring into existence • *The government is going to **establish*** a new office that will help people pay their medical bills.

explorer *n* a person who travels to places where no one has ever been to find out what is there • *During the 1400s, European **explorers** went to many places in Asia and North and South America.*

handsome *adj* attractive; usually used to describe men • *Don't you think Brad Pitt is very **handsome**?*

historian *n* someone who studies or writes about history • *A British **historian** claims he found a new play by Shakespeare inside an old book.*

make up *v* to invent a story that isn't true • *Every night she **makes up** a story to tell the children before they go do sleep.*

publish Ⓐ *v* to make information available to the public, usually as a book, magazine, or newspaper • *The newspaper will **publish** a story about the family who died in the fire.*

prove *v* to show that something is true • *This test will **prove** that there are dangerous chemicals in the water.*

spice *n* a substance from plants, which is used to give a special taste to food • *Mexican and Chinese cooks use different **spices** in their food.*

trace Ⓐ *v* to find the origin of something • *The police are trying to **trace** where they letter came from.*

trader *n* a person who buys and sells things • ***Traders** traveled from China to the Mediterranean, buying and selling many different things.*

voyage *n* a long trip, especially by ship • *The **voyage** across the Atlantic Ocean lasted a month or more.*

widespread Ⓐ *adj* affecting or including a lot of places or people • *The **widespread** crime in the city has made people afraid.*

UNIT 2 • READING 3

Hoaxes

area Ⓐ *n* part of a country, city, town, etc. • *The houses in this **area** cost less than the houses in the center of town.*

assist Ⓐ *v* to help • *I looked around but there was no one to **assist** me.* **assistance** Ⓐ *n* help • *If you get lost, you can ask a police officer for **assistance**.*

cave *n* a large hole in the side of a mountain or under the ground • *Early humans often lived in **caves**, which give them some protection from the weather.*

collect *v* to ask people to give you money for something • *The students are going to **collect** food and money to give to people in need.* **collection** *n* money that people give for a special purpose, a person in need, or an organization • *They started a **collection** to help soldiers coming home from the war.*

contact Ⓐ *n* communication with someone • *I have had no **contact** with him since we were in school.*

create Ⓐ *v* to make something or exist • *I am going to **create** something new and delicious for dinner.* **creation** Ⓐ *n* a process in which someone makes something happen or exist • *After the **creation** of the new government, the prime minister will speak on television.*

curiosity *n* the feeling of wanting to know or learn about something • *Most children have a strong sense of **curiosity** so they ask a lot of questions.*

deception *n* a statement or action that makes someone believe something that is not true • *She was very honest and so did not want to participate in the **deception**.* **deceive** *v* to make someone believe something that is not true • *She did not want to **deceive** him, but she could not tell him the truth.*

joke *n* a story or trick that is said or done in order to make people laugh • *When he told the **joke** for the second time, no one laughed.*

occur Ⓐ *v* to happen, often without being planned • *Experts predict that a big earthquake will **occur** in California in the next 50 years.*

profit *n* money that you make when you sell something • *The new business began to make a **profit** in its second year.*

reveal Ⓐ *v* to give someone information that is surprising or that was previously secret • *I will not **reveal** the password for my computer.* **revelation** Ⓐ *n* a piece of information that is discovered although it was intended to be kept secret • *The **revelation** about the actor's secret life came after this death.*

tool *n* a piece of equipment that use with your hands to help you do something • *You need to use a special **tool** to open the box.*

UNIT 3 • READING 1

How Do Advertisements Work?

achieve Ⓐ *v* to succeed in doing something, usually by working hard • *In order to **achieve** our goal, we will all need to work through the weekend.*

athlete *n* a person who is very good at a sport and who competes with others in organized events • *Many high school **athletes** do not continue with their sport after they graduate.* **athletic** *adj* strong, healthy, and good at sports • *The company was looking for strong, healthy, **athletic** people who like to work outside.*

aware Ⓐ *adj* to know about something • *He was so interested in the lecture that he was not* ***aware*** *that two hours had passed.* **awareness** Ⓐ *n* the mental state of knowing about something • *This newspaper article with increase public* ***awareness*** *of the problem.*

customer *n* a person who buys things • *Yesterday only five* ***customers*** *came into the store and none of them bought anything.*

direct *adj* saying clearly and honestly what you think • *It is usually a good idea to be* ***direct*** *when you have something difficult to say.* **directness** *n* the quality of being clear and honest in your speech and behavior • *His* ***directness*** *surprised everyone; they were expecting someone quiet and shy.*

effective *adj* successful or achieving the result that you want • *This medicine is very* ***effective*** *so you should feel better very quickly.*

emotional *adj* showing strong feelings or making people have strong feelings • *People often feel very* ***emotional*** *when they read the ending of the book.* **emotion** *n* a strong feeling, such as love or anger • *It is important to control your* ***emotions*** *when you are in a dangerous situation.*

encourage *v* to make someone more likely to do something • *I hope you* ***encourage*** *your friends and family to visit Puerto Rico. It is a wonderful place!*

envious *adj* wishing you had what someone else has • *He was* ***envious*** *of other people who were more successful.* **envy** *n* the feeling that you wish you had something that someone else has • *I still feel* ***envy*** *when I think of my rich school classmates.*

figure *n* a number that expresses an amount • *I hope we can agree on a* ***figure*** *for the sale of the car.*

goal Ⓐ *n* something that you want to get or achieve • *The* ***goal*** *of the program is make sure every student is ready for college.*

principle Ⓐ *n* a basic idea or rule for how something works • *To understand how a plane flies, you must understand the* ***principles*** *of physics.*

rational Ⓐ *adj* based on facts and not affected by emotions • *Even* ***rational*** *people sometimes make foolish decisions.*

UNIT 3 • READING 2

The Psychology of Price

anchor *n* the first piece of information a person gets about something that sets a standard used to judge other information; or, a heavy object that is dropped in the water to keep a boat from moving • *They dropped the* ***anchor*** *near an island and went swimming near the boat.*

bargain *n* something sold for a price that is lower than usual or lower than its value • *This dress was 60 percent lower than the original price—a real* ***bargain****!*

cross out *v* to draw a line through something you have written, usually because it is wrong • *I am going to* ***cross out*** *my first answer and write the correct one above it.*

design Ⓐ *v* to make or draw plans for something • *A famous architect will* ***design*** *the new museum building.*

effect *n* a change, reaction, or result that is caused by something else • *The weather will not have any* ***effect*** *on our plans.*

fundamental Ⓐ *adj* relating to the most important or main part of something • *The* ***fundamental*** *idea behind our program is that every human being is important.*

item Ⓐ *n* one thing in a set or on a list • *There were seven* ***items*** *on her shopping list.*

menu *n* a list of food and drinks that you can order in a restaurant • *Everything on this* ***menu*** *looks great, but I think I will order the chicken.*

profitable *adj* making or likely to make a profit • *In order to be* ***profitable****, a business must make more money than it spends.*

reduce *v* to make something less • *You should* ***reduce*** *the temperature so the food will not burn.*

sale *n* a time when a store sells goods at a lower price than usual • *Let's wait until there is a* ***sale*** *so we can save money.*

sign *n* a symbol or message in a public place that gives information • *The* ***sign*** *says the store is open from ten until six o'clock.*

symbol Ⓐ *n* a sign or object that is used to represent something else • *The* ***heart*** *is a symbol of love.*

tag *n* a small piece of paper or plastic with information on it that is fixed to something • *The* ***tag*** *inside of the shirt explains the best way to wash it.*

trick *n* an effective way of doing something • *The* ***trick*** *to opening the door is to push and turn at the same time.*

value *n* how much money something could be sold for • *The* ***value*** *of this house has increased in the last ten years.*

UNIT 3 • READING 3

Guerrilla Marketing

community Ⓐ *n* the people who live in particular area • *Everyone in* ***community*** *is worried about the increase in crime here.*

give away *v* to give something to someone without asking for money • *He* ***gave away*** *all of his books and furniture when he moved to a new city.*

hug *v* to put your arms around someone, usually as an expression of affection • *He always* ***hugs*** *his children before they go to sleep.*

lack *n* not having something, or not having enough of something • ***Lack*** *of rain has been a big problem this summer; everything is very dry.*

method Ⓐ *n* a way of doing something, often one that involves a system or plan • *There are many different* ***methods*** *for cooking rice.*

military Ⓐ *n* the armed forces — the army, navy, or air force — of a country • *Many countries require young men to serve in the* ***military****.*

mob *n* a large group of people that is often violent or not organized • *An angry **mob** burned cars and buildings last night.*

perform *v* to entertain people by singing, dancing, etc. • *The schoolchildren will **perform** a play for the holiday.*

population *n* all the people living in a particular area • *The **population** of Karachi is growing very quickly.*

post *v* to make information known to the public, or to put it on the Internet so other people can see it • *The government will **post** information about the new program on the Internet.*

professional Ⓐ *n* a person who has a job that needs skill, education, or training • *Today, there are many jobs available for health **professionals**.*

promote Ⓐ *v* to advertise something • *The company plans to **promote** its new product on television and the Internet.*

regular *adj* usual or normal • *My **regular** lunch is just a salad, but today I among going to have pizza.*

share *v* to use, experience, or enjoy something with others • *Let's **share** this exciting news with everyone else!*

similar Ⓐ *adj* looking or being almost the same, although not exactly the same • *These two pictures look very **similar**, but there are some small differences.*

strategy Ⓐ *n* a plan you use to achieve something • *We need to decide on a new business **strategy** because the one we are using now is not working.*

UNIT 4 • READING 1

Taste – The Least Understood Sense

aspect Ⓐ *n* one part of a subject, situation, etc. • *There is one **aspect** of this project that I do not understand.*

bump *n* a round, raised area on a surface • *He hit his head on the door and now he has a big **bump**.*

cell *n* the smallest living part of an animal or a plant • *There are 37 trillion **cells** in the human body.*

complex Ⓐ *adj* having a lot of different but connected parts in a way that is difficult to understand • *This is a very **complex** problem so it will take some time to solve it.*

dissolve *v* to make a solid thing become part of a liquid • *Salt and sugar will **dissolve** in water.*

distinct Ⓐ *adj* different and separate • *You can see two **distinct** colors on the bird's wings.*

essential *adj* very important and necessary • *Water is **essential** for human life.*

identify Ⓐ *v* to find and recognize someone or something and say who or what it is • *We found a snake that we cannot **identify**.*

message *n* a short piece of information that is sent somewhere • *I sent a **message** to him yesterday but he has not answered.*

perception Ⓐ *n* the ability to notice something • *The game of tennis requires excellent visual **perception**.*

protein *n* food such as meat, cheese, fish, or eggs that is necessary for the body to grow and be strong • *Milk has a lot of **protein**—about eight grams in one glass.*

role Ⓐ *n* the job someone or something has in a particular situation • *What you eat plays an important **role** in your health.*

saliva *n* the liquid that is made in your mouth • *Your **saliva** helps to keep your mouth wet.*

signal *n* a set of energy waves that carry a sound, picture, or other information • *Your eyes and ears send **signals** to your brain, and then your brain sends signals to your muscles.*

survival Ⓐ *n* the fact of continuing to live or to exist • *The **survival** of early humans depended on their ability to find and preserve food,*

vitamin *n* one of a group of natural substances in food that you need to be healthy • *Fruits and vegetables contain many important **vitamins**.*

UNIT 4 • READING 2

Taste and Color

appetite *n* the feeling that makes you want to eat • *After I swim, I always have a big **appetite**.*

attractive *adj* beautiful or pleasant to look at • *The hotel has a beautiful view of the ocean and the rooms are also very **attractive**.*

determine *v* to find out the facts or truth about something • *Officials are trying to **determine** the cause of the fire.* **determination** *n* the process of finding something out • *Experts will make a **determination** of the value of the painting.*

display Ⓐ *n* a collection of things arranged for people to look at • *The museum has is a **display** of items from ancient Egypt* **display** Ⓐ *v* to show something or a collection of things for people to see • *She is going to **display** her paintings at the community center.*

expectation *n* the feeling or belief that something will happen • *We began this project with the **expectation** that we could finish it in six months.* **expect** *v* to think that something will happen • *We **expect** the package to arrive by tomorrow.*

major Ⓐ *adj* more important or more serious than other things or people of a similar type • *Spanish is the **major** language of most South American countries.*

normal Ⓐ *adj* usual, ordinary, and expected • *It is **normal** to cry when you are very sad.*

packaging *n* the paper, box, etc., that something is inside • *There is so much **packaging**; I can't find what is inside the box!*

reaction Ⓐ *n* something you say, feel, or do because of something that has happened • *When you touch something very hot, the usual **reaction** is to pull your hand away.*

reject Ⓐ *v* to refuse to accept or agree with something • *If the university **rejects** his application, he will work for another year.* **rejection** Ⓐ *n* the act of refusing to accept or agree with something • *I applied for the job, but I received a letter of **rejection** from the company.*

respond Ⓐ *v* to say or do something as an answer or reaction to something • *The teacher asked a question and waited for the children to* ***respond***. **response** Ⓐ *n* something said or done as a reaction to something that has been said or done • *There has been a very positive* ***response*** *to the new movie.*

rotten *adj* something that is old and no longer good • *If you leave the bananas for too long, they will all be* ***rotten***.

vision Ⓐ *n* the ability to see • *His* ***vision*** *was getting worse so he had to get glasses.*

UNIT 4 • READING 3

Why Do Some People Hate Broccoli?

adult Ⓐ *n* a person who has finished growing and is now not a child • *At the party,* ***adults*** *sat at one table and children sat at another table.*

cautious *adj* taking care to avoid risks or danger • *He is very* ***cautious*** *in his business and does not like to take any risks.*

combination *n* a mixture of different people or things • *The food at the restaurant is a* ***combination*** *of French and Mexican flavors.*

competitive *adj* wanting to win or to be more successful than other people • *She is very* ***competitive*** *and becomes angry when she does not win.*

consistent Ⓐ *adj* always happening or behaving in a similar, usually positive, way • *The temperature in Bogotá is very* ***consistent****—about 68 degrees every day.*

criticize *v* to say that something or someone is bad • *It is important to be able to learn when other people* ***criticize*** *your work.*

decline Ⓐ *v* to become less in amount, importance, quality, or strength • *The price of oil is expected to* ***decline*** *this year.*

gene *n* a part of a cell that is passed on from parent to child and that controls particular characteristics • ***Genes*** *determine characteristics like eye and hair color.*

individual Ⓐ *n* a single person or thing, especially when compared to the group or set to which it belongs • *There are two prices, one for groups and one for* ***individuals***.

personality *n* the way you are as a person • *We have very similar* ***personalities*** *so we never fight.*

pregnant *adj* expecting a baby • *When a woman is* ***pregnant****, she needs to be careful about what she eats and drinks.*

require Ⓐ *v* to need or demand something • *Opening this door* ***requires*** *a lot of strength,*

risk *n* danger, or the possibility that something bad might happen • *During the summer, the* ***risk*** *of forest fires is higher.*

sensitive *adj* easily affected by things in the environment • *She is very* ***sensitive*** *to noise, so she closes all the windows at night.*

specific *adj* used to refer to a particular thing and not something general • *I asked you to meet with me for a* ***specific*** *reason.*

variation Ⓐ *n* a difference in amount or quality • *There is a lot of* ***variation*** *in color and size among the fish.*

UNIT 5 • READING 1

Oceans – An Economic Resource

apart *adv* separated by a space or period of time • *Two buses arrived, just a few minutes* ***apart***.

century *n* a period of 100 years, especially used in giving dates • *My grandfather was born a* ***century*** *ago.*

civilization *n* human society and all its social organizations • *The timeline for western* ***civilization*** *began about 2500 years ago.*

cotton *n* a plant that produces a soft, white substance used for making thread and cloth • *I like to wear* ***cotton*** *clothing in the summer because it is very cool.*

dramatically Ⓐ *adv* very suddenly or noticeably • *This year, the winter was* ***dramatically*** *colder than the year before.*

goods *n pl* items that are made to be sold • *The company buys* ***goods*** *from China and Korea.*

maritime *adj* relating to ships or sea travel • *During the eighteenth century, Great Britain was leader in* ***maritime*** *trade.*

massive *adj* very big • *There is a* ***massive*** *storm coming, with strong wind and heavy rain.*

necessity *n* something you need • *If you visit Chicago in winter, a warm coat is a* ***necessity***.

oxygen *n* a gas that is in the air and that humans and animals need to live • *Water is made of* ***oxygen*** *and hydrogen atoms.*

period Ⓐ *n* a length of time • *There was a* ***period*** *of economic decline before World War II.*

quarter *n* one of four equal parts • *A* ***quarter*** *of my pay goes to taxes.*

rapidly *adv* happening or moving very quickly • *Technology changes so* ***rapidly****; it is difficult to know what is coming next.*

recover Ⓐ *v* to improve after a period of difficulty or trouble • *The economy is beginning to* ***recover*** *after five difficult years.*

resource Ⓐ *n* something that a country, person, or organization has that they can use • *Brazil has many natural* ***resources****, including gold, iron, and wood.*

species *n* a group of animals or plants that share similar characteristics • *There are about ten thousand different* ***species*** *of birds in the world.*

UNIT 5 • READING 2

The Role of Oceans in Weather and Climate

absorb *v* to take in a liquid, gas, or chemical *This cloth can* ***absorb*** *a lot of water.* • **absorption** *n* the process by which a substance or object takes in a liquid, gas, etc., and makes it part of itself • *This equipment can measure the* ***absorption*** *of water and* CO_2.

consequence Ⓐ *n* the result of an action or situation, especially a bad result • *Forest fires are usually a* ***consequence*** *of human activity.*

constantly Ⓐ *adv* happening a lot or all the time • *We are* ***constantly*** *trying to improve our service to customers.*

cycle Ⓐ *n* a series of events that happen in a particular order and are often repeated • *The seasons come and go in a yearly* ***cycle****.*

distribute Ⓐ *v* to give something out to people or places • *Wind* ***distributes*** *the seeds from the trees.* **distribution** *n* the activity or work of supplying something or giving something out to people • *The new manager is in charge of* ***distribution*** *of our products to stores.*

energy Ⓐ *n* the power that comes from the sun, electricity, gas, etc. • *We get* ***energy*** *from oil but also from the sun and wind.* **energize** *v* to make something more active • *The good news will* ***energize*** *everyone and help us keep working.*

evaporate *v* to cause a liquid to change into a gas or vapor • *The rain on the ground will* ***evaporate*** *when the sun comes out.* **evaporation** *n* the process of changing from a liquid to a gas • ***Evaporation*** *occurs more quickly when it is hot.*

flood *n* a large amount of water covering an area that is usually dry • *Heavy rain has caused* ***floods*** *all over the country.*

global *adj* relating to the whole world • ***Global*** *trade depends on a healthy economy.*

permanent *adj* continuing forever or for a long time • *I have worked at many places for a short time, but now I am looking for a more* ***permanent*** *position.*

reverse Ⓐ *v* to change a situation or change the order of things so that it becomes the opposite • *Scientist don't believe we can* ***reverse*** *the process of global warming.* **reversal** Ⓐ *n* a change to the opposite of something • *In the last five years, there has been a* ***reversal*** *in the population decline.*

solar *adj* relating to, or involving the sun • ***Solar*** *energy has become much less expensive in recent years.*

violent *adj* sudden and causing great damage or hurt • *There was a* ***violent*** *explosion at the chemical factory.*

UNIT 5 • READING 3

The Health of Our Oceans

acidity *n* the amount of acid that is in a substance • *Lemons are high in* ***acidity****.*

destructive *adj* causing a lot of damage • *The* ***destructive*** *storm tore the roof off our house.*

disrupt *v* to interrupt something and stop it continuing in its usual way • *I don't want any phone calls or visitors to* ***disrupt*** *the meeting.*

dolphin *n* a sea mammal that looks like a large, grey fish with a pointed mouth • *From the ship, we could see the* ***dolphins*** *swimming in the water.*

estimate Ⓐ *v* to guess the cost, size, value, etc., of something • *I* ***estimate*** *that the bicycle will cost about $150.*

jellyfish *n* a sea animal with a clear body with tentacles that can sting • *Watch out for all of the* ***jellyfish*** *in the ocean today.*

lobster *n* a sea animal that has a shell covering on its body, two large claws, and eight legs • ***Lobster*** *is very expensive so we only eat it on my birthday.*

mammal *n* an animal that gives birth to babies, not eggs, and feeds its babies on milk from its body • *Human beings, monkeys, and dogs are all* ***mammals****.*

organism *n* a living thing • *Higher global temperatures can have a negative effect on many different* ***organisms****.*

pollution *n* damage caused to water, air, etc., by harmful substances or waste • *Cars that use gasoline are one of the major causes of air* ***pollution****.*

shellfish *n* sea creatures that live in shells and are eaten as food • *Shrimp, crab, and lobster are all types of* ***shellfish****.*

shrimp *n* a small, pink, sea animal that you can eat, with a curved body and shell • *Fried* ***shrimp*** *is his favorite thing on the menu.*

source Ⓐ *n* where something comes from • *Cheese is a good* ***source*** *of protein.*

toxic *adj* poisonous • ***Toxic*** *chemicals are killing many fish and other animals that live in the ocean.*

volume Ⓐ *n* the amount of something, especially when the amount is large • *The* ***volume*** *of traffic on the roads continues to grow.*

whale *n* a very large sea animal that looks like a large fish but it breathes air through a hole at the top of its head • *Some* ***whales*** *weigh more than 150 tons (150,000 kilograms).*

UNIT 6 • READING 1

Scribes – A Tradition

alive *adj* continuing to exist • *Although the river is covered with ice, the fish below are still* ***alive****.*

cook *n* someone who prepares food • *The school* ***cook*** *makes lunch for the children every day.*

document Ⓐ *n* a piece of paper with official information on it • *This* ***document*** *shows information about where and when he was born.*

especially *adv* very; particularly • *There is a lot of coal in Brazil,* ***especially*** *in the south of the country.*

fill out *v* to give written information, especially by completing a form • *Before his interview, he had to* ***fill out*** *three forms.*

frequent *adj* happening often • *The patient said she has* ***frequent*** *headaches — more than two a week.*

function Ⓐ *n* the purpose or duty that is part of someone's job • *The* ***function*** *of heart is to move blood around the body.*

immigrant Ⓐ *n* a person who comes to live in a different country • *Many* ***immigrants*** *from Somalia live in this area.*

literacy *n* the ability to read and write • ***Literacy*** *is very high in South Korea; more than 97 percent of the population can read and write.*

mechanical *adj* relating to or operated by machines • *The accident occurred as a result of* ***mechanical*** *problems on the train.*

post office *n* a place where you can buy stamps and send letters and packages • *She mailed the package at the* ***post office***.

record *n* information that is written on paper or stored on a computer so that it can be used in the future • *He keeps of* ***record*** *of all the money that he spends.*

technology Ⓐ *n* a particular way in which science is used for practical purposes • ***Technology*** *has changed the way we communicate.*

text message *n* a written message sent from one cell phone to another • *He sent a* ***text message*** *to say he was arriving late.*

tradition Ⓐ *n* a custom or way of behaving that continued for a long time in a group of people or a society • *It is a community* ***tradition*** *to share food during the holiday.*

valuable *adj* very useful • *Although our business was not successful, the experience was* ***valuable***.

UNIT 6 • READING 2

Communication in Natural Disasters

agency *n* a government department or international organization • *The function of this* ***agency*** *to assist people who have nowhere to live.*

aid Ⓐ *n* money, food, or equipment that is given to help a country or a group of people • *Many countries sent* ***aid***, *mostly food and blankets, to Nepal after the earthquake.*

communicate Ⓐ *v* to share information with others by speaking, writing, moving your body, or other signals • *People who cannot hear use their hands to* ***communicate***. **communication** *n* the process by which messages or information is sent from one place or person to another • *Text messages became a popular form of* ***communication*** *in the beginning of the twenty-first century.*

damage *n* harm or injury • *Yesterday's floods caused a lot of* ***damage*** *to homes and businesses.* **damage** *v* to harm or break something • *Drinking a lot of juice and soft drinks can* ***damage*** *your teeth.*

earthquake *n* a sudden movement of the Earth's surface, often causing damage • ***Earthquakes*** *occur frequently in Chile, China, and Japan.*

equipment Ⓐ *n* a tool or object used for a particular activity or purpose •.*They used special* ***equipment*** *for climbing the tall mountain.* **equip** Ⓐ *v* to give someone with the skills or tools they need to do a particular thing • *We have borrowed enough money to build and* ***equip*** *a new factory.*

information *n* facts about a situation, person, event, etc. *The police are asking for* ***information*** *about the two men in the photograph.* • **inform** *v* to tell someone about something • *We will* ***inform*** *you about the test results next week.*

panic *n* a sudden strong feeling of worry or fear that makes you unable to think or behave calmly • *The loud sound of the guns caused* ***panic*** *and everyone began to run.*

request *n* a question which politely or officially asks for something • *We will respond to your* ***request*** *for information within one week.* **request** *v* to politely or officially ask for something • *Students can* ***request*** *books from other libraries.*

rumor *n* a statement that a lot of people are talking about although they do not know if it is true • *There is a* ***rumor*** *that the President made a secret trip last week, but no one really knows.*

supply *n* the amount of something that is ready to be used • *The* ***supply*** *of medicine in the country is dangerously low.*

victim *n* a person who has suffered from a disaster, illness, or violence • *Many* ***victims*** *of the disaster lost everything.*

volunteer Ⓐ *n* a person who does work for no pay in order to help others • *She worked as a* ***volunteer*** *in a hospital on weekends.*

UNIT 6 • READING 3

How Do Social Networks Affect Our Daily Lives?

anonymously *adv* doing something without giving your name. • *The money was given* ***anonymously***, *so we cannot thank anyone for it.*

billion *number* 1,000,000,000 • *More than a* ***billion*** *people in the world are hungry.*

concerned *adj* worried • *I am* ***concerned*** *about your health. You don't look well.*

depressed Ⓐ *adj* very unhappy, often for a long time • *After his wife's death, he became very* ***depressed***.

enormous Ⓐ *adj* extremely large • *There is an* ***enormous*** *amount of interest in the new smartphone.*

expand Ⓐ *v* to increase in size or amount • *Next year the company will* ***expand*** *to Canada and Mexico.*

interact Ⓐ *v* to talk and do things with other people • *Some people prefer to* ***interact*** *on the telephone or online.*

magnify *v* to make something look larger or more important • *The new law will* ***magnify*** *the problems we already have.*

make fun of *phr v* to make a joke about someone or something in an unkind way • *The little boy always cries when other children* ***make fun of*** *him.*

network Ⓐ *n* a group of people who know each other, or computers that are connected together so they can share information • *All of the computers in the office are connected in a* ***network***.

offline *adj* not connected to the Internet • *I was* ***offline***, *so I did not receive the email message.*

reflect *v* to show or be a sign of something • *Our actions usually* ***reflect*** *what we are feeling.*

site Ⓐ *n* an area on the Internet where information about a particular subject, organization, etc., can be found • *Several* ***sites*** *can give you information about places to see in Kyoto.*

substitute Ⓐ *n* someone or something that is used instead of another person or thing • *You can use milk as a* ***substitute*** *for cream.*

team Ⓐ *n* a group of people who play a sport together against another group of players • *He plays on the basketball* ***team*** *at his school.*

vacation *n* a period of time when you are not at home but are staying somewhere else for enjoyment • *This year we plan to go to Croatia on our summer* ***vacation****.*

UNIT 7 • READING 1

The History of Currency

banknote *n* a piece of paper money • *In the United States, all the* ***banknotes*** *are green.*

barter *v* to exchange goods or services for other things or services, without using money • *Some communities use a* ***barter*** *system, in which people exchange bread for fish, for example.*

convenient *adj* easy to use • *Driving my car is more* ***convenient*** *than taking the bus.*

credit card *n* a small plastic card that you can use to buy something and pay for it later • *She did not have enough money with her so she paid with a* ***credit card****.*

currency Ⓐ *n* the units of money used in a particular country • *The official* ***currency*** *in much of Europe is the euro.*

dominant Ⓐ *adj* main or most important • *English is the* ***dominant*** *language of the business world.*

economic Ⓐ *adj* relating to trade, industry, and money • *The* ***economic*** *situation is improving so people in the country are spending more money.*

electronically *adj* using the Internet or another electronic communication system • *I can pay all of my bills* ***electronically*** *so I never have to mail them.*

financial Ⓐ *adj* relating to money or how money is managed • ***Financial*** *experts can give you advice about the best way to save your money.*

forward *adj* something is making good progress • *The project is moving* ***forward*** *quickly and will be finished soon.*

key *adj* very important in influencing or achieving something • *For the test, just study the* ***key*** *ideas and forget about the details.*

medium of exchange *n* something that is used to pay for goods or services • *Money is one* ***medium of exchange****; gold is another.*

rare *adj* not common; unusual • *White tiger are very* ***rare****; there are only 200 in the world.*

resolve Ⓐ *v* to solve or end a problem or difficulty • *We need to* ***resolve*** *this problem before we can move to the next step.*

somewhat Ⓐ *adv* slightly • *It is* ***somewhat*** *colder today than yesterday so I am wearing a sweater.*

wallet *n* a small, flat container for paper money and credit cards • *I left my* ***wallet*** *at home so I have no money with me.*

UNIT 7 • READING 2

Counterfeit Money

apparent Ⓐ *adj* able to be seen or understood • *His happiness was* ***apparent*** *from the smile on his face.*

cashier *n* someone whose job is to receive and pay out money in a store, bank, etc. • *After I finished shopping, I went to the* ***cashier*** *and paid for everything.*

cloth *n* material made from cotton, wool, etc., and often used to make clothes • *She bought two yards (1.83 meters) of* ***cloth*** *to make a dress.*

counterfeit *adj* made to look like the real thing in order to trick people • *The police said that the store was selling* ***counterfeit*** *watches.*

extremely *adv* very, or much more than usual • *The weather has been* ***extremely*** *cold so everyone is staying inside.*

fake *adj* not real, but made to look or seem real • *The real painting was worth millions of dollars, but the* ***fake*** *painting was worth nothing.*

feature Ⓐ *n* an important part of something • *This smart phone has several new and useful* ***features****.*

handle *v* to touch, hold, or pick up something with your hands • *If you pick up these objects or* ***handle*** *them, you might break them.*

microscope *n* a piece of scientific equipment that uses lenses to make very small objects look bigger • *If you look at it under a* ***microscope,*** *you can see a lot of the small details.*

purchase Ⓐ *n* something that you buy • *She paid for her* ***purchases*** *with a credit card.*

regional Ⓐ *adj* relating to a particular area in a country • *There are* ***regional*** *differences in how people talk.*

scanner *n* a piece of equipment that copies words or pictures from paper into a computer • *I can make an electronic copy of this document with my* ***scanner****.*

slightly *adv* a little • *My sister is* ***slightly*** *taller than me — only half an inch (1.25 centimeters).*

treasury *n* the government department that controls a country's money supply and economy • *The* ***treasury*** *department is responsible for printing money.*

three-dimensional *adj* having length, depth, and height • *New technology makes the people in the movie seem* ***three-dimensional****.*

ultraviolet *adj* light that cannot be seen by humans • ***Ultraviolet*** *light allows you to see things you cannot usually see, but it can also damage your skin.*

UNIT 7 • READING 3

Money, Art, and Identity

appropriate Ⓐ *adj* suitable or right for a particular situation or person • *This film is for adults; it is not* ***appropriate*** *for young children.*

architecture *n* the design and style of buildings • *The **architecture** of this building has features from ancient Greece.*

colony *n* a country or area controlled in an official, political way by a more powerful country • *The United Kingdom had **colonies** all over the world, including Asia to Africa.* **colonize** *v* to send people to live in and govern another country • *In the science-fiction movie, people from Earth **colonize** other planets.*

hero *n* someone who does something brave or good that people respect or admire them for • *Everyone is calling him a **hero** because he saved two children in a fire.*

highlight Ⓐ *v* to emphasize something or make people notice something You should ***highlight*** important facts and ideas when you are reading your textbook. • **highlight** Ⓐ *n* the best or most important part of something • *Visiting Egypt was the **highlight** of our trip, especially the pyramids.*

gate *n* the part of a fence or outside wall that opens and closes like a door • *You must ring the bell at the **gate** in order to enter.*

landmark *n* a building or structure that you can easily recognize, especially one that helps you know where you are • *The most famous **landmark** in China is the Great Wall.*

refinery *n* a factory where substances, such as sugar, oil, etc. are made pure • *The largest oil **refinery** in the world is in India.* **refine** Ⓐ *v* to improve an idea, method, system, etc., by making small changes • *We need to **refine** our ideas before we present them to our director.*

replace *v* to start using another thing or person instead of the one that you were using • *Some people wonder if the metric system will ever **replace** the old system of measurement in the United States.* **replacement** *n* the thing or person that replaces something or someone • *One of the teachers left her job last week so we need to find a **replacement**.*

responsible *adj* to be the person or organization whose duty is to deal with someone or something • *You will be **responsible** for the business while I am away.*

structure Ⓐ *n* a building or something that has been built • *Only a few **structures** were still standing after the earthquake.* **structure** Ⓐ *v* to arrange something in an organized way • *We are going to **structure** our organization very differently in the future.*

tower *n* a very tall, narrow building, or part of a building • *The church has a tall **tower** with a bell.*

tropical *adj* from or in the hottest parts of the world • ***Tropical** areas usually have hot, wet weather for most of the year.*

UNIT 8 • READING 1

Who Benefits from Space Exploration?

adapt Ⓐ *v* to change something so that it is suitable for a different use or situation • *They are going to **adapt** the book and make it into a movie.*

analyze Ⓐ *v* to examine the details of something carefully in order to understand or explain it • *We need to **analyze** the situation carefully before we make any decision.*

crack *n* a line on the surface of something that is damaged • *I have a **crack** in my tooth so I am going to the dentist this morning.*

crystal *n* a clear rock that forms in nature • *Sugar and salt are both in the form of a **crystal**.*

fascinate *v* to interest someone a lot • *He likes to visit ancient places because history **fascinates** him.*

gravity *n* the force that pulls objects toward a planet or that makes objects fall to the ground • *On earth the force of **gravity** is stronger than it is on the moon.*

investigate Ⓐ *v* to try to discover all the facts about something, especially a crime or accident • *Officials are going to **investigate** the cause of the fire.*

mineral *n* a valuable or useful substance that is dug out of the ground • *Quartz is one of the most common **minerals** on Earth.*

planet *n* a large, round object in space that moves around the sun or another star • *Earth is one of eight **planets** that go around the sun*

program *n* an officially organized system of activities that help people achieve something • *The children go to a **program** after school where they play games a do homework.*

project Ⓐ *n* a carefully planned piece of work that has a particular purpose • *She has been working on a science **project** for weeks.*

survey Ⓐ *n* a set of questions that you ask a large number of people so you can learn about their opinions • *We did a **survey** of our students to find out their opinions.*

technique Ⓐ *n* a particular or special way of doing something • *Doctors are using a new **technique** with patients who have memory problems.*

tire *n* a thick, round piece of rubber filled with air, that fits around a wheel • *It is dangerous to drive if the **tires** on your car are old and worn.*

vehicle Ⓐ *n* something such as a car or bus that takes people from one place to another, especially using roads • *You need to take a different driving test for each kind of **vehicle**: cars, trucks, and buses.*

whereas Ⓐ *conj* compared with the fact that • *Job opportunities for graduates with engineering degrees are increasing, **whereas** the number of positions for arts graduates is going down.*

UNIT 8 • READING 2

Living in Space

bacteria *n pl* very small living things that sometimes cause disease • *Different kinds of **bacteria** live on our skin and in our mouths.*

challenge Ⓐ *n* something that is difficult and that tests someone's ability or determination v • *Although it was a* ***challenge****, he was able to finish his university studies in less than three years.*

chef *n* a skilled and trained cook who usually works in a restaurant or hotel • *The* ***chef*** *at the hotel restaurant is famous all over the world.*

float *v* to stay in the air, or move gently through the air; also to stay on the surface of a liquid instead of sinking • *If you lie flat, you can* ***float*** *on the water.*

lie down *v* to move into a position in which your body is flat, usually in order to sleep or rest • *I am going to* ***lie down*** *and rest for a while.*

practical *adj* suitable or useful for a situation which may involve some difficulty • *Studying nursing is very* ***practical*** *because there are lots of jobs.*

resemble *v* to look like or be like someone or something • *The two sisters* ***resemble*** *each other so much that some people think they are twins.*

rinse *v* to wash something in clean water in order to remove dirt or soap • *You should* ***rinse*** *fruit and vegetables before you eat them.*

spit *v* to force out the liquid in your mouth • *If you don't like the taste, you can* ***spit*** *it out.*

squeeze *v* to press something firmly; also to press a lemon, orange, etc. to get juice from it • *I am going to* ***squeeze*** *these oranges to make juice.*

sunrise *n* the time when the sun appears in the morning and the sky becomes light • *The time of* ***sunrise*** *changes every day here.*

terrible *adj* very bad, of low quality, or unpleasant • *This restaurant is* ***terrible****; I am never coming back.*

threat *n* someone or something that is likely to cause harm or damage • *Global warming is a* ***threat*** *to many species of plants and animals.*

toothpaste *n* a substance that you use to clean your teeth • *He forgot to take* ***toothpaste*** *on his trip so he got some at the hotel.*

tie *v* to fasten something with string, rope, etc. • *The boy bent down to* ***tie*** *his shoes.*

tube *n* a long, thin container for a soft substance, that you press to get the substance out • *He squeezed a small amount of medicine out of the* ***tube*** *and put it on his skin.*

UNIT 8 • READING 3

Health Effects of Living in Space

accustomed *adj* if you are accustomed to something, you have experienced it often enough for it to seem normal to you • *The student from Venezuela was not* ***accustomed*** *to this cold weather.*

adjust Ⓐ *v* to change something slightly so that it works better, fits better, or is more suitable • *You need to* ***adjust*** *the mirror so you can see the cars behind you.* **adjustment** Ⓐ *n* a slight change that you make to something so that it works better, fits better, or is more suitable • *The does not quite fit so we will need to make an* ***adjustment****.*

balance *n* the state of having your weight spread in such a way that you do not fall over • *He lost his* ***balance*** *and fell on the ice.* **balance** *v* to be in a position where you will not fall to either side, or to put something in this position • *Some people can* ***balance*** *heavy things, such as books or water, on their heads when they walk.*

cancer *n* a serious disease that is caused when cells in the body grow in a way that is uncontrolled and not normal • *After many years of smoking, he developed* ***cancer*** *in his lungs.*

circulatory *adj* relating to the system that moves blood through the body and that includes the heart, arteries, and veins • *Exercise can improve the health of your heart and the rest of your* ***circulatory*** *system.*

contribute Ⓐ *v* to help or cause something to happen; also to give something, especially money, in order to provide or achieve something together with other people • *Many different factors, including genes and diet,* ***contribute*** *to your health.* **contribution** Ⓐ *n* something that you do to help produce or develop something, or to help make something successful • *Everyone has made an important* ***contribution*** *to the success of the project.*

effortless *adj* achieved without a • any special or obvious effort • *Although dancers were working hard, their movements looked* ***effortless****.*

fluid *n* a liquid • *You should drink plenty of* ***fluids*** *when it is hot outside.*

long-term *adj* continuing a long time into the future • *After you finish your studies, what are your* ***long-term*** *plans?*

monitor Ⓐ *v* to watch something carefully and record the results. • *Doctors will* ***monitor*** *the patient until she is out of danger.* **monitor** Ⓐ *n* a machine, often in a hospital, that measures something such as the rate that your heart beats • *The* ***monitor*** *can measure your heart and breathing rate.*

muscle *n* one of many pieces of tissue in the body that are connected to bones and which produce movement by becoming longer or shorter • *I did a lot of exercise so my* ***muscles*** *are very tired and sore.*

radiation *n* energy from heat or light that you cannot see; often refers to the harmful energy of sunlight, a nuclear reaction, etc. that in large amounts can be very dangerous • ***Radiation*** *from the sun keeps our planet warm.* **radiate** *v* to send out heat or light • *Light* ***radiates*** *from the window in the bedroom.*

upset *v* to cause problems for something • *She is crying because the bad news really* ***upset*** *her.*

Index to Key Vocabulary

Words that are part of the Academic Word List are noted with an Ⓐ in this appendix.

Improving Your Reading Speed

Good readers read quickly and understand most of what they read. However, like other skills, reading faster is a skill that requires good technique and practice. One way to practice is to read frequently. Read about topics you are interested in, not just topics from your academic courses. Reading for pleasure will improve your reading speed and understanding.

Another way to practice is to choose a text you have already read and read it again without stopping. Time yourself, record the time, and keep a record of how your reading speed is increasing.

These strategies will help you improve your reading speed:

- Before you read a text, look at the title and any illustrations. Ask yourself, *What is this reading about?* This will help you figure out the general topic of the reading.
- Read words in groups instead of reading every single word. Focus on the most important words in a sentence – usually the nouns, verbs, adjectives, and adverbs.
- Don't pronounce each word as you read. Pronouncing words will slow you down and does not help you to understand the text.
- Don't use a pencil or your finger to point to the words as you read. This will also slow you down.
- Continue reading even if you come to an unfamiliar word. Good readers know that they can skip unfamiliar words as long as they understand the general meaning of the text.

Calculating Your Reading Speed

After you have completed a unit in this book, reread one of the readings. Use your cellphone or your watch to time how long it takes you to complete the reading. Write down the number of minutes and seconds it took you in the chart on the following pages.

You can figure out your reading speed; that is your words per minute (wpm) rate by doing the following calculation:

First, convert the seconds of your reading time to decimals using the table to the right.

Next, divide the number of words per reading by the time it took you to complete the reading. For example, if the reading is 525 words, and it took you 5 minutes 50 seconds, your reading speed is about 90 words per minute (525 ÷ 5.83 = 90).

Record your wpm rate in the chart on the following pages.

Seconds	Decimal
:05	.08
:10	.17
:15	.25
:20	.33
:25	.42
:30	.50
:35	.58
:40	.67
:45	.75
:50	.83
:55	.92

UNIT	READING TITLE	NUMBER OF WORDS IN READING	YOUR READING TIME minutes:seconds 00:00	READING SPEED (WPM)
Unit 1 Human Behavior	Procrastination	613	_____:_____	
	Memory and New Technology	594	_____:_____	
	Lying	766	_____:_____	
Unit 2 Fact or Fiction	Fact or Fiction – Science	627	_____:_____	
	Fact or Fiction – History	611	_____:_____	
	Hoaxes	746	_____:_____	
Unit 3 Marketing	How Do Advertisements Work?	552	_____:_____	
	The Psychology of Price	585	_____:_____	
	Guerrilla Marketing	705	_____:_____	
Unit 4 Taste	Taste – The Least Understood Sense	617	_____:_____	
	Taste and Color	500	_____:_____	
	Why Do Some People Hate Broccoli?	723	_____:_____	

UNIT	READING TITLE	NUMBER OF WORDS IN READING	YOUR READING TIME minutes:seconds 00:00	READING SPEED (WPM)
Unit 5 Oceans	Oceans – An Economic Resource	603	____:____	
	The Role of Oceans in Weather and Climate	666	____:____	
	The Health of Our Oceans	839	____:____	
Unit 6 Communication	Scribes – A Tradition	586	____:____	
	Communication in Natural Disasters	637	____:____	
	How Do Social Networks Affect Our Daily Lives?	736	____:____	
Unit 7 Money	The History of Currency	668	____:____	
	Counterfeit Money	616	____:____	
	Money, Art, and Identity	720	____:____	
Unit 8 Space	Who Benefits from Space Exploration?	547	____:____	
	Living in Space	523	____:____	
	Health Effects of Living in Space	728	____:____	

REFERENCES

UNIT 1, READING 1

Partnoy, Frank. *Wait: The Useful Art of Procrastination*. New York: Public Affairs, 2013. Print.

Perry, John. *The Art of Procrastination: A Guide to Effective Dawdling, Lollygagging, and Postponing*. New York: Workman, 2012. Print.

UNIT 1, READING 2

Sparrow, B., J. Liu, and D. M. Wegner. "Google Effects on Memory: Cognitive Consequences of Having Information at Our Fingertips." *Science* 333.6043 (2011): 776–78. Web.

Vincent, James. "Is Facebook Making Us Forget? Study Shows That Taking Pictures Ruin Memories." *The Independent*. Independent Digital News and Media, 10 Dec. 2013. Web. 29 June 2015.

UNIT 1 SKILLS AND STRATEGIES 2

"Honest Tea." *Honest Tea*. Honest Tea, 19 Aug. 2014. Web. 01 July 2015.

UNIT 1, READING 3

Ariely, Dan. *The (Honest) Truth About Dishonesty: How We Lie to Everyone — Especially Ourselves*. New York: Harper Perennial, 2013. Print.

Lickerman, Alex, MD. "Why We Lie." *Psychology Today*. Sussex Publishers, LLC, 8 Mar. 2010. Web. 29 June 2015.

Rose, Lacey. "Lying Is Good For You." *Forbes*. Forbes Magazine, 24 Oct. 2005. Web. 29 June 2015.

UNIT 2, READING 1

Toothman, Jessika. "10 Completely False 'Facts' Everyone Knows." *HowStuffWorks*. HowStuffWorks.com, 26 Sept. 2012. Web. 29 June 2015.

Vedantam, Shankar. "Persistence of Myths Could Alter Public Policy Approach." *Washington Post*. The Washington Post, 04 Sept. 2007. Web. 29 June 2015.

UNIT 2, READING 2

Smith, Patrick. "12 Common History Myths, Debunked." *BuzzFeed*. N.p., 19 Feb. 2014. Web. 29 June 2015.

Troy, Eric. "CulinaryLore.com." *Marco Polo and His Chinese Pasta: Legend or Fact?* CulinaryLore, 28 Mar. 2012. Web. 29 June 2015.

UNIT 2 SKILLS AND STRATEGIES 4

Barfield, Tom. "Nigerian Scam Emails 'deliberately Implausible'" *The Telegraph*. Telegraph Media Group, 21 June 2012. Web. 01 July 2015.

Furness, Hannah. "One in Ten People Fall Victim to Scams, Investigation Finds." *The Telegraph*. Telegraph Media Group, 16 July 2012. Web. 01 July 2015.

UNIT 2, READING 3

Mydans, Seth. "The Tasaday Revisited: A Hoax or Social Change at Work?" *The New York Times*. The New York Times, 12 May 1986. Web. 30 June 2015.

Pegg, David. "25 Greatest Scientific Hoaxes in History." *List25*.com, 16 July 2012. Web. 30 June 2015.

Radford, By Benjamin. "A Savage Hoax: The Cave Men Who Never Existed." *LiveScience*. TechMedia Network, 25 June 2008. Web. 30 June 2015.

"The Birth of Bigfoot." *Museum of Hoaxes*. Web. 30 June 2015.

UNIT 3, READING 1

Baker, Jenni. "Eurozone Woes Continue to Dampen Global Ad Spend Forecast." *M&M Global*. 1 Oct. 2012. Web. 30 June 2015.

Danesi, Marcel. *Why It Sells: Decoding the Meanings of Brand Names, Logos, Ads, and Other Marketing and Advertising Ploys*. Lanham: Rowman & Littlefield, 2008. Print.

Fowles, Jib. "Advertising's 15 Basic Appeals." *Cyberpat.com*. Web. 30 June 2015.

Gooch, Liz. "Advertisers Seek to Speak to Muslim Consumers." *New York Times*. New York Times, 11 Aug. 2010. Web. 30 June 2015.

Wimbush, Patrice D. "Top Five Appeals That Advertisers Use to Sell a Product." *Houston Chronicle*. Demand Media, n.d. Web. 30 June 2015.

UNIT 3, READING 2

Lindstrom, Martin. "The Psychology Behind The Sweet Spots Of Pricing." *Fast Company*. Mansueto Ventures, LLC, 27 Mar. 2012. Web. 30 June 2015.

O'Reilly, Terry:. "Geography As Branding: An Encore Presentation." *Under The Influence with Terry O'Reilly*. CBC/Radio Canada, 22 Apr. 2015. Web. 30 June 2015.

Poundstone, William. *Priceless: The Myth of Fair Value (and How to Take Advantage of It)*. New York: Hill and Wang, 2010. Print.

Torabi, Farnoosh. "Pricing Psychology: 7 Sneaky Retail Tricks." *CBSNews*. CBS Interactive, 2 May 2011. Web. 30 June 2015.

UNIT 3 SKILLS AND STRATEGIES 6

Shackleton, Lane. "The Orabrush Story: How a Utah Man Used YouTube to Build a Multi-million Dollar Business." *Official Google Blog*. Google, 15 Nov. 2011. Web. 01 July 2015.

UNIT 3, READING 3

Grainger, Jesse. "47 Outrageous Viral Marketing Examples over the Last Decade." *Ignite Social Media*. 28 June 2009. Web. 30 June 2015.

Humbert, Mirko. "20 Creative Guerilla (sic) Marketing Campaigns." *Designer Daily: Graphic and Web Design Blog*. N.p., 02 Mar. 2011. Web. 30 June 2015.

Walker, Rob. "Meet America's Top Guerilla (sic) Marketer." *Fast Company*. Mansueto Ventures, LLC, 01 Nov. 2008. Web. 30 June 2015.

UNIT 4, READING 1

Andrews, Julie D. "What Is Mouthfeel?" *TheBlot Magazine*. 31 Jan. 2014. Web. 30 June 2015.

Parkes, Simon. "The Science of Taste." *BBC News*. BBC, 13 Aug. 2012. Web. 30 June 2015.

"Nervous System — Taste." *BBC News*. BBC, 24 Sept. 2014. Web. 30 June 2015.

UNIT 4, READING 2

Murphy, Cheryl G. "Looks Can Taste Deceiving: How Color Can Affect Taste." *Scientific American*. Scientific American, a Division of Nature America, Inc., 29 Oct. 2013. Web. 30 June 2015.

Poon, Linda. "Tasting With Our Eyes: Why Bright Blue Chicken Looks So Strange." *NPR*. NPR, 16 Apr. 2014. Web. 30 June 2015.

UNIT 4 SKILLS AND STRATEGIES 8

Fleming, Amy. "Are you a 'supertaster'?" *Word of Mouth Blog*. The Guardian, 12 Feb. 2013. Web. 1 July 2015.

Harris, Rob. "Why Do Some Animals Have More Taste Buds?" *Animals*. Demand Media, Web. 01 July 2015.

Hemsley, Susan. "Do Animals Taste the Same Things as Humans?" *Ask an Expert (ABC Science)*. ABC, 12 Aug. 2010. Web. 01 July 2015.

Mauer, Lilli, and Ahmed El-Sohemy. "Prevalence of Cilantro (Coriandrum Sativum) Disliking among Different Ethnocultural Groups." *Flavour*. Biomed Central Ltd., 2 May 2012. Web. 01 July 2015.

UNIT 4, READING 3

Abbasi, Jennifer. "Love of Spicy Food Is Built Into Your Personality." *Popular Science*. 6 Dec. 2012. Web. 30 June 2015.

Albers, Dr. Susan. "Are You a Supertaster? Mindless Eating and Your Taste Buds." *The Huffington Post*. TheHuffingtonPost.com, 17 Nov. 2011. Web. 30 June 2015.

Callaway, Ewen. "Genes Give Africans a Better Sense of Taste." *New Scientist*. Reed Business Information Ltd, 2 Jan. 2009. Web. 30 June 2015.

Jacobson, Rebecca. "The Bitter Taste of Genetics." *PBS*. PBS, 23 Dec. 2010. Web. 30 June 2015.

Nagourney, Eric. "Why Does My Food Have Less Flavor?" *The New York Times*. The New York Times, 05 Dec. 2012. Web. 30 June 2015.

UNIT 5, READING 1

Levitt, Tom. "Overfished and Under-protected: Oceans on the Brink of Catastrophic Collapse." *CNN*. Cable News Network, 27 Mar. 2013. Web. 30 June 2015.

"History of Fishing." *Wikipedia*. Wikimedia Foundation. Web. 30 June 2015.

"The Ocean — National Geographic." *National Geographic*. Web. 30 June 2015.

"The Water Cycle : Feature Articles." *The Water Cycle: Feature Articles*. Web. 30 June 2015.

UNIT 5, READING 2

Stewart, Robert. "The Ocean and Climate." *Our Ocean Planet*. Dept of Oceanography, Texas A&M University, 21 Dec. 2012. Web. 30 June 2015.

"Sea Level Rise — National Geographic." *National Geographic*. Web. 30 June 2015.

"The Role of Ocean Currents in Climate." *PBS LearningMedia*. Web. 30 June 2015.

UNIT 5 SKILLS AND STRATEGIES 10

Astazia, Randy. "11 Islands That Will Vanish When Sea Levels Rise." *Business Insider*. Business Insider, Inc., 12 Oct. 2012. Web. 1 July 2015.

Duff, Mark. "New Plan to 'lift' Sinking Venice." *BBC News*. BBC, 22 Nov. 2005. Web. 01 July 2015.

UNIT 5, READING 3

Allen, Leslie. "The Big Idea: Noisy Ocean." *National Geographic Magazine*. NGM.com. Web. 30 June 2015.

Barry, Carolyn. "Plastic Breaks Down in Ocean, After All — and Fast." *National Geographic*. National Geographic Society, 20 Aug. 2009. Web. 30 June 2015.

Watson Wright, Wendy. "Oceans Could Be 150% More Acidic by 2100." United Nations Educational, Scientific and Cultural Organization, 23 Jan. 2012. Web. 30 June 2015.

"Ocean Acidification — National Geographic." *National Geographic*. Web. 30 June 2015.

"Reviving Our Oceans." *Natural Resources Defense Council*. N.p., 4 Oct. 2011. Web. 30 June 2015.

UNIT 6, READING 1

Duval Smith, Alex. "The Scribe of Bamako." *Magazine Monitor*. BBC News, 13 Feb. 2014. Web. 30 June 2015.

Giridharadas, Anand. "The Ink Fades on a Profession as India Modernizes." *The New York Times*. The New York Times, 25 Dec. 2007. Web. 30 June 2015.

Tracy, William. "Scribe." *Saudi Aramco World*. Web. 30 June 2015.

Wing, Linda. "Wong Chong Mun: Hero to His Son." *Angel Island Immigration Station Foundation*. Web. 30 June 2015.

UNIT 6, READING 2

Bowers, Andy. "Danah Boyd Discusses It's Complicated." *Slate.com*. 27 Feb. 2014. Web. 30 June 2015.

Hampton, Keith. "Social Media as Community." *The New York Times*. 18 June 2012. Web. 30 June 2015.

Hampton, Keith, Lauren Sessions Goulet, Lee Rainie, and Kristin Purcell. "Social Networking Sites and Our Lives." *Pew Research Center Internet Science Tech RSS*. 15 June 2011. Web. 30 June 2015.

Mullins, Justin. "Can Facebook Make You Sad?" *BBC*. Feb. 2014. Web. 30 June 2015.

"Social Networks: Global Sites Ranked by Users 2015 | Statistic." *Statista*. 2015. Web. 30 June 2015.

UNIT 6, READING 3

Popova, Maria, and Flora Lichtman. "Arbiter of 'Interestingness' Navigates The 'Net." *Talk of the Nation*. NPR, 17 Aug. 2012. Web. 30 June 2015.

UNIT 7 SKILLS AND STRATEGIES 13

Russell, Helen. "Welcome to Sweden — the Most Cash-free Society on the Planet." *The Guardian*. 12 Nov. 2014. Web. 1 July 2015.

UNIT 7, READING 1

Mudd, Douglas. *All the Money in the World: The Art and History of Paper Money and Coins from Antiquity to the 21st Century*. New York: HarperCollins, 2006. Print.

"The History of Money." *NOVA*. PBS Online, 26 Oct. 1996. Web. 30 June 2015.

"The History of Money (Infographic)." *Infographics Zone*. 2014. Web. 30 June 2015.

UNIT 7, READING 2

Brain, Marshall. "How Counterfeiting Works." *HowStuffWorks*. N.p., 19 Mar. 2004. Web. 30 June 2015.

"100 Euro Banknote." *CurrencyGuide.eu*. Web. 30 June 2015.

"Anatomy of a $100 Bill." *NOVA*. PBS, 8 Jan. 2002. Web. 30 June 2015.

"Feature Great Historical Counterfeits." *PBS*. PBS. Web. 30 June 2015.

"Know Your Money - Counterfeit Awareness." *United States Secret Service*. United States Government. Web. 30 June 2015.

UNIT 7 SKILLS AND STRATEGIES 14

Kestenbaum, David. "Why A Principal Created His Own Currency." *NPR*. NPR, 14 Dec. 2012. Web. 01 July 2015.

UNIT 7, READING 3

Mudd, Douglas. All the Money in the World: The Art and History of Paper Money and Coins from Antiquity to the 21st Century. New York: HarperCollins, 2006. Print.

Perlberg, Steven. "16 Foreign Banknotes that Look Way Cooler than the Boring American Dollar." *Business Insider*. Business Insider, Inc, 30 June 2013. Web. 30 June 2015.

Phillips, Matt. "Here Are the Nine Most Beautiful Banknotes in the World." *Quartz*. 21 June 2013. Web. 30 June 2015.

Standish, David. *The Art of Money: The History and Design of Paper Currency from Around the World*. San Francisco: Chronicle, 2000. Print.

UNIT 8, READING 1

Adamu, Zaina. "Exploring Space: Why's It so Important?" *CNN.com*. CNN, 20 Oct.2012. Web. 30 June 2015.

Carrington, Daisy. "Is a Virgin Galactic Seat worth $250,000?" *CNN*. Cable News Network, 16 Aug. 2013. Web. 30 June 2015.

Townshend, Mindy. "5 Things We Have Thanks to Space Exploration." *Care2.com*. 29 Mar. 2015. Web. 30 June 2015.

Space Future — Space Tourism. Web. 30 June 2015.

UNIT 8, READING 2

Palca, Joe. "Why Astronauts Crave Tabasco Sauce." *NPR*. NPR, 23 Feb. 2012. Web. 30 June 2015.

Poisuo, Pauli. "10 Fascinating Facts About Living In Space." *Listverse*. 13 July 2013. Web. 30 June 2015.

Watson, Stephanie. "How Space Food Works." *HowStuffWorks*. HowStuffWorks.com, 19 Feb. 2008. Web. 30 June 2015.

"Sanitation in Orbit." *PBS*. PBS, 1999. Web. 30 June 2015.

"Space Sleep." *HumanSpaceFlight*. NASA, n.d. Web. 30 June 2015.

UNIT 8 SKILLS AND STRATEGIES 16

Cain, Fraser. "How Cold Is Space?" *Universe Today*. N.p., 02 July 2013. Web. 01 July 2015.

Dismukes, Kim. "Behind the Scenes: People." *Behind the Scenes: People*. NASA, 23 June 2003. Web. 01 July 2015.

"Astronauts Answer Students' Questions." *ETC: A Review of General Semantics* 65.3 (2008): 289–90. *NASA Education*. National Aeronautics and Space Administration. Web. 1 July 2015.

"Space Wear." *HumanSpaceFlight*. NASA, 2 Apr. 2003. Web. 01 July 2015.

UNIT 8, READING 3

Ferrell, Keith. "Space: The New Medical Frontier / NASA Spinoffs Milestones in Space Research." *U.S National Library of Medicine*. 2007. Web. 30 June 2015.

Mann, Adam. "Blindness, Bone Loss, and Space Farts: Astronaut Medical Oddities." *Wired.com*. Conde Nast Digital, 23 July 2012. Web. 30 June 2015.

"Chris Hadfield Readjusts to 'Earthling' Life." *YouTube*. WorldNews&EverythingAboutLife, 18 May 2013. Web. 30 June 2015.

"Known Effects of Long-term Space Flights on the Human Body." *Discovery Channel*. Web. 30 June 2015.

Credits

The authors and publishers acknowledge the following sources of copyright material and are grateful for the permissions granted. While every effort has been made, it has not always been possible to identify the sources of all the material used, or to trace all copyright holders. If any omissions are brought to our notice, we will be happy to include the appropriate acknowledgements on reprinting and in the next update to the digital edition, as applicable.

Illustrations
Jim Atherton

Photography

T = Top, C = Centre, B = Below, L = Left, R = Right, B/G = background

p. 1: ©Kimberry Wood/Getty Images; p. 6: ©Philip J Brittan/ Getty Images; p. 13: ©Thailoei92/Shutterstock; p. 14: Hinterhaus Productions/DigitalVision/Getty Images; p. 33: ©Digital Vision/Getty Images; p. 38: ©Room the Agency/ Alamy; p. 45: (T) Pictures from History/Universal Images Group/Getty Images; (B) PHAS/Universal Images Group/ Getty Images; p. 55: TED ALJIBE/Staff/AFP/Getty Images; p. 56: RichLegg/E+/Getty Images; p. 65: Siegfried Layda/The Image Bank/Getty Images; p. 69: (T) ©Stasique/Shutterstock; (C) ©Zero Creatives/Getty Images; (B) ©Icsnaps/Shutterstock; (BR) ©Alp Images/Shutterstock; p. 77: Eivaisla/iStock/ Getty Images Plus/Getty Image; p. 87: ©Hindustan Times/ Getty Images; p. 88: ©Amble Design/Shutterstock; p. 97: ©Beauty Photographer/Shutterstock; p. 110: ©Bitt24/ Shutterstock; p. 116: ©Arunas Gabalis/Shutterstock; p. 131: ©Barry Downard/Getty Images; p. 153: (L) ©Julia Kuleshova/Shutterstock; (R) ©Jason Swain/Getty Images; p. 163: ©BraunS/Getty Images; p. 167: ©Daseugen/ Shutterstock; p. 168: ©Radiokafka/Shutterstock; p. 169: ©LiliGraphie/Shutterstock; p. 195: ©Steve McAlister/ Getty Images; p. 208: (T) ©Kokhanchikov/Shutterstock; (B) Davidhills/iStock/Getty Images Plus/Getty Images; p. 216: ©Daniel Sambraus/Getty Images; p. 217: (T) ©Imac/ Alamy; (C) ©Image Broker/Alamy; (B) ©Yuliyan Velchev/ Shutterstock; p. 225: ©Shutterstock; p. 230: ©Vadim Sadovski/Shutterstock; p. 231: ©Victor Habbick Visions/ Science Photo Library/Getty Images; p. 237: ©Yoshikazu Tsuno/Getty Images; p. 239: Bettmann/Getty Images; p. 247: Space Frontiers/Stringer/Archive Photos/Getty Images.

Text

M&M Global for the table on p. 71 from 'Eurozone woes continue to dampen global ad spend forecast' by Jenni Baker, *M&M Global*, 01.10.2012. Copyright © M&M Global 2012;

Telegraph Media Group Limited for the graph on p. 136 adapted from 'All seafood will run out in 2050, say scientists' by Christopher Clover, *The Telegraph*, 03.11.2006. Copyright © Telegraph Media Group Limited 2006;

International Telecommunication Union for the graph on p. 175 adapted from 'ITU_Key_2005-2015_ICT_data. xls', Internation*al Telecommunication Union*. Copyright © International Telecommunication Union 2015.